D1163237

PÈRE LAGRANGE
AND THE
SCRIPTURES

Père Marie-Joseph Lagrange, O.P.

Père Lagrange
AND THE
SCRIPTURES

TRANSLATED FROM THE FRENCH BY

Richard T. Murphy, O.P.

S.T.D., SS. PROLYTA.

THE BRUCE PUBLISHING COMPANY
Milwaukee

Imprimi potest: VERY REV. PETER O'BRIEN, O.P., Provincial
Nihil obstat: REV. JOHN A. SCHULIEN, S.T.D., Censor deputatus
Imprimatur: ✠ MOSES E. KILEY, Archbishop of Milwaukee
August 1, 1946

33320

BX
4705
L253
O34

Copyright, 1946
Richard T. Murphy, O.P.
Printed in the United States of America

MATRIBUS MEIS

CONTENTS

PREFACE TO THE AMERICAN EDITION

NOT uncommonly many outside the Catholic Church, and occasionally some insufficiently enlightened minds within it, seem to think that a scholar cannot at one and the same time be a loyal son of the Church and a genuine, scientific biblical critic. Evidence of the existence of such opinion may be seen not only in the explicit statements which appear in print from time to time to that effect, but also from the manner in which the writings of even the more eminent Catholic biblical scholars are ordinarily passed over as unworthy of notice by independent critics. Those who understand the principles which guide Catholic critics realize that such an opinion is in reality unfounded. The truth about it is illustrated in a concrete way by the work of Catholic scholars who have distinguished themselves in an outstanding manner in the subjects of biblical criticism.

These essays, a synthesis of the exegetical and historical work of Reverend Père Lagrange, founder of the *École Biblique Internationale* of Jerusalem, afford evidence that he, a faithful son of the Church, was also a genuine biblical critic. Written by specialists who have themselves attained eminent places in the ranks of French scholarship, they were published in the French language in 1935 in connection with the fiftieth anniversary of the ordination of Père Lagrange to the priesthood. Consequently they do not include a consideration of some of the more technical works produced after that date on the subject of biblical criticism, namely, his *Critique textuelle du Nouveau Testament,* the *Critique Historique, les Mystères: l'Orphisme,* and subsequent articles of critical value in the *Revue Biblique.* Nevertheless they afford an excellent summary of the earlier productions of P. Lagrange and give concrete proof both of his virtue and of his scholarship.

Père Lagrange esteemed it the highest privilege to be a member of the Catholic Church. A high judgment of the value of Christian faith and of all that the possession of it involves was undoubtedly the reason which led him in early manhood, when he was fully acquainted with the legitimate pleasures of the world and when his revered parents were seemingly looking forward to a distinguished legal career on his part, to consecrate himself to God in the service of the priesthood and in the life of a religious order. Convinced as he was that the Catholic Church was an institution divinely founded and left in the world as the custodian and authoritative interpreter of God's supernatural revelation to mankind, he dedicated himself to the lifelong advocacy and defense of that conviction. It was not his intention at any time to depart from the official teaching of the Church, the representative of Christ on earth. With childlike humility, when the legitimacy of some of his opinions was questioned, he stated that he recognized fully that there might be errors in his writings, but that nothing was further from his thought than to present them in a spirit of disobedience to ecclesiastical tradition or to the decisions of the Biblical Commission. Among the papers found after his death was his "spiritual testament," in which he affirmed: "I have always had the intention in all my studies of contributing to the good — I mean to the reign of Jesus Christ, to the honor of the Church, to the good of souls."

Père Lagrange was nevertheless a genuine biblical critic in the full sense of that term. The principles which he followed are those of the ordinary critical scholar plus those which he derived from the Christian faith. He worked under the light of human reason and of divine revelation. He did not fear that any contradiction of truth would result from the application of the principles of sound criticism. Accepting the office of the Church as the divinely guided teacher in matters of faith and morals, he recognized that on the part of the teaching authority of such a society there would be unusual care not to accept, even in matters only remotely related to religion, any claim to truth unless it was properly justified, and moreover a conservatism in the guardianship of truth possessed by it. A traditional interpretation handed down in such a society is from the viewpoint of criticism more apt to be right in matters in which the society is vitally interested than are the results obtained by individual minds, however powerful their efforts may be. The manner in which P. Lagrange was able to go back into the history of Israel and of Christianity and to enter into the minds of writers of the Old and of the New Testament, with the aid of tradition and of all the modern helps supplied by recent investigation of a linguistic, archaeological, and historical nature, made him a critic whose conclusions are always worthy of most serious consideration.

It is a commonplace to recall that the faith of Catholics does not rest primarily on the Scriptures. Christian faith comes ordinarily through the Church, which was anterior to the Scriptures of the New Testament. The Catholic recognizes the divine purpose and teaching of Sacred Scripture and is grateful for the assistance which the voice of the Church gives him concerning the meaning of it. But it is not commonly recognized that in practice the limitation placed upon his liberty of interpretation by the Church is comparatively very slight. The number of passages whose meaning has been directly defined by the authority of the Church is not large; the number of cases in which the interpretation of the Fathers is binding on him by reason of their being morally unanimous witnesses of the Church in a matter of faith and morals is relatively small. Practically, the commentaries of the Fathers offer more of a directive to his thought than a positive ruling of faith. The Catholic exegete is aware that, as a few swallows do not make a summer, so likewise the citation of the concerted opinion of a few Fathers does not make an interpretation binding on him; and the opinions of even distinguished theologians do not necessarily constitute the official teaching of the Church. And so the Catholic critic is conscious of both the liberty which results in such matters, and the necessity which generally lies upon him of depending ultimately on principles which are based on human reason itself — the same principles of interpretation which are used in the understanding of ordinary literature. The Catholic critic is therefore ordinarily obliged to employ the use of the same principles of rational criticism as are employed by critics outside the Church.

Lack of recognition of the divine inspiration of the Scriptures and attenuation of the doctrine concerning it have rendered their defense by the old-fashioned, purely theological methods of less avail with the general public than was formerly the case. Valid though the traditional methods are in teaching the faithful, they have become less practicable in the defense against unbelievers. For this reason P. Lagrange was led to resort to the employment of the so-called Historical Method in the study of the Scriptures and of allied subjects. So great was his faith in the divine character of the Bible that he was persuaded that on the ground of historical criticism the value of the Sacred Scriptures as historical documents would be fully vindicated. He therefore descended into the arena of historical criticism and strove valiantly in their defense in that field.

His endeavors in this regard have not always been looked upon with favor. The manner in which the publication of his series of lectures on the application of the principles of the Historical Method to the books of the Old Testament was received by many Catholic scholars might make one think that the use of the method was in itself illegitimate. P. Lagrange felt that the Catholic exegete was at liberty to employ that method. In view of the adverse criticism concerning his conferences on the Historical Method and the Old Testament, it is interesting to recall that after the publication of those conferences he was given singular tokens of unusual favor by Pope Leo XIII. P. Lagrange himself was, of course, aware of the limitations of the Historical Method. He made other scholars conscious of its impotence beyond certain bounds. He had therein the advantage over his adversaries of the light of the Church, guiding his interpretation.

Although it was particularly in the application of the Historical Method to the books of the New Testament that this disquietude was felt in some quarters, P. Lagrange went ahead courageously with a spirit of faith and, in conjunction with the theological viewpoint, made the application of the Historical Method to the study of the Gospels in his series of commentaries. The resultant product has been almost universally accepted as exceedingly successful in showing not only the theological meaning of the texts but also their value and trustworthiness as historical documents. The Historical Method, thus employed, frustrates the attempt to separate the Scriptures and the living Church. It was in the Church that the New Testament was written and the Church has the knowledge of its meaning.

The learned world is seemingly becoming more and more aware of the merits of the writings of P. Lagrange. He is becoming better recognized as a textual, literary, and historical critic of eminence. Adversary and friend alike have testified to his merits in this regard. For instance, the well-known French opponent of the divine origin of Christianity, M. L. Couchoud, confessed (*Hibbert Journal,* January, 1939, p. 195) that "the four commentaries on the Gospels of Père Lagrange are works of honest and solid scholarship," even though Couchoud could not consistently accept the convictions of Père Lagrange concerning the dates of the composition of the Gospels. Reverend P. A. Vaccari, S.J., of the Pontifical Biblical Institute at Rome, declared (*Verbum Domini,* 1937, p. 128) Père Lagrange to be "magister magistrorum." He was so because, unlike some of his contemporaries, he never wrote in a spirit of disregard of ecclesiastical tradition, because in addition to that great aid of intellectual sobriety he made use of his liberty to employ all the help which modern science affords. The past half century has seen a return in reasonable critical circles to traditional positions. It is not too much to say that Père Lagrange has played a large part in promoting this respect for the voice of tradition.

But it is not only in the ranks of the critics that the work of P. Lagrange has been felt. As testified by M. Guitton in Chapter V of this volume, the influence of the learned Dominican is strongly active among French intellectuals and particularly in university circles of the graduate and undergraduate students who live in an atmosphere of skepticism, generated by unsound philosophical systems and often productive of disastrous consequences in religious matters. Even though many of these university students are unable to follow the technical treatises of P. Lagrange, they are benefited by his more popular works such as that on *The Gospel of Jesus Christ,* his small volumes on *The Meaning of Christianity According to Luther and His Followers,* on *Christ and Renan,* and on *M. Loisy and Modernism.* Likewise they are assisted indirectly by the feeling of assurance, derived from P. Lagrange's reputation, that the scriptural basis on which, along with Sacred Tradition, the edifice of our Catholic faith is founded remains solid and unshaken.

In the hope that a better knowledge of the work of P. Lagrange may help to produce in our own country a similar influence, the translation of the outlines of his works contained in this volume has been made by Reverend Richard T. Murphy, a former student at the Dominican Biblical School at Jerusalem. The task of translation, which Father Murphy has accomplished in a praiseworthy manner, has been prompted undoubtedly by a sense of gratitude toward his distinguished confrere. To his implicit tribute of admiration and respect the writer of this preface to the American edition is pleased humbly to add his own statement of affection and thanks to the memory of the venerable and erudite biblical critic.

EDWARD J. BYRNE

St. Bernard's Seminary
Rochester, N. Y.

PREFACE

ON DECEMBER 22, 1933, in the quiet of the convent of St. Stephen's, Jerusalem, Père Lagrange celebrated the fiftieth anniversary of his ordination to the priesthood. Throughout many long years in religion, this son of St. Dominic had rendered to God a life in which the two outstanding characteristics of the founder of the Dominican Order found expression: a burning love for the Church, and a tender devotion toward the Blessed Virgin. At the same time, as a disciple of St. Thomas Aquinas, he could offer to God the magnificent fruit of the *talents* he had been given, a lifetime fruitfully spent in wholehearted dedication to the pursuit of truth in the error-strewn field of scriptural studies. This eager explorer of Palestine and pioneer in the labyrinthine thickets of independent or hostile criticism had accomplished a scientific work which was impressive to men who knew the field; he had displayed in all its light the solidity of the scriptural bases upon which, along with tradition, the sacred edifice of our faith rests.

Such a work had been sorely needed, for in the course of the nineteenth century the holy books of both Old and New Testaments had been subjected to the most rude assaults. Their origin, composition, historical value, in fact everything about them, had been put to the test by a criticism which, though learned, was also extremely severe. The facile imaginings of Renan are nothing compared to this enormous marshaling of archaeological, linguistic, and historical knowledge used to discredit altogether the documents of Christian revelation; by constant mutilations it tended eventually to ruin the text itself. Some who logically followed the destructive movement to its conclusion have today reached the point where they deny the human existence of Christ. In very truth, reason unguided by sound method ends in nonsense.

P. Lagrange was not intimidated by the extent and power of the attack. Certain of the inspiration of the Holy Scrip-

7

tures as taught by his faith, he perceived that the truth would
have to concentrate — if it were to triumph — not on a defensive scattered over each of the positions under attack, but
rather on a distinct effort of Catholic thought. It would have
to be possessed of a well-informed science, which, combining
with an accurate and intelligent method, could take up the
whole problem afresh and bring it to reliable conclusions.
In this spirit he founded, in 1890, the *École Biblique* of Jerusalem, where he molded a company of learned disciples who
in time became his collaborators. With their help he undertook, in 1892, the publication of the *Revue Biblique*. This
gave wide publicity to the works of the school, and received
lively encouragement from Pope Leo XIII in a letter dated
September 17, 1892. Since that date, its patient task of research, investigation, and positive contribution to the worthy
vindication of our sacred books has never been interrupted,
even during the World War.[1] The hard-won results of this
inquiry are enshrined in the large volumes of the *Études
Bibliques,* published under the direction of P. Lagrange since
1903. Excellent works have been published by other Catholic
scholars of renown independently of the *Études Bibliques,*
but this collection is unquestionably the most complete ensemble, or, may we say, *summa* of scriptural knowledge produced in our age. P. Lagrange would be the last to assert
that it must be accepted in all its details, for only the Church
is infallible; but no one can deny that it attempted to
demonstrate the divine transcendence of our holy books, and
succeeded.

For a long time, Scripture professors — I speak from experience — and those interested in such studies either out of
curiosity or anxiety of conscience, have realized the enormity
of the task P. Lagrange set himself, and fully appreciate the
service he has done them. But how many others know nothing
about him?

For this reason the *Nouvelle Journée* was happily inspired
in consecrating this volume to him. It contains articles
written by authors particularly well qualified to speak on

"The Old Testament and Semitism," on "The New ¡Testament and Christian Beginnings," on "P. Lagrange the Hellenist," on "The Comparative History of Religions and the Revealed Religion," and on "The Influence of P. Lagrange." We are certain that readers will be surprised to discover how important a work the founder of the *École Biblique* did, and will add their homage to ours.

If in his laborious old age P. Lagrange had heard from the lips of our Lord these words heard by his master, St. Thomas, in ecstasy at Salerno: "Well hast thou written of Me; what reward wilt thou have?" the memory we cherish from our brief visit with him in his convent at Jerusalem in 1912, assures us that he, too, would have replied: "Nothing but Thyself, O Lord!"

ACHILLE, CARD. LIÉNART
Bishop of Lille

CHAPTER I

THE OLD TESTAMENT — SEMITISM

PÈRE LAGRANGE'S work on the Old Testament and Semitism is considerable. In the following pages I have tried to give a bird's-eye view of it, without however restricting myself to a mere listing of positions. The first section treats of inspiration, key question dominating all exegesis. The second deals with the work of Moses, a delicate subject because of the various problems it raises, but one which by that very fact is more likely to give a good idea of his method. After these two fundamental studies, a third and final section will indicate briefly other works of his which treat of the Old Testament and Semitism.

I. INSPIRATION

One of the most difficult studies of theology is the question of inspiration. It is a speculative research which supposes a profound knowledge of both traditional doctrine and the texts of the Bible. Catholic critics, fearing lest they stumble, often dare not launch out into this research, where they feel less at ease than they do in the explanation of facts; or perhaps, since they are so accustomed to positive studies, they do not always give to speculation the honor which it rightly deserves. However, it sometimes happens that theologians do not attach sufficient importance to criticism, and often brush it aside without troubling to see if their own deductions cover all the facts. The study of inspiration, which in final analysis must take into account the inspired book as such, implies necessarily a union of theology and criticism. What makes P. Lagrange so important is the fact that he was a thorough master in both fields.[1]

The Bible is an inspired book; it has God for its author. There, in a simple formula, is a résumé of the teaching of the Church. But how explain it?

Before the studies of P. Lagrange, the system of Franzelin had enjoyed a considerable vogue.[2] For Franzelin, the starting point was the notion of author. What is required that God be the author of the Scriptures? The Cardinal endeavored to draw a neat distinction between the formal and material elements of the inspired book (*ratio formalis et ratio materialis*). The formal element contained the thoughts and came from God; the material element contained, broadly speaking, the words used. Inspiration was necessary for the thoughts; assistance was sufficient for the words. As for the thoughts, the book was previously conceived by God and then suggested to the writer. This results in something close to dictation, for God communicates the book already made, at least as regards the thoughts, to the author charged with its wording. A dualism such as this engenders considerable difficulties on the score of the intellectual operations of the inspired author. How, then, explain the use of documents which is supposed by the Bible itself? These documents existed and were known to the inspired author before they formed a part of the Bible, and God did not have to suggest them. How conceive a thought without the words which express it? There are differences between some historical accounts which report the same event; if God had conceived and suggested the book already made, an exegete would feel bound to see everywhere, of necessity, the same thoughts, and the individuality of authors would be reduced to the mere usage of words.

Well armed with his knowledge of St. Thomas, P. Lagrange took a stand against Franzelin, and led biblical studies out of the *impasse* in which they were languishing. Instead of beginning with the notion of author, he analyzed the very notion of inspiration. The formula: God is the author of the scriptures, is rigorously true.

It "rests upon this other [formula]: the canonical books were written under the inspiration of the Holy Ghost. The notion of inspiration will then have to be examined in itself, but it must nevertheless be conceived in such a manner as to include this conclusion: God is the author of these books."[3]

It was the terminology of the Vatican Council that suggested this approach to P. Lagrange: "The Church considers them (these books) as sacred and canonical . . . because, having been written under the inspiration of the Holy Ghost, they have God for their author."[4] It is enough to know the laws of subordinate propositions to appreciate the correctness of this.[5]

Keeping in mind the explanation given by the eminent Thomist, Cardinal Zigliara, P. Lagrange began his analysis of inspiration.[6] He clearly distinguished it from revelation, in contrast to which inspiration is not necessarily conscious and implies no communication of ideas. God, of course, can reveal things to His inspired writer, but the notions of revelation and inspiration are distinct. God gives no new knowledge by inspiration; He acts upon the will, moving it to write, and upon the intellect by enlightening it. In virtue of this divine light, of the grace which elevates his spirit, the inspired author formulates a judgment of divine certitude upon things which he can know naturally.

Everything affirmed in virtue of this light will enjoy the infallibility of divine truth itself. God is the cause of this judgment which is certainly true; it is therefore God who utters it, who speaks and who teaches.[7]

It may happen that God does not suggest or furnish any idea, but simply gives a grace which is productive of a judgment of divine truth, and therefore, of an infallible judgment. As P. Lagrange understands it, inspiration is incompatible with error. Throughout the preparation and execution of the whole work, the sacred writer remains under God's action; the radiance of the divine light extends to the entire composition, even to the words. Not that verbal inspiration is dictation. Each author possesses his own ideas and style, and yet in the divine light the thoughts and words are chosen correctly. Aside from the fact that the ideas and the words are so intimately connected, the author is unceasingly moved by God during the writing, in such a manner that no element which is absolutely his own can be singled out. All is God's, and at the same time all is man's. God is the principal cause, and the hagiographer, or sacred writer, is a special kind of instrumental cause. The inspired writer remains free, preserves his intellectual activity, works, forms judgments, makes affirmations, and does everything other authors of books do, but he is at every moment moved by God. The divine action penetrates, but does not impede the man in any way, "either in the free choice of expressions, or in the unobstructed formation of his concepts."[8] A Thomist would say: God creates both "being" and "being free." And in the present case God is indeed author, for He moves the hagiographer throughout the whole of the writing and causes judgments by His light.

Such sound Thomistic notions enabled P. Lagrange to establish a sound theological doctrine fitting admirably into the teaching of the Church. His considerable influence has given new life to the question; to be convinced of this one has only to open a few treatises on inspiration.[9]

It is evident that the system of St. Thomas has prevailed, and that it is not easy to free it from the rut into which Franzelin had led it. Some find it difficult to admit that they have come around, more or less, to the explanation of P. Lagrange. Franzelin's system survives among a number of disciples who preserve much of his terminology and some of his spirit, recognizing as they do so that inspiration does not necessarily imply a communication of divine thoughts. If not a few authors mix the theories of Franzelin and Lagrange, it is because they see the insufficiency and difficulties of Franzelin's system; and if they still maintain that the book was composed and suggested by God, it is because as Molinists they cannot conceive of divine causality as anything but a collaboration, which is not sufficient to make God the author of the book. Thomists have no need to bother with suggestion, for divine causality, as they understand it, is total in its way, but does not for all of that impede the free action of the writer. Basically the debate hinges on the question of divine concursus.[10]

The principle of inspiration is a necessary guide for the Catholic exegete who must tackle the facts. P. Lagrange was exceptional in that he collated his explanation with the exegesis of texts and the findings of critics; and he was not afraid to deal with difficulties which many authors would pass by in silence. His doctrine of inspiration, which does justice to principles and the needs of the faith, enabled him to answer various problems which were raised by criticism. Here, then, is the touchstone:

Harmony will be established between tradition and modern science by grouping the newly ascertained facts under the ancient principles. Routine will be astonished at the changes in conclusions, but true theologians know that the progress of dogma is effected precisely in this manner: that ancient principles are clarified or developed by new and contingent notions.[11]

Study of the inspired text leads to an understanding of the object and the manner of inspiration, for reasoning is active in the analysis of its concept.

P. Lagrange was always careful of his texts. He took pains to read them just as they stood, and to respect them. He remarks:

It is not for us to determine what God should have done or what He should fitly have done, but humbly to ascertain what forms a part of His work. These are not questions which any man can resolve as he will; he must abide by what emerges from the facts.[12]

This concern for facts has not always been understood. P. Lagrange has been reproached for explaining the holy books as one would explain other books. It is quite necessary to look upon the sacred books as books proposed to men by other men; that is, by men who speak in God's name, according to the rules of human speech. Not for a moment did P. Lagrange forget that the book was of divine origin, and that a divine institution, the Church, had been entrusted with it and given the right to interpret the divine teaching. Inspiration extends to everything in the book, even to the words; but the inspired author is not always affirming. The Bible is not a collection of theses. The author does not always teach in the name of God. Furthermore, there can be, in the mind of the sacred writer, false ideas as well as true ones, but by reason of inspiration, the object of affirmation can be only the true idea. "Until a judgment has been formed, there is neither error nor truth." It is the task of an exegete to investigate the meaning of the judgments of these inspired authors, that is, to examine what he is teaching. For this P. Lagrange formulated this rule:

Everything that is taught in the Bible, God teaches; but He teaches only what is taught by the sacred writer, who in turn teaches nothing but what he wishes to teach.

This is very simple, but very fruitful, for it supposes that inspiration does not change the meaning of the terms, nor the character of the propositions, nor the literary genus of the books; and it is only by studying the sense of the terms, the character of the propositions and the literary genus of the books that we can know the thought and intention of the author.[13]

This method marked a vigorous reaction against the prevailing tendency of seeing everywhere in the Scriptures the affirmations of God. On this point P. Pesch agrees with P. Lagrange: "Nothing is proposed to be believed except what God wishes to propose as true by the words of the hagiographer." Then, approaching the delicate point, he does not hesitate to affirm that "the inspired writer can even have false opinions; it may even happen that from his manner of speaking we may surmise what true or false opinions he had in his head."[14] It was this that P. Lagrange maintained against P. Brucker.[15]

But can this position be maintained, after the decree of the Biblical Commission concerning the state of mind of Paul and the Apostles concerning the second coming? "All that the hagiographer affirms, expresses, and insinuates must be held as affirmed, expressed, and insinuated by the Holy Ghost."[16] P. Bea sums it up briefly: "In other words, the words by which the hagiographer expresses his judgments, with that shade of meaning in which he expresses them, are the words of God,"[17] and consequently are the judgments of God. Only the judgments, therefore, which the sacred writer expresses as certain, are certain judgments of God. Moreover, it is enough to point out that a conjecture concerning the state of an author's mind is not at all the same thing as an expression or even an insinuation of the author. If people have to guess about what I think, then I have not insinuated it clearly. Inspiration does not supply for the ignorance of the inspired writer. Always we return to the same point: the truth of the judgments must be saved, leaving only the objects of the judgments to be determined by exegesis. In such investigations P. Lagrange was always careful to exclude texts whose interpretation has been settled by the Church, but such texts are few and the task of the exegete remains immense.

For more than three centuries the question of the Bible and natural sciences has preoccupied scholars. It was around 1507 that Copernicus began to publish his epoch-making works. The encyclical *Providentissimus Deus* (1893) marked the end of a long controversy: in questions of natural sciences, the sacred authors, like ordinary men, spoke according to appearances; they were not teachers of science. There can then be no question of scientific errors in the Bible, since it contains no scientific teaching. Men, however, are slow to change, and although Leo XIII had declared that God had no intention of teaching men truths of natural science, many books on apologetics and manuals of Scripture were for a long time weighted down with what was called concordism, and with a pseudo-scientific kind of exegesis. Since the Pope had settled the question, P. Lagrange did not concern himself with it, except for drawing out several instructive lessons from the past mistakes, and reacting against those who were still bent on finding teachings about cosmography in the Bible.[18]

Difficulties no longer came from science, but from history. In the nineteenth century the advances of historical criticism, and the immense archaeological and epigraphical documentation unearthed by excavations in Egypt and western Asia, had revealed the Old Testament in a new light. A solution had been found for the problems created by the earth's position in space; still awaiting an answer were the problems which dealt with the place of humanity in time, the development of Israel's history, and the relationship between the Bible and the literature of Assyria, Babylon, and Egypt. In

this field, up to now unexplored by Catholics, it was a difficult business and a delicate one to determine the judgments
of the sacred writer. However, since the best interests of
countless souls and consciences were at stake as a result of
these new problems, P. Lagrange spared no pains to find the
solutions. Where the fighting is fierce, a man stands in a
perilous place, but it is there he can best serve.

When dealing with history, remarked P. Lagrange, it is
important to determine first of all the literary genus.[19] Some
books may be historical in appearance but not in fact. "A fic-
titious history can be more useful than a true one." To both
these literary genera, details and precision are common. The
Church can indeed pronounce upon the literary genus of a
book, but when the Church says nothing, exegetes must form
their own judgments, based on respect for tradition and a
critical spirit, and try to determine the literary genus, wholly
submissive to what the ecclesiastical magisterium may in the
future determine.[20] In this difficult matter P. Lagrange was
always most reserved, and before publishing in the *Revue
Biblique* M. Cosquin's extremely interesting article on "Le
livre de Tobie et l'histoire du sage Ahicar," he submitted it
to M. Vigouroux.[21]

The Bible contains a true history "whose prestige has been
greatly increased and whose defense has been made easier by
modern discoveries."[22] This history, remarks P. Lagrange,
reproduces the substantial truth of words and facts. "God
teaches only what the historian wishes to teach." When accounts of the same words and facts are variously rendered in
different books, care must be taken of the authors' free will,
different purposes, and knowledge, rather than having recourse to a forced harmony. The method of P. Lagrange provides startling confirmation of the substantial reality of the
facts, for thus we have many witnesses for it instead of one.
These remarks are applied to the Gospels and to some texts
of the Old Testament. As for the historical books of the Old
Testament, the manner in which the Semites wrote history
must be taken into consideration. They not infrequently
compiled narratives from very ancient sources, which they

transcribed purely and simply, completing one by the other. The articles published in the *Revue Biblique* by M. Guidi and by Msgr. (now Cardinal) Tisserant are most instructive in this regard.[23]

In many historical books of the Old Testament, criticism reveals written sources which antedated the author and were reproduced, in the Semitic manner, without citation. These documents, at times divergent, are occasionally copied bodily from beginning to end; at other times they are carefully blended.

P. Lagrange was one of the first to indicate that a utilization of documents by an inspired author would work to the advantage of a defense of the Bible. He wrote:

To paint the picture as black as possible, suppose two passages were really contradictory by categoric affirmation. The simplest way out of the difficulty and of exonerating the principal author from all reproach of error is precisely to suppose that he reproduced textually his sources. . . . In the composition which gives the documents in question the character of an inspired work, they only figure as affirmations of the author to the extent he himself wished them to figure. Citing a letter of the Spartans (1 Mach. 12:19–23), he does not intend to guarantee its truthfulness. If indeed he does place two contradictory accounts of the same fact on the same page, it is impossible to suppose that he took the responsibility for both versions, and that he taught both of them.

P. Lagrange then gives us his own opinion:

Most of the time, perhaps always, the contradiction will be merely apparent. It is much simpler to demonstrate that there is no contradiction between two pages which do not emanate from the same author, than between two which issue from the same pen. Two authors were possessed of different points of view, ideas, different purposes, and that explains much. No more forcing of harmony: the divergence is quite natural; we have only to find now a general harmony in the thought of the author of the whole.[24]

The documents utilized by the sacred writer can be profane or already inspired. If profane, he can make them more or less his own. If he does approve a profane page and make it his own while acting under the light of inspiration, he thereby makes it a work of God. This page, "human in its elements, in its origin . . . became divine, as guaranteed by God and as inserted in His book by a special act of His will."[25]

In each case the citation must be examined in order to determine the measure in which the sacred writer covers it with his authority. The document he utilizes can be inspired.

To transcribe and develop a sacred work is certainly permissible and can be the result of inspiration. To bring into harmony even some inspired works, and to this end reduce them to certain proportions, is not disrespectfully to dissect them, but rather to use them as they were definitely destined to be used by divine Providence.[26]

Aside from the cases where there is a noticeable dependence between two books of the Bible, it is impossible to pass judgment on the inspired character of the documents. The dogma of inspiration demands only that the last redactor have been inspired.

On the other hand, once the sacred book was composed, it could have been added to and touched up by a later inspired author. Exegesis of the Old Testament has for long been tied up with the classic concept of the book written at one sitting and in an entirely personal fashion. Actually the "entire Bible was written under divine inspiration, but according to the literary processes of the Orientals."[27] In the explanation of some of the historical books, a thorough knowledge of these processes is of considerable importance in determining the judgments of the sacred writer, a fact which is being more and more recognized. Many Catholic authors admit written sources in several books, Genesis, Judges, and Samuel, for example, and solve many difficulties with the help of these principles.

Finally, P. Lagrange thought it possible to admit, for certain sections of the Old Testament only, an intermediate literary genus standing between parabolic history, which does not teach actual fact, and history properly so called. In this intermediate genus there would be, simultaneously, facts and popular traditions, history and an appearance of history.

Facts having a connection with dogma must, of course, be considered as historical.[28] He had in mind the first chapters of Genesis, which contain facts of history, and all of whose details are not to be taken literally.[29] Known as the "theory of historical appearances," this system had already been put forth by P. Cornely[30] and was further developed by P. de Hummelauer.[31] In the encyclical *Providentissimus Deus*, having first spoken of the sciences, Leo XIII wrote at the beginning of the next paragraph a tiny phrase which was to become famous: "The principles here laid down will apply to cognate sciences, and especially to history."[32] Both P. Lagrange and P. de Hummelauer believed that the text expressed the thought of P. Cornely; the prefect of the Congregation of Studies, Cardinal Satolli, was of the same mind.[33] A controversy arose. When finally the *Spiritus Paraclitus*, September 15, 1920, gave an authentic interpretation to Pope Leo's phrase, P. Lagrange had already renounced his own interpretation of the *Providentissimus Deus*.[34] The authentic interpretation was that the historical value of the Scriptures must be defended, not that questions arising from history should be treated just as those which concern the sciences.[35] It must be added that, in laying down this important rule, Benedict XV did not deny the existence — though naturally the cases are rare and well established — of books or passages of the Scriptures which have only the appearance, not the proper nature of history: *nimis facile ad citationes, quas vocant implicitas, vel ad narrationes specie tenus historicas confugiunt.*[36] What is condemned is the abuse, not the prudent use.

Compared with the burning questions of history, the question of the senses of the Scriptures seems to be peaceful. Following St. Thomas, P. Lagrange makes allegory a part of the literal sense. All Scripture has a literal sense; it is the sense the author wished to express and which flows from the very words; and the exegete must seek it out and explain it.

A book which boasts of God as its author can have a meaning beyond the grasp of the sacred writer, and so P. Lagrange admitted a sense which was "in some way supraliteral."

Belief in the inspiration of the Scriptures leads to the admission that they contain more than the obvious and purely literal sense. At any rate, since there is one author of the whole of Scripture, one thought of His may be explained by another. We can go further. The Revealer of tradition is the same as the Author of the Scriptures; a scriptural idea then can be commented upon by the truths of Tradition.

This does not mean that the text is to be joined to any sort of thought — that would be rabbinical — but to a thought "truly drawn from Scripture or from Tradition." P. Lagrange carefully pointed out that only the Church, custodian of all revelation, can determine this supraliteral meaning to a text. In such a case the explanation "would go beyond the obvious and grammatical meaning. . . . May not a simple exegete point it out?"[37] This fruitful suggestion helps bring out the harmony of divine teaching, and neatly links the authority of the Magisterium with freedom of scientific research.

Like St. Thomas, his master, P. Lagrange placed the spiritual sense in things, and not in the words.

God controls history, and knows to what part of His plan in the future a past event corresponds. In relating a first fact, He does not forget what meaning it has in relation to a second fact. He gives it a special meaning, really willed by Him. One event prefigures another. As for the hagiographer, he does not know without a special revelation, "what the things of which he speaks prefigure in the future."[38]

II. THE WORK OF MOSES

While he busied himself with the question of inspiration, from the outset of his career P. Lagrange produced a series of studies on the important question of the work of Moses, upon which almost all Old Testament history depends. To be cited immediately among these studies are "Les sources du Pentateuque," text of the famous conference delivered at the scientific Congress of Catholics at Fribourg,[39] "L'hexaméron,"[40] "L'innocence et le péché,"[41] "Le code de Hammourabi,"[42] besides other studies of the fine points.[43] Some of these points were taken up again or were treated in La méthode his-

torique. These publications provide the elements for a vast synthesis dealing with the origins of the Pentateuch, primitive history, and Mosaism. Rather than analyze each of these, we shall sketch out a synthesis drawn from his articles, and shall treat successively of literary and historical criticism. To proceed otherwise might cause the reader to lose his way in the details, and might leave the great directive lines without proper emphasis.

A. *The Literary Criticism*

To the question: Is Moses author of the legislation which bears his name, P. Lagrange did not hesitate to reply in the affirmative. But he proposed a distinction between the substance of the legislation and the redaction of the laws, between the author as understood by the ancients, and the literary author of the moderns. The modern conception was quite unknown to the Semites, as M. Guidi has shown.[44]

That the Pentateuch contains different drafts of the same laws, even the most important ones, is evident to anyone who opens the Bible. The Ten Commandments, basis of all else, appear once in Exodus (20:1–17) and again in Deuteronomy (5:6–18). The short Code of the Alliance in Exodus (20:23 – 23:19) is a sort of first draft of Deuteronomy. Leviticus contains especially laws considered from a priestly point of view.

This being so, then the question is: Did Moses himself outline these successive redactions, or were they separated by intervals of time, measured not by the life of one man but by that of a people? The direct literary activity of Moses is not held necessary by the Biblical Commission, which allows for the collaboration of secretaries, men who were not merely scribes, but collaborators whose temperaments, dispositions, and knowledge would — if we wish to use this hypothesis to explain the differences of style and outlook — have left their mark upon the work.

Does Catholic tradition, that is, a genuine ecclesiastical tradition, which enjoys equal authority with Scripture, oblige us to believe that Moses at least inspected, and approved with his signature, all these different expressions of his legislation?

P. Lagrange did not think it happened this way, because such a literary approbation was not necessary to make Moses truly the author of a set of laws which proceeded from him. Successive editings, implying modifications in details, and even additions in harmony with the principles, do not substantially alter the *corpus juris*. Justinian's *Institutiones* certainly differ more from those of Gaius than Deuteronomy does from the most ancient texts of the Pentateuch, and yet it is only a summary of Roman Law. Furthermore, the coming of Christianity introduced a new principle into this [Roman] law, whereas the Mosaic legislation built upon the same foundations, and applied the same principles.

Determined never to undertake a study contrary to an ecclesiastical tradition, P. Lagrange raised the preliminary question of the limits within which a Catholic exegete could work. He did not, as a matter of fact, ever propose an absolute solution for the problem of the origin of the Pentateuch. He was convinced, and said so, that critical studies made it impossible to maintain the view inherited from the Jews that Moses had drawn up the entire Pentateuch as it now is. More clearly still did he point out that the system of Wellhausen was not a critical solution based upon a knowledge of the Orient. Between these two absolute systems, he thought there was room for a moderate opinion which would recognize the antiquity of the Israelite legislation in its substance and promulgation by Moses, but which would distinguish in the Pentateuch different editorial strata in great part posterior to the famous lawgiver.

He himself never found time to elaborate this moderate position. He believed his duty lay in preparing the soil for it, by pointing out the weakness of the two opposing systems, and by showing that the new solutions would not spell the ruin of the faith, but rather would lead to a more intelligent understanding of a literary history which suggests, through the extraordinary character of the law of Israel, a supernatural intervention in which the Catholic Church believes.

The solution planned by him is a corollary to his distinction between the historical and literary traditions:

Moses is the legislator of Israel. Mosaism is at the bottom of the whole history of the Chosen People. There we have the historical tradition. Moses drew up the Pentateuch we possess. That is the literary tradition.[45]

Both traditions have been and are still violently attacked by the critics. P. Lagrange became the defender of the historical tradition. Without Moses, Israel's whole history is inexplicable; and the teaching of the Bible is formal.

If the Bible has misrepresented that history, it is no longer the history of salvation. Faith is threatened when the great facts of the Kingdom of God become uncertain. Moreover . . . all the arguments of a wise historical criticism compel us to attribute to Moses the historical role which tradition assigns to him.[46]

P. Lagrange was unwilling, however, to grant the same weight to the literary tradition. Difficulties raised by the critics appeared to him to demand the documentary theory.

The first author to admit the use of documents in Genesis was a Catholic, John Astruc (1684–1756).[47] Astruc's theory has been extended to the whole of the Pentateuch by the independent critics. Briefly, their theory calls for four documents: $J, E, D,$ and $P,$ generally supposed to have been drawn up as follows: J — ninth century, in Judea; E — somewhat later, in the kingdom of Israel; D — seventh century, in Judea; and P — during the Babylonian exile.[48] They are supposed to have been united later: first J with $E,$ then J and E with $D,$ and finally after the Babylonian exile, $J, E,$ and D with $P.$ At the close of the past century this theory, with a few variations in detail, was almost universally admitted. At the same time it was so complicated with dangerous, subjective theological opinions and attacks upon religion, that it appeared to be completely suspect.

At this juncture Leo XIII uttered words of encouragement to Catholic scholars, and especially to P. Lagrange, who was convinced that the moment had come for the baptism of criticism, to do for criticism what St. Thomas had done for Aristotle, that is, to reject its dross but welcome whatever good it contained, and to make that good serve the faith.[49] Like St. Thomas, he was inspired by apostolic zeal.[50]

The reasons advanced to justify the plurality of written sources were well known, so P. Lagrange did not pause to make up his list of them. He alludes to doublets,[51] speaks of the numbers which concern the tribes, the army, etc., and of the evolution of the law. In his commentary on Numbers, P. de Hummelauer declared that the numbers were really exaggerated, and concluded that some pious but stupid scribe (scriba aliquis inepte pius) had multiplied the numbers by 100.[52] As P. Lagrange remarked, this would have led to mistakes involving hundreds of thousands, but the units would have been preserved.

> . . . the independent critics will not be convinced. . . . They will not fail to say that such huge numbers are part of the style, and in a given document are bound up with the core of the story.[53]

Developing his point concerning the divergences between laws which deal with the same subject, he said:

> For a long time now, those who insist on harmonizing them propose solutions which are singly possible, but, when taken together, constitute a moral impossibility. Once let it be admitted that legislation does evolve, and the very appearance of a contradiction disappears.[54]

The difficulty is only too well known to Catholics. M. Vigouroux held for a succession of laws, framed however by Moses himself, and many of them drafted ahead of time by prophetic vision. P. de Hummelauer similarly admitted some sort of evolution, which he thought should come to an end with Moses. In his *Genesis* he discovered documents tracing back to Adam, Noah, and Abraham,[55] and in his *Exodus* and *Numbers* he found laws going back to the patriarchs. P. Lagrange asked, however: "Is Moses the legislator because he laid the foundations, or because he crowned the edifice? That is the question."[56] For his part, he did not hesitate to answer that Moses was the beginning.

But do not the Scriptures always say: "God said to Moses," and thus seem to imply that, if Moses did not draw up the law, he did enact it? Was it, then, the priests who deceived the people by signing Moses' name to their own laws? P. Lagrange replied that it was the duty of the priests to interpret the law and to resolve practical questions (Deut. 17:9–11). Thence arose a jurisprudence which in turn became a text of law. It would be wrong to speak of deceit. It was natural enough, by a legal fiction known also to the Romans,[57] to extend the old law to cases unforeseen by it.

To Moses, God revealed what He judged fitting for him to know. . . . What He did at Sinai He could do later on. . . . The formula, God said to Moses, means simply: here is a law which issues from divine authority in the spirit of the first lawgiver.[58]

But do not the facts of Scripture and tradition seem to oppose any theory of documents which does not leave Moses as the drafter of the whole Pentateuch? These questions were treated by P. Lagrange in his conference at Fribourg, and the following is a digest of his remarks to that very well-informed audience.

What saith the Scripture? Both Old and New Testaments state that Moses wrote down some laws and facts, thus establishing the fact of a Mosaic legislation. But they do not state that Moses wrote all; nor do they allow of any clear distinction between laws made by him and those which came later on.[59]

From the historical, but less so from the literary point of view, tradition is very firm. Many of the Fathers, P. Lagrange went on to say, held that after the exile God had inspired Esdras to reproduce the holy books lost during the Babylonian captivity, particularly the Law of Moses.[60] From that time on, in the opinion of these Fathers, it was on the authority of an inspired Esdras that the authority of the Pentateuch rested.

The idea, a product of Judaism, crops up in an apocryphal work, 4 Esdras, and in the Talmud (Sanhedrin 21 b). The restoration of the Pentateuch by the famous scribe was plainly designed to trace every syllable of it back to Moses; but does not this artifice, which is no longer believed, seem to have been designed to conceal the memory of an editorial revision carried out at this time?

The Fathers were more than once led into error by Jewish rabbinical influences. P. Lagrange recalls the story of the seventy locked in their cells, a legend which some of the most important Fathers thought to be true, and one which led them to admit the inspiration of the Greek version,[61] and then remarks:

The Jews thought they knew all about their origins and infected some of the Christians with their brashness. Exaggerations of their traditions should make us suspicious of it. They traced the origin of the vowel points back to Sinai, and concocted the idea of the Great Synagogue. . . . It is high time we distinguish more clearly the apostolic tradition from that of Jewish opinion.[62]

Concerning Numbers, he observed:

It would be taking a decisive stand to replace a late Jewish interpretation with a Catholic interpretation which follows more certain data. This could not be done without difficulty because of the deep-rooted attachment to these judaic infiltrations.[63]

He then suggested the use of a profoundly modified documentary theory, and it is worth consideration. He maintained against the critics both the value and antiquity of the Elohist (*E*), which is anterior to *J*,[64] and is attributed without grounds to the northern kingdom.[65] Memories approaching the time of the Exodus and texts written by Moses (cf. Exod. 17:14; 24:4), as well as other items,[66] were contained in this source upon which P. Lagrange relied much and which he vigorously defended against Winckler's attacks. It recounts miracles; these are not legends and marvelous tales, but interventions of God, who thus accredited the mission of Moses and the true religion.[67]

Deuteronomy, when compared to the Code of Alliance (Exod. 21 — 22:19), marks the end of an evolution. Some authors felt obliged to hold that Moses had brought about this change in the space of forty years, but not P. Lagrange. "Is it likely, that, once the Law was given by God on Sinai, He transformed it after forty years, and then immobilized it for centuries?" Deuteronomy burns with the spirit of the prophets, and was definitively drawn up shortly before Josias.[68]

P, the fourth document, dates from the time of the exile. "Shall anyone say," asked P. Lagrange, "that an account separated from the facts by centuries is unworthy of belief? Such an admission would place Moses in a bad light in regard to the history of the patriarchs," for Abraham lived five or seven hundred years before Moses, or almost as many years as Moses lived before the Babylonian Exile. Once the authority of this document is granted, we have a *new witness* which fits in with the other witnesses on essential points; and this is a criterion of truth, since this document had to have its own still more ancient sources.[69] The genuineness of the important facts is not called into question but is guaranteed, critically by the other sources, and theologically by inspiration, for these facts form a part of the history of salvation and are bound up with dogma. The differences are not important in themselves; "we may wonder if God really desired to teach them to us, or if He employed them as material elements of a higher teaching." Why could not the priestly code idealize the past as Ezechiel idealized the future? In both cases God could have desired to forecast the new law.[70] Nothing would be posterior to Esdras.[71]

Such is the critical position proposed by P. Lagrange for the consideration of Catholic exegetes.[72] The study of documents forms an introduction to that of the history they relate.

B. *The Historical Criticism*

Since it must eventually come into contact with history, itself the basis of theological interpretations, literary criticism is nothing more than the preparation for a more certain historical criticism.

In his classes, P. Lagrange often criticized the shortcomings of a bookish sort of criticism which consisted in the mere analysis of texts, oblivious to the advantages which history, archaeology, and geography could offer. In other words, he leaned toward the comparative method, but he was not the first to employ it. M. Vigouroux had really opened the way with his books on the Bible and modern discoveries. But he was too much concerned in finding confirmations of the Bible. P. Lagrange's purpose was also to help souls in their adherence to the Christian faith, but he was clearly convinced that *all* truth contributes to the support of the integral truth of Christianity; and we must first of all acquire the truth. No truth, even one whose relation to the faith we do not see, is indifferent. To set out, in exegesis, with the intention of confirming the Bible might perhaps lead to a vain attempt to prove the routine conclusions. The first objective should be to understand, not to confirm, the Bible. Know much, so as to understand better, might well have been P. Lagrange's motto.

He thought that, in the field of history, knowledge would reveal itself by the use of the comparative method of dealing with the facts, previous to any dissection and reconstruction of the texts. The realism which is so efficacious in art is a *must* for history. Certainly the texts must be consulted, but the place of honor should be given to texts which are not the interpretation or arrangement of facts, but rather a reflection of them. Inscriptions are an example; the facts can sometimes be grasped from the ruins and the sites. In such a large field, however, ideas also are facts (*res*), and they are the object of history, precisely as they were understood in antiquity. Here again the realistic and the comparative methods join forces, and both rest upon literary criticism. They guarantee its progress.

We will now clarify the theory of P. Lagrange by stating some of his conclusions as indicated in articles on Creation, the Fall, Primitive and Patriarchal History, and the Exodus from Egypt, for the Pentateuch ends before the entry into the Promised Land.

1. THE ACCOUNTS

a) Creation

For the good reason that there is no concordance between the days and periods, P. Lagrange dismissed concordism. Moreover, in the first of the two accounts of creation, the days are ordinary days;[73] they represent, as St. Thomas had pointed out, a logical order, and constitute an artificial framework designed to inculcate the sanctification of the Sabbath. As for the tenor of the story, P. Lagrange draws a distinction between the facts and their modalities.

In Genesis, some real facts are affirmed and taught in the proper sense of the word: an all-wise God created the world; creation is good, because it conforms to the idea of its Creator; and man, by reason of his resemblance to God, holds a place high over other creatures. These facts were revealed to Israel. P. de Hummelauer held that Genesis recorded the visions and revelations of Adam, and that they were altered among other peoples. In mitigated form, such concordism still crops up from time to time, but P. Lagrange denounced it, from the very start, as fanciful. How had such truths come to Israel, entirely worked out as P. de Hummelauer believed, and by what intermediary?[74]

It is a fact that details of the biblical account have some resemblance to the cosmogonies of Phoenicia and Chaldea.[75] From the literary similarities, unbelieving critics conclude that Genesis is completely myth and legend. A better answer than an appeal to a meaningless traditionalism (for these striking similarities are unparalleled outside the Semitic world, and concern only details) is that the similarity is not one of ideas, but of literary dress or expression. The great Babylonian poem of creation depicts gods who are born from chaos, and who struggle against evil forces; and the concept of the world in the Phoenician cosmogony leads to atheism. On the contrary, the biblical text, with its pure monotheism, is without parallel from the religious and moral point of view. Once again, revelation is the most reasonable explanation of such transcendence. However, this is not the case for the literary expression. That is why all the accounts present the same popular touch, and in the Hexameron, as well as in the Phoenician cosmogony, there is the same order of beings, although, in the Babylonian poem, man first, and then the animals, are created by Marduk.

Thus "the Mosaic account of creation is unique in its

teaching because it comes from God," but "its structure is like that of the other cosmogonies because such a format is the fruit of the Semitic genius." No direct dependence, therefore, but a surrounding Semitic influence. What admirable divine pedagogy!

This is indeed the teaching of the Father who instructs his children concerning the truths necessary for salvation. In order to sink these truths into their minds, He chooses images either inoffensive in themselves, or else carefully purified of whatever they might contain contrary to the truth, but images to which they are accustomed.[76]

b) *The Fall*

Here P. Lagrange applied the same principles of exegesis[77] and clearly distinguished the teaching from its literary expression.

The history of the fall is a true history, but not everything in it must be taken literally. Our first parents sinned and lost their privileges. Analyzing this, he says:

It is impossible . . . not to be struck by two facts: the perfect conformity of this teaching with Catholic dogma, and the absence of a necessary bond between this teaching and certain details which serve as the vehicle of the account. It is curious that some people will not recognize the popular character of the expressions, because they do grasp their depth and reality, while others, because they recognize the face of the old legends, do not feel how tragic and serious is their tone.[78]

One by one, P. Lagrange studied the circumstances which form the dress of the teaching, e.g., the parade of the animals before Adam, the trees, the sword, etc. P. de Hummelauer held that the story of Adam's rib need not be believed; these things could have occurred in a vision! P. Lagrange was familiar with this exegesis, but still, he said, "we will have to choose between vision and parable."[79]

The fact of the fall was known by revelation. Humanity is too ancient to have retained a clear memory of the exact story which our memory preserves for us; and, anyhow, there was no tradition in the pagan world "expressly recalling the history of original sin, either as regards the fundamentals, or as regards the circumstances."

The details of the story recall many characteristics of the Assyro-Babylonian texts. "We move in the Semitic world, in the same circle of symbols: a delightful resting place of the gods, sacred trees of life and knowledge, and the marvellous power of the serpent." The Church does not command that all the details of the story must be taken literally, even when an important theological doctrine could be based upon the presentation of the facts.

We do not find it unworthy of God to teach us this truth [concerning the Fall] in a very simple manner, along with the marks transmitted by popular imagination, and used by the inspired author as symbols. Nor are we desirous that souls be lost because they refuse to believe what the Church does not even ask them to believe.[80]

Concerning the rivers of paradise, P. Lagrange soberly remarks that "the Bible is to be explained by the geography of the ancients, even if it is less exact, and not by the most modern maps."[81]

c) Primitive History

It was long believed that the Bible contained a primitive history which extended from the origins of mankind down to Abraham.

Moses was easily a much earlier writer than any other, and well-informed too, for his witnesses went back to the first days of mankind in an unbroken line. For Christian apologetics, this was one of the firm positions, and not only Bossuet, but Pascal also, took his stand upon it: "Sem who saw Lamech, who saw Adam, at least saw Abraham, who saw Jacob, who saw those who beheld Moses."[82]

Discoveries in prehistory, as revealed by finds in Egyptian and Chaldean excavations, have changed all that. Here as elsewhere, P. Lagrange worked for a solution which would take into account the exigencies of doctrine and also the newly discovered facts.

In this primitive history he made it a point to single out and distinguish the historical character of original sin, as has already been shown. The fact is "based upon the unshakable foundation of revelation." But "abstracting from this dogmatic point . . . why not allow to this primitive history its own peculiar character, even though men of bygone days may not have understood it sufficiently?"[83] If God did not reveal sciences to His people, because such things were unprofitable for them as far as salvation was concerned, "there is room to believe the same of the revelation of history, which was not important to him, except insofar as it was needful for salvation."[84]

P. Lagrange was fully aware of the biblical problem raised by the antiquity of the human race. Oral tradition does not preserve the memory of facts across so many thousands of years. Doubtless it could, with extraordinary fidelity, conserve the names of places for centuries, but at times it either forgets some facts, or else adapts and transforms them. Rich imaginations vie with faithful memories in the tales entwined around place names. Indeed, concluded P. Lagrange, history is a sister to writing.[85]

Israel is young, compared to other peoples of prehistoric times. Genesis, introducing Israel to the world, said nothing about oriental history previous to Abraham, or of the great kingdoms of Egypt and Chaldea, although the official history of the Hebrews will coincide very well with that of the Assyrians, to take but one example. In biblical primitive history, all the proper names are Hebrew names. The first men had other names. There is no point in postulating a translation, for "syllables no longer correspond to syllables, nor apparently does sense match sense."[86] The sacred writer tells of the origin and progress of civilization; he speaks of the great inventions, and often the name of the inventor corresponds to the name of the invention.[87] The sobriety of the account is admirable. Yet, if a person were to call attention to certain legendary touches in the story of the deluge, tower of Babel, or ruin of Sodom, such traits are not noted for themselves, but are the expression of a religious and moral teaching. What the author intends to teach is the holiness of God and the ugliness of sin.[88]

There is nothing in the Bible that is not "superior to what we find anywhere else; everything befits the dignity of the inspired Scriptures." But why search in it for "a history of humanity, or even of one of its branches, since there is hardly one single event for every thousand years, and even then we should not know where to place it"?[89]

d) *Patriarchal History*

While P. Lagrange never had occasion to compose a broad sketch of this period, still he would not tolerate the theory that the personal histories of Abraham, Isaac, and Jacob were the relations of the ancient tribes artificially concealed.

"A new history truly began when Abraham was called by God in Chaldea to become the father of the Chosen People"[90] and it was the history of their first ancestor and model.

That Abraham's parents were polytheistic pagans is recorded in Josue 24:2. From this plain statement, P. Lagrange drew two conclusions: (1) We cannot state precisely what the tradition was whose religious truth Abraham had absorbed; the Bible does not favor traditionalism any more than profane history does. Revelation began again with Abraham. (2) We must be careful not to speculate about the transcendent faith of the patriarchs. He then quotes St. Cyril of Alexandria, "who was never suspected of rationalism," and who had perceived the poverty of the patriarchal ideas in religion.[91] Their ideas about God may have been primitive, but they are remarkable just the same. Yahweh is one, austere; there is for Him neither idol nor goddess. After a brief analysis of the patriarchal as compared to contemporary religions, P. Lagrange concluded that it would be inexplicable without the special intervention of God. "The triumph of this simple cult over the enervating but splendid cults of a more refined civilization" impressed him still more with this idea of divine intervention. After that, the prophets developed their tradition by fighting for it.[92] Revelation had progressed by degrees, and the first shoots of the religion of Israel appeared with Abraham.

P. Lagrange was quick to point out how the life of this famous patriarch fitted into history. From 1897 on, he stressed the importance of the discovery of the name of Chedorlaomer on a brick in the museum of Constantinople, and how this could be used advantageously to defend the historical character of Genesis 14. He thought it quite probable that Amraphel of this chapter was to be identified with Hammurabi. The patriarchal period "is very historical."[93]

e) *Exodus and Mosaism*

At the conclusion of Genesis, Abraham's descendants were a tribe, the tribe of Jacob. From the first chapter of Exodus, a people emerges. Between the two books there is a gap. P. Lagrange praised P. de Hummelauer for disputing the current Jewish opinion, which does not stem from the ancient tradition, viz., that they were all descended from Abraham. He wrote:

For P. de Hummelauer the whole tribe of Manasses had scarcely any of Manasses' blood in its veins. The same holds for Juda, in whose midst the tribe of Caleb, a stranger, appears (Comm. in Num., 215ss). With a discretion that must be appreciated historically, the Bible is silent on the question of the immediate origins of the people. . . . The ancient tradition presents us at the beginning of Exodus with the people of Israel, but affirms nothing about its formation. Of course there is a choice group which claimed to know its genealogy, but there was likewise a mixed people.[94]

Rational criticism rejects as legendary the story of Exodus. The supernatural, and miracles, are held to be mythology. In this connection P. Lagrange made three important remarks: First, no one denies facts of profane history simply because marvels accompany them. Ishtar revealed herself to Assurbanipal before he crossed a river; through the personal intervention of Amon, Ramses II won the famous victory of Qodchou. Herodotus and Livy could distinguish facts from the added nimbus of apparitions and prophecies. On the other hand, in Exodus the supernatural is anything but an embellishment. It appears here in a form met with nowhere else,

that, namely, of a miracle performed by a man before a people, for the purpose of awakening or confirming their faith and attaching them to God. This it is which distinguishes Yahweh's action from that of other gods. Everywhere else divine intervention is merely a brilliant disguise of natural causes, or a caprice of the imagination.

Finally, P. Lagrange adds,

if a miracle were the fruit of the imagination and the growing product of popular tradition, then patriarchal history would contain more of miracles than it would of Moses. But it does not contain them, at least no miracles performed by the hand of man; they make their appearance with Moses as supremely befitting the final establishment of a supernatural religion.

His conclusion:

Miracles under these conditions are not without historical probability. If they are reported by history worthy of the name, they have to be believed.

At this point, P. Lagrange insisted upon the great value of the document E (Elohist), and attained to a very solid apologetic, much more conservative than was at one time believed.[95]

We have already seen that, for P. Lagrange, Moses was the great lawgiver of Israel. Very often he reacted against the long-popular tendency to "belittle the actions of great men, so as to attribute everything to the hidden, instinctive, development of the people."[96] Against negative criticism, he defended the part played by Moses. No doubt,

it always will be very difficult to say exactly what Moses did write personally, but there can be no gainsaying the tradition which represents him as Israel's lawgiver, and we will never consent to abandon it, for literary quibbling will never destroy the great facts of history.[97]

Much more must be attributed to Moses than the Code of Alliance (Exod. 21—23, 19).

The Torah is a collection of laws concerning sacrifices, the priesthood, the distinction between pure and impure things, vows, impurities contracted by contact with the dead or with lepers, matrimonial alliances, heredity, agricultural customs, the law of blood, etc. Would any one care to say that, if Moses did not write the Torah, all this is posterior to Moses? A hundred times better to say that all this is a thousand, or two thousand years, anterior to him. All of these usages, in part common to all Semites, and partly proper to nomadic or semi-nomadic Semites, were known and approved by God's representative, Moses. Especially did he impress upon all hearts the memory of the blessings of Yahweh.[98]

The discovery of the Code of Hammurabi brought startling confirmation to these views. After the publication of the text by P. Scheil, O.P., Père Lagrange published his own study of the famous code in the *Revue Biblique*[99] in which he pointed out that the law of the great Babylonian king was centuries older[100] and superior to the Hebrew code from the point of view of material civilization, but inferior to it from a moral and religious point of view. In some cases there are close resemblances. Thanks to this marvelous discovery, wrote P. Lagrange, we can now examine the civil legislation of the Hebrews in its full historical light.[101]

Many commentators, both ancient and modern, have thought that the Jewish law was divinely revealed. In that case it should be perfect, yet some of its precepts are inferior in comparison to Greek or Roman law, both products of worldly wisdom. Faced with this, Origen abandoned the literal sense and took refuge in allegory. Calmet concluded that the Scriptures contained secret senses. On the other hand, many of the Fathers admitted some adaptation of strange customs out of divine condescension. After recording this history of exegesis, P. Lagrange shows how a knowledge of the Babylonian code opens the way to a deeper understanding of God's way of acting. Israel had its customs and Moses did not overlook them. The Law did not fall ready-made from heaven. God used things as they were, but in accordance with His justice and holiness. "As a matter of fact, He was not concerned about introducing the refinements of civilization through the law, but He did exclude all rottenness from it." A comparison of the two codes gives an accurate idea of the large part due to the divine intervention, which in religious and moral matters is incontestable; it penetrates into the domain of even civil customs, without, however, destroying or disturbing them.[102]

After this necessary observation, P. Lagrange surveys the development of the Jewish law. It would be contrary to divine Providence, which destroys none of the normal modes of being, to fix the Hebrews fast in an inflexible law, for then "we would have a real misconception to deal with, namely, that progress in religion (which no one denies) took place without exercising any influence upon customs, or that the progress in customs was paralyzed by an inflexible law, or that it would have been forbidden to notice any development in the laws."[103] So just are these observations, and so great are the critical difficulties,[104] that no one now holds that Moses drew up the entire law.[105]

One of the big questions in the Pentateuch, especially in Exodus, is that of the divine names. P. Lagrange wrote on this subject also.[106] Some texts on the use of the word "Yahweh" are hard to explain without an appeal to the distinction of documents. In *J*, God is from the very beginning called Yahweh; in *E*, Yahweh becomes a divine name after the episode of the burning bush (Exod. 3:11–14); and in *P*, it is said that the patriarchs did not know God by the name of Yahweh (Exod. 6:3). *P* is related to *E*. To these apparent divergences, some Catholic authors have evolved unsatisfactory responses, while some independent critics held that the cult of Yahweh was a later borrowing from the Qenites who inhabited the region of Horeb. P. Lagrange rejected the Qenite hypothesis:

It contradicts everything we know about the religious East. Stronger peoples never adopted the religion of inferior peoples. If the Qenites were annexed to Israel, as tradition has it, it was they who, entering into the orbit of Israel, adopted Israel's religion.

Tradition speaks of a theophany on Mt. Horeb. There are differences in the texts. P. Lagrange explains first that tradition did not insist upon the universal use (i.e., by all Israelites) of the name Yahweh and, finally, that a people does not create the name of its God.

The simplest answer is that Moses proposed and explained to the clans who were destined to become a people, a divine name which they already knew. Perhaps it was already in existence in the tribe of Levi. Moses' mother Jochabed bears a name which indicated the worship of Yahweh.[107]

The sensational discovery at Tell el-Amarna, in Egypt, of correspondence carried on between the Canaanite kings and the chancery of the Pharaohs of the fourteenth century B.C., heralded the dawn of a new day for biblical scholars. The correspondence mentions the Khabiru who were then invading Palestine. Khabiru may mean 'Abiri, and many authors, especially M. Loisy, identified them with the Hebrews. All that was necessary was to push back the date of the Exodus; and this might possibly be the answer. However, armed with sound critical and historical sense, P. Lagrange rejects the identification[108] and his observations still prevail. The 'Abiri have not yet invaded our textbooks.

2. GEOGRAPHY

P. Lagrange had perforce to apply his realistic method to geography. He had found and brought into being the Dominican *École Biblique* at Jerusalem (1890), for the purpose of developing and facilitating biblical knowledge by study on Palestinian soil. He himself took the initiative, and it bore much fruit. Knowledge of the sacred places and of the customs confers undeniable advantages on a student of Scripture; so the Dominican school became the model for many others.[109]

In Germany the search for the sources of the Pentateuch was carried so far that history dissolved into thin air because of the continued dissections of the texts and subdivisions of sources whose value was considered suspect. The leader of the critical school, Wellhausen, declared that topographical discussions were a waste of time, and said: "Where Sinai is, we do not know, and the Bible is hardly consistent in the matter. The discussion of the question I recommend to dabblers."[110] Would-be topographers had the Israelites marching across desk maps in quite fantastic itineraries. Cades, Mt. Hor, and other places, were located according to dubious traditions. We now have these places accurately located, but it was not always so; and credit for the immense progress is due to the trips of P. Lagrange, for these marked a really decisive point in the study of the Exodus. The same trips are now made by many professors and students; but these men are followers, not pioneers. It is well to recall this.

A few explorers had already crossed the desert. Palmer, a member of the English Ordinance Survey of Sinai (winter 1868–1869 and 1869–1870), and Trumbull (1881), had been successful in identifying the site of Cades, but their lack of critical biblical knowledge left the localization open to dispute. There was need of a methodical, scientific expedition, and P. Lagrange, becoming explorer, undertook it. In 1893 he made his first trip to Egypt and Sinai, returning to Jerusalem by way of the Negeb. Then, in 1896, he again covered the same territory. Starting from Suez on February 15, he arrived at Serbal and Jebel Musa on the 22nd and 24th; at Cades on March 11; and a few days later, on March 18, reached Jerusalem. The account of this voyage, jotted down day by day as it was being made, appeared in the *Revue Biblique*.[111] Learned topographical discussions, sections devoted to Semitic philology, and erudite investigation alternate with descriptions of grandiose landscapes and tales of picturesque scenes, for when he wished to do so, P. Lagrange, like Pierre Loti, could paint with rich colors.

In the autumn of 1896 he explored Petra, the famous Edomite and Nabatean city. The *École Biblique* had been commissioned by the Academy of Inscriptions and Fine Arts to explore this city and to keep an eye out for an inscription mentioned by ancient travelers and needed for the Corpus of Semitic Inscriptions. It was found by Père Vincent, a member of the expedition, after many days of search. The success of the trip was proved by many useful topographical observations and a rich harvest of texts.[112] Marquis de Vogüé warmly congratulated Fathers Lagrange and Vincent in the name of the Academy.[113]

In 1897, the *Institut de France* authorized P. Lagrange to undertake new epigraphical researches at Petra. The rich booty taken constituted an important contribution to the knowledge of the Nabatean language, history, and religion.[114]

Today trips to Sinai, Cades, and Petra are easy. Automobile roads are maintained by the Egyptian and English governments, and almost complete security is assured by posts of soldiers along the routes. Amman, resting place for tourists going to Petra, boasts a Cook's Hotel with latest conveniences. When P. Lagrange made his trips things were much different: there were long, difficult trips on camel,[115] exposed to all kinds of dangers, to the razzias of robbers or to tribal attacks, in an almost wholly unexplored country. Provisions to last a month had to be carried and immense fatigue was accepted as a matter of course. The ever suspicious Bedouins were not quick to show these strangers the places they asked to see. During the first voyage to the desert, the hostility of the Arabs prevented the biblical caravan from visiting Cades, although they passed close to it. They succeeded in visiting it, after long palavers, in 1896.

But if these trips are now more easily made, they are not nearly so instructive. No more do the voyagers live the life of the desert, slowed down to the measured tread of camels, involving many camps and unhurried contact with the Bedouins. It is not so easy today to attune one's soul to that of the ancient nomads.

From 1898 to 1900, P. Lagrange published the results of his studies concerning the itinerary of the Hebrews. He fixed the landmarks.[116]

Cades, Mt. Seir, and Mt. Hor are to be located, not to the east, but to the west of the Araba and south of the Negeb, contrary to the Jewish tradition represented by Josephus and Onkelos, also to the *Onomasticon* of Eusebius and that of St. Jerome, and, finally to the Moslem tradition. The location of Cades is certain today. Near Cades, which is bathed by an ever flowing spring, are other water places: 'Ain Qusaima, 'Ain Qouderat, 'Ain Nouelleh. Chipped flint instruments and enclosing walls point to prehistoric installations and ancient cultures. More to the north, P. Lagrange explored ancient ruins of Canaanite cities which barred the route of the Hebrews; unfortunately these ruins were destroyed during World War I.[117] Some of his identifications, proceeding from south to north, are these: Mosera (Moseroth), where Aaron died, is Nouelleh; Beeroth is Birein; and Rehoboth, of Genesis 26:22, is Roueibeh.

Punon, which is Fenan today, where the incident of the

brazen serpent took place (Num. 33:42; cf. chap. 21), is another great landmark of the Exodus from Egypt. P. Lagrange discovered and explored the site during the second voyage to Petra. The people of Shobek, north of Petra, told him of a place called Fenan, but no one had ever troubled to look it over. The current opinion had located it to the east of Petra, but actually it was to the northwest.

The names sound exactly alike (Punon and Fenan); and the sound has persisted despite Hellenistic transformations. The site moreover is noteworthy because of the mines.

Synthesizing data gathered from the Septuagint, tradition, and the map of Madaba,[118] P. Lagrange was firmly convinced of this identification. During the persecutions, especially that of Diocletian, many Christians were condemned to the mines and died martyrs' deaths here.

Today three shepherds watch, all unknowing, over these heroic memories and repeat, without comprehending, the name of the old Edomite tribe: Kharbet Fenan! It is true that they have not preserved the memory of the passage of the Israelites, but they are witnesses to the tradition.[119]

Many moderns have tried to locate the mount of God, Sinai, at Jebel Araif, near Cades, or else to the east of the Araba. But, as P. Lagrange has demonstrated, the tradition is firm, and the famous mount must be located at the southern extremity of the peninsula. Knowledge of the actual places, along with the study of tradition, led him to prefer Jebel Musa to the Serbal as being Sinai.

The Bible refers to the Mount of God as Horeb, or as Sinai. P. Lagrange noted that Horeb is used in E and D (except for the canticle of Deut. 33:2), and Sinai in J and P. It is the same mountain, he explained. Horeb may have been called Sinai because of the near-by desert of Sin, or because of the lunar god, Sin, perhaps already adored at that time by the nomads, as he was later on by the Arabs.

It is easy to see that Sinai, being only a name, was applied to the place ordinarily called Horeb, and also that the use of this name was avoided when affinities with a polytheistic cult were known.[120]

The topographical explorations of P. Lagrange brought out the historical value of the Exodus from Egypt, for the topographical details of the Bible correspond to places too well to have been imaginations after the fact.

C. Conclusion: Impressions

Such, in résumé, were the great contributions of P. Lagrange to the study of Moses and his work. His unbiased search for the truth was favorable to apologetics. Some looked upon criticism as a terrible arm raised against the faith, but P. Lagrange did not favor such an absolute rejection of a criticism which does raise real problems. He took from it whatever appeared reasonable and advantageous to the attackers, corrected it, and, with the help of criticism itself, victoriously defended both the Scriptures and the faith. The tables were turned, for the truth contained in the doctrines taught by the Scriptures was not watered down in the least; rather the history of salvation and the reality of Mosaism were brought out into strong relief.

Yet the new position was a startling one, and P. Lagrange naturally became the object of much criticism. The Patriarch of Jerusalem, Msgr. Piavi, denounced to the Propaganda his article on the sources of the Pentateuch, but was advised to keep out of the whole affair. P. Lagrange was quite sure that the article in question, along with others, had been sent to the Holy Office for investigation.[121] No unfortunate consequences followed the complaint. Leo XIII never tired of encouraging the learned scholar. In spite of denunciations and opposition, he named P. Lagrange a member of the Biblical Commission in January, 1903, and, a few days later, instructed the Dominican Master General to summon him to Rome. The trip from Jerusalem to the Eternal City was made with some misgivings, but the welcome which awaited him there put him completely at ease. The Holy Father chose the *Revue Biblique* as the official organ of the Biblical Commission for all Acts published expressly in the Pope's name.[122] Certainly this was not a blanket approval of everything written in the pages of the *Revue*, but it was a kindly, reassuring gesture of favor. More than that, the Pope planned to establish a biblical institute in Rome and to summon P. Lagrange to a place in it.[123]

Some time later, P. Lagrange was anonymously attacked in an article in the *Civiltà Cattolica,* in which broad hints were dropped to the effect that Leo XIII, in his denunciation of dangerous temerity on the part of some Catholic authors, had wished to include P. Lagrange.[124] It would have been strange if the Pope had not in mind Loisy and his pseudonyms which gave the impression that he was a whole school. This time, though he had never before replied to any of the venomous attacks upon him, P. Lagrange took up his pen, for it was his orthodoxy that had to be defended. He recalled Leo XIII's kindnesses toward him, and the zeal of the *Civiltà Cattolica* for the new criticism, up to 1903. Then he concluded simply with the text of a letter Cardinal Rampolla had written to him from Rome. He had offered his humble objections to the project of the Sovereign Pontiff, for, he wrote: "It seemed hard to tear the *Revue Biblique* from the Holy Land which gave it life, and to sacrifice the School of Jerusalem to the new Roman Institute." Cardinal Rampolla replied on June 22, 1903, that his objections had been overruled, and added: "You need fear no evil results, either for the *Revue,* or for the School at Jerusalem, or for your Order. The Holy See has no other intention in this matter than that of showing both you and the Order a sign of its benevolence and esteem. As for the Institute of Higher Biblical Studies, it is clear that your Paternity is not acquainted with all the details. I can assure you, in advance, that you will be fully satisfied when you understand the steps taken by the Holy Father."[125]

Next came the Modernist crisis. The documentary theory was invoked by innovators in a manner far different from that admitted by P. Lagrange, for now even the documents were looked upon with suspicion, or their worth was denied, or their date was drastically lowered. Dogmas and the story of salvation were held to be mere ideas of those times, without objective reality. Moses' part was completely denied. Naturally such proceedings caused anxiety in the authority charged with the care of the Scriptures. P. Lagrange pointed out very well, in his book criticizing Loisy's stand on the gospel and the Church,[126] how some authors destroyed the faith under the pretext of defending it. Faced with the abuses to which the documentary theory of the composition of the Pentateuch had led, and seeing the confusion spread by such abuses in the ranks of both clergy and faithful, the Biblical Commission took action. It recalled and strictly applied to the question of the Pentateuch the principles which must govern the progressive evolution of Catholic doctrine.

It is not *de fide* that Moses wrote the whole Pentateuch, but the opinion is one of those common traditional ones which should not be changed without clearly demonstrable reasons. The Commission, therefore, not underestimating the serious arguments proposed by the critics against the composition of a great part of the Pentateuch by Moses himself, declared that these arguments were not of such value as to justify abandonment of the traditional view. To the question: "Are the arguments proposed by the critics in attacking the Mosaic authenticity of the holy books designated by 'Pentateuch,' of such weight that they provide the right to affirm that these books have not Moses for their author, but were composed from sources which were in large part posterior to Moses?" it replied in the negative.[127] The Commission does not rule out the theory that Moses used secretaries. To the question: "Can it be admitted without prejudice to the authenticity and substantial integrity of the Pentateuch, that in the course of so many centuries, some modifications have occurred: such as additions by an inspired author after the death of Moses, or glosses and interpolated explanations in the text . . ." it replied: Yes, *salvo iudicio Ecclesiae*.[128] Additions or modifications which were added to Moses' *opus,* therefore, are not ruled out by the Commission which, in this response, seems even to invite a new study of the question. P. Lagrange did not feel himself qualified to propose, in a closely reasoned and comprehensive survey, his own distinction between the substantial authenticity of Mosaic legislation and the modifications which under divine guidance developed in the course of time. Finally, the *new* scholars attacked the essential foundation of our faith, the New Testament; hence P. Lagrange turned his attention in that direction.

His studies on the Pentateuch did not occupy his attention to the exclusion of many other questions, as will be clear from the following section.

III. OTHER WORKS

A. *Old Testament*

In 1900, P. Lagrange had launched the project of a complete scriptural commentary designed to meet the scientific needs of our times.[129] The famous collection known as the *Études Bibliques* was the result, and today is recognized as one of the outstanding encyclopedias in its field; year by year it has grown under the active direction of its founder. He himself contributed the first volume of the series: *Le livre des Juges*.[130] In this volume P. Lagrange applied the critical method which we have studied in connection with his studies on the Pentateuch. A translation of the original text, first established with full use of all the resources of textual criticism, occupies the top of the page, and the commentary covers the lower portion. Not that the Vulgate, the official text of the Latin Church, is rejected; in order to be better understood, the Word of God must be made known in its primitive form.[131]

The commentary is philological, geographical, and historical. Copious notes of literary and historical criticism follow in the form of "excursus" after each chapter or number of chapters. Judges, as it stands, is stated to be later than the solemn promulgation of Deuteronomy (621) by Josias; but it is composed of ancient documents which go back to the beginnings of the Israelite royalty. In the text, signs in parentheses single out the sources at a glance. The technical side is more developed than the theological; this was done, not to sacrifice principles to accidentals, or theology to philology or geography, but to divide the work, and to avoid any excess.

Such a study of the sacred text is a great service to theologians and spiritual authors.[132]

The *Revue Biblique* published many other articles by P. Lagrange. He treated many very diverse subjects chosen from the Old Testament, with a competence indicative of his learning.

A comparison of two commentaries on the Psalms — Calmet's (1734), and Fillion's (1893) — showed him where criticism stood, for Fillion was in many places not as far advanced as Dom Calmet. The insufficiency of the current teaching of Scripture was already a source of grave concern for many; and men who carry on their apostolate in intellectual circles can still sense this anxiety.[133]

P. Lagrange adopted Van Hoonacker's proposal that Nehemias precede Esdras.[134] The discovery, a few years later, of the Aramean Jewish papyri, at Elephantine, shed new light on Israelite life in Palestine and Egypt at this period. At once P. Lagrange began to study the texts, and soon journeyed to the island of Elephantine to visit the excavations. His explanations of the famous papyri have become classic.[135]

One of the outstanding miracles of the Old Testament is its messianism, a great fact which holds its unique position "despite all the inquiries of historians of religion. There we see a promise of God which was kept, i.e., a predicted fact."[136] P. Lagrange contributed a number of detailed studies concerning messianic prophecies.[137] The publication of Sully-Prudhomme's *La vraie religion selon Pascal*[138] clearly insinuated that the progress of criticism might well ruin the argument Pascal had drawn from messianic prophecy, so P. Lagrange grasped the opportunity to check the reasoning of the apologist philosopher, to see which of his arguments had lost their value and which remained solid. In this way, he furnished the basis for an argumentation whose real, probative value cannot be ruled out of court by modern criticism.[139]

Next comes the important book of Daniel. The interpretation which P. Lagrange gave to it is clear and satisfactory; it gains new adherents still.[140] The difficult problem of the book's composition is taken up in a later work,[141] where he proposed that the ancient edition of the book had been re-edited at the time of Antiochus Epiphanes — a middle position which meets the difficulties raised by literary and historical criticism.[142]

The *Méthode historique* gives a few general ideas concerning the theology of the Old Testament. A fundamental distinction divides the Old and New Testaments: "In the New Testament, dogma has reached a definitive stage"; it may still develop and become better known, but there is no new revelation. This is quite different from the Old Testament, in which revelation was granted morsel by morsel, and where the essential elements of dogma developed. God tempered the light; step by step He prepared Jewish thought to receive the revelation of Christ, who brought man's religious life "to a truly new phase." There is, consequently, no need to search out all of the New Testament in the Old, but the successive steps can be noted. In Israel's religious history there are four of these steps: the period of the Patriarchs, that of Moses, that of the Prophets, and the post-Exilic period. These are the landmarks in the development of dogma and theology, and each of them corresponds to God's actions and revelations.[143] P. Lagrange's studies on some of the particular points of this development appeared in the *Revue Biblique*.[144]

Two of the topographical studies are especially important. The first is a study localizing the old city of Jerusalem at the time of David. For centuries it was thought to have been situated on the large hill to the west, now called Sion. Studying the texts on the spot, P. Lagrange pronounced from among the probable sites in favor of the tiny hill Ophel, to the south of the actual city. It is difficult for us to appreciate the excitement this caused; objections and attacks came from every side. Where would Solomon have put his cavalry? The hill seemed too small for the mighty glory of the past. But later excavations have proved P. Lagrange correct; the name Sion was first applied to Ophel, then to the grown city, and afterward to the high hill to the west.[145]

Another, less publicized debate arose concerning the site

of Sodom. Some authors maintained that Sodom and the ancient Pentapolis were to the north of the Dead Sea. Professors of the Roman *Institutum Biblicum,* it is true, had found there the remains of a very ancient Canaanite city. Following his methodical way, however, P. Lagrange clearly demonstrated by a study of both text and terrain that Sodom and the Pentapolis should be located south of the Dead Sea,[146] and those who held the contrary view prudently withdrew.

A more complete idea of P. Lagrange's activity in the Old Testament would entail mention of his lengthy reviews, in the *Revue,* of many books written in many languages. In the course of these reviews he refuted many errors, and proposed explanations of texts and difficulties too numerous to mention in this chapter.[147]

B. *Semitism and Judaism*

We introduce here the works of P. Lagrange on Semitism and Judaism only to illustrate his realistic and comparative method. The essential lines have been indicated.[148]

The *Études sur les religions sémitiques* are a veritable *Summa* which reflects the religious atmosphere of the oriental world out of which the Hebrews came, and in which they lived. Famous Babylonian and Phoenician myths, pantheons, beliefs, and rites are examined in their proper perspective. It is a work in which the Bible remains entirely in the background, but it is wonderfully clarified nonetheless. Israel's religion is seen "in its true light, as something both historical and divine." Comparisons can be made to bring out its "striking religious and moral superiority, especially that germ of progress which it bears in its bosom — sure signs of revelation."[149] Similarities of traditions and rites serve only to heighten the contrast of ideas. This, after his articles "L'Hexaméron" and "L'innocence et le péché," which study the details,[150] was the best possible reply to the *Pan-Babylonianism* which insisted on explaining specifically biblical ideas as the result of Chaldean influences.[151]

Again, the Old Testatment milieu was further made

known by the many inscriptions deciphered and published with commentary by P. Lagrange as quickly as they were discovered.[152]

Two volumes, *Le Messianisme chez les Juifs* and *Le Judaisme avant Jésus-Christ,* bring out the Israelite ambitions and ideas in the time of our Lord, and appear as parallel works to the studies of the Greek world which will be mentioned further on. These latter treat of the Hellenistic milieu, both religious and intellectual, into which the primitive Church stepped and lived and grew.

What were the Jewish ideas concerning the Messias? Loisy pictured Christ as the mere mouthpiece of the common messianic and eschatological hopes of his day. Many Catholic authors adopted and now hold this view. They describe the hope of the Jews as something unique; then they show how this hope was realized by Jesus. Thus the cool reception of the Redeemer by the Jews becomes quite inexplicable, and nonbelievers who put their trust in natural evolution can raise the objection that Christ's messianism contains nothing original, for He did nothing more than to realize the expectations of His milieu.

P. Lagrange made a special study of Jewish messianic ideas over and above the indications given in the Scriptures. He sought out the ideas circulating in the minds of Christ's contemporaries concerning the person, work, and time of the Messias, and attempted to find the relationships which existed between the messianic and apocalyptic ideas. He thumbed through Josephus and Philo, read apocryphal apocalypses and ancient rabbinic writings, and studied the Jewish history of the first century. At the end of his enormous literary investigation, he wrote that Jewish theology

was incapable of contemplating the Messias as God without taking away His humanity, and then His only functions would be to judge and preside over the world to come; nor could it consider the human Messias without leaving God out of the picture, in which case He would be the Savior of Israel only. . . . Everywhere questions are raised, but nowhere are there answers acceptable to all.[153]

In His messianic and eschatological teaching, Christ did
not begin with the common faith of His times, for such a
thing did not exist.

True, most of His ideas were actually current, but He grouped
them in a solution so simple that it bears the stamp of His
divinity, especially when it is compared to the prophecies it so
harmoniously realizes.[154]

The bulky *Judaisme avant Jésus-Christ* is not a rehash
of the previous volume, but rather a new and considerable
work, in which history, literature, and the great themes of
Palestinian and Egyptian Jewish theology of the first century
B.C. are brought together for study. P. Lagrange did not
linger over the multiple details already handled by Schürer;
his immediate interest was to trace out the central lines, to
disclose the religious condition of Jews contemporary with
Christ. All this aids our understanding of the origins of
Christianity. To clarify these beginnings, one chapter is devoted to outside influences which were thought to have
affected Judaism after the Babylonian exile.

Merely to consider all that P. Lagrange wrote on inspiration, critical method, the Old Testament, and the Semitic
and Jewish world is to be impressed by a learned and vast
work. Yet this is not all. As Ryckmans of the University of
Louvain said: "His glory consists in having been the champion of truth, in having consecrated his life to the realization
of the ideal of Leo XIII: *ne veritatis impar sit cum errore
concertatio.*"[155] Through him Catholic criticism was restored
to dignity, and to him many Catholics owe their faith.

The Dominicans of the *École Biblique* are friars and
preachers. P. Lagrange left his silent cell, the library, or the
classroom to go to choir for Office. He frequently spoke in
the pulpit of the charming basilica of St. Stephen's during
Advent and Lent. Every month a rosary procession wended
its way through the garden. Evenings and mornings, close
to the tomb of St. Stephen, in the restored basilica where
fifth-century monks once chanted the psalms, there comes

the sound of the divine Office, the Church's prayer. Every night the *Salve Regina,* the procession to the altar of our Lady, and the prayer to St. Dominic, *O Lumen Ecclesiae,* fill the soul with a sense of God's peace. The life of prayer animates the life of study. Intimate friends of Père Lagrange know well the source whence the great master drew his energy.

J. CHAINE
Professor of the Faculté
Catholique de Lyon, France

CHAPTER II

THE NEW TESTAMENT — BEGINNINGS OF CHRISTIANITY

I. PRINCIPLES AND METHOD

THE commentary on the gospel according to *Saint Mark,* published in 1910, was the first of P. Lagrange's great New Testament works. Then came in succession the *Epitre aux Romains* (1916); *aux Galates* (1918); *Evangile selon S. Luc* (1921);[1] *S. Matthieu* (1923); *S. Jean* (1925); the *Synopsis Evangelica* (1926); and, in 1928, the *Evangile de Jésus-Christ,* a synthesis and crown worthy of the great commentaries. It was the second half of his career that saw the appearance of the scientific works on the New Testament. He had, of course, always been interested in the gospels, and as early as 1895 had written two important articles dealing with the sources of St. Luke and with the Infancy of Christ.[2] Still, his own preference, and that of his colleagues, was for the Old Testament, for the history of Israel was being revealed in a new light by studies about the Semitic milieu and by Palestinian archaeology. Another reason was that the burning "Biblical Question," in all its obvious Old Testament bearing, had just been thrown sharply into focus.[3]

It was, however, the urgent need of combating Modernism that caused him to turn to the study of the New Testament. Historical criticism, as applied to the gospels by most of the German critics, led to a conception of Christian beginnings which was contrary to that of the traditional faith. Loisy's works were a brilliant attempt to reconcile his own conception, which he believed to be scientifically necessary, with the essential principles of Catholicism. Historical problems, of capital importance for the faith, were raised concerning the life and teaching of Jesus Christ, concerning Paul's part in primitive Christianity, and many others concerning the origins of Christian theology and worship. Only a critical examination of the New Testament, one armed with all the latest information gleaned from the background in which Christianity was born, would lead to fruitful discussion. Step by step, in the *Revue Biblique,* P. Lagrange followed the latest developments of the modernist crisis in the field of exegesis. He undertook the necessary critical study — it was indeed necessary, for the insufficiencies of the orthodox exegesis, which had lost touch with the real progress in biblical science in the fifty preceding years, were all too evident.

This fact became still more evident when Renan, in his *Vie de Jésus* and in later works on the origin of Christianity, introduced the conclusions of the German exegetes to French readers. Almost all of those who undertook to refute Renan betrayed a regrettable lack of familiarity with the methods and data of New Testament criticism; naturally this weakened considerably the efficacy of their refutations. Realization of this weakness led eventually to a more progressive French Catholic exegesis which can be seen in the works of Vigouroux, Lesêtre, Fouard, and Le Camus, to name only the best-known writers in the revival. Their extensive and thorough learning helped them to reconstruct satisfactorily the historical and geographical framework of the New Testament, but at the same time not enough space was given to genuine criticism; and this is indispensable for a solid discussion of the theories of rationalistic exegesis. Much progress was realized, however, toward the end of the century, and the *Revue Biblique* played a large part in it; yet, Catholic scholars were usually ill-prepared to venture upon the plane of criticism, where independent exegesis, poring over the gospels and apostolic writings, was determined to apply the same scientific methods which had proved so fruitful in the general study of ancient history and writings.

In 1900 P. Lagrange clearly pointed out the work that awaited willing workmen, and traced out a plan and program for a complete commentary on the Holy Scriptures; this he proposed to begin in order to meet "with the needs of our time, and for the utility of Catholic studies."[4] He insisted vehemently upon the need of using the original texts, rather than the Latin Vulgate, as a basis; this would be the job of textual and literary criticism, and would provide scientific bases for the commentary. He urged that the commentary be complemented by works of a general nature on geography, history, archaeology, biblical theology, etc. The volumes which have already appeared are inspired by such ideas, and in these works one sees how the historical method is applied to the study of the Scriptures.

Where the New Testament is concerned, the application was extremely delicate, and the Catholic exegete found his liberty limited. Aside from the question of biblical inspiration, dogma is seldom directly and specifically interested in the historical interpretation of the Old Testament, for there are few dogmatic facts in biblical history. On the other hand, the preparatory and progressive nature of revelation before the coming of Christ excuses the interpreter from seeking out in the Church's dogmatic definitions a rule of interpretation for the study of the "theology of the Old Testament." It is, finally, a rare thing to find the Fathers agreed to such an extent that their interpretation becomes a tradition which must be accepted by Catholic exegetes to the curtailment of their liberty. But the New Testament is different. Literary and critical questions, such as the authenticity of the gospels and apostolic epistles, or how the gospels were composed, may indirectly pertain to faith.

To suppose that when a book is inspired, i.e., is the product of the Holy Spirit, its author is not so important, is to forget that we are not dealing here with the book of Job (as St. Gregory was), a sublime poem whose date does not make much difference, but with witnesses to the miracles and teaching of the very Author of our Faith.[5]

The fourth gospel, for example, has quite another human value if it is the work of St. John, intimate disciple of Christ and eyewitness of what he writes, than it would have if it is the work of some third-generation Christian.[6]

Scientific exegesis and Catholic dogma meet most frequently where historical criticism properly so called is applied to the New Testament, i.e., wherever discussion centers around historical facts related by the evangelists, and wherever the doctrinal texts, which both gospels and apostolic writings contain, are interpreted literally. How can the rights of the authoritative Church, charged with maintenance of Catholic dogma, be reconciled with the legitimate and necessary scientific liberty of exegetes and historians? This was the fundamental problem raised by Modernism and the modernist crisis.[7]

P. Lagrange seized the chance to clarify his position, and proceeded to trace out a middle way between (1) an *excessive conservatism,* for which traditional interpretations were final (this overlooked the progress realized by historical science), and (2) a *radicalism* which advocated the suppression of all contact between a critical and a literary interpretation of the Scriptures. Loisy's critical studies of the New Testament led him to attempt a reconciliation of the most radical positions with the profession of Catholicism; his procedure was to separate absolutely history and faith. He held that the historical Christ could be entirely different from the Christ of faith, and still more different from the Christ of theology. How disengage the figure of this historical Christ? By criticism of the gospels and apostolic writings, in which everything that proceeded from the exaggerations of faith was to be deleted. Such faith, he declared, exerted from the beginning a great influence upon Christian tradition, and led finally to the dogmatic definitions and theological formulas of the Church.

In the first of his conferences at Toulouse (1902), P. Lagrange explained his position in the matter of the relationship between critical exegesis and Church dogma.[8] He took up the subject anew in a detailed commentary[9] on the *Lamentabili* of Pius X, which condemned a great number of propositions set forth and proposed by Modernism in the name of criticism and history. Modernism attempted to resolve the conflict between dogmatic authority and scientific liberty. How? By a rigorous distinction between science and faith, and by complete independence in these fields. The decree of the Holy Office brings out the sheer impossibility of this rigorous distinction; for there are mixed questions, and in this field history cannot contradict dogma. No one who wishes to remain a Catholic can hold, as historically and demonstrably true, any proposition in contradiction with the dogmatic declarations of the Church. P. Lagrange thought a restatement of these principles would dispel the confusion and would lead to the abandonment of a conclusion which, as stated, was impossible. But he had to show that the intervention of the Church, e.g., as here in the decree of the Holy Office, would permit sufficient liberty for a critical and historical research. He first pointed out that history may find itself limited by other than dogmatic truths.

When all the known witnesses have agreed upon the date of an eclipse, no historian would write that the eclipse took place on a day contrary to the calculations of astronomers, calculations which he might not, perhaps, be in a position to verify. Not that astronomy prevails over history, but it does prevent the historian from erring.

Thus it is, for the believer, with Catholic dogma. However, the Church does not oppose to historical facts a purely speculative dogma produced out of thin air. "Actually she upholds the value of documents, which alone can serve as a basis for history and for the facts contained therein." On the other hand, she does not oblige historians to furnish positive proof of a dogmatic truth, because written documents are not the sole resource of the Church, as regards divine acts; there is also tradition.

It can happen that the historical interpretation of a text does not correspond to everything the Church draws out of it, for the Church considers it in its relation to tradition. It would be to misunderstand the freedom of history, not to allow it to be satisfied with a minimum of critical exegesis. No one demands any more than this, on condition that it does not impose this exegesis as a negation of the complete sense fixed by the Church.[10]

The exegete who believes is not bound by his faith to find the actual dogmas of the Church, with all their theological precision, in the pertinent New Testament texts. The

Church admits a real progress in dogma, that is, in the understanding of the revealed truth and in the very formula in which it is proposed. Theologians take an actual dogma as the object of their study: the exegete, however, tries to grasp it in its origin, historical precision, and scriptural expression. It would be asking too much to demand that his analysis should terminate in exactly the same results as that of a theologian, even when he tries to determine the exact meaning of texts in their literal and historical aspects.

In the eyes of a believer, this partial limitation of an exegete's independence in a critical study of the Scriptures, and especially of the New Testament, is quite justifiable. It is further so from a human point of view, according to P. Lagrange; and he developed this idea at length in his two first conferences at Toulouse, where he said:

I maintain that in using the science of criticism without losing sight of the authority of the Church, our method is sound, since it is one of the primary canons of criticism that the environment should be taken into account, and it is precisely in the Church that we have the environment in which the Scriptures appeared. . . . When a Catholic critic firmly resolves never to read into the text anything contrary to Catholic dogma, if this act of docility is a dictate of his faith, it is at the same time in full agreement with the dictates of human prudence. It is impossible ever to understand documents without knowing the society from which they sprang, and here we are dealing with documents coming from a society which has a fixed belief, and texts which regulate that belief. It cannot be claimed on the authority of documents that the faith, to the rise of which they have contributed, or which at least they have contributed to maintain, is no longer the faith of *the* one society distinguished above all others by its attachment to its doctrinal tradition.[11]

It was some thirty years ago that P. Lagrange developed this idea, and it still merits attention; for non-Catholic exegetes are in the habit of assigning the principal role in the origin of the New Testament to the primitive Christian community.[12]

The need of adherence to ecclesiastical, and principally to dogmatic tradition, far from being a source of annoyance for critics and historians, is rather a safeguard. This is quite

evident from the vagaries of independent exegesis of the New
Testament and in the field of comparative Christianity. The
point is clearly brought out by P. Lagrange in a series of
conferences on *Le sens du christianisme d'après l'exégèse
allemande*,[13] given at the Catholic *Institut* of Paris in
1917–1918.

In the first conference, P. Lagrange showed how the
Church, considered from a merely human point of view,
possesses all the necessary elements and method for a proper
exegesis of the New Testament. The Church *is* in the correct
state of mind, namely, that in which the sacred writers lived.
She rests upon an uninterrupted tradition, and upon the synthesis of all the elements governed by her; she provides good,
sound, and clear exegesis, that of common sense.[14] P. Lagrange outlined the various systems which arose in Germany
for the purpose of interpreting the gospels and apostolic
writings; systems often mutually conflicting in many of their
basic assumptions, and which, despite the erudition and
exertion of their authors, in the main constituted *magni
passus extra viam*. Broken loose from all tradition, radical
German exegesis naturally tended to *Unilateralism,* to *Sys-
tematism;* and in the end these systems crumbled, for they
were built up upon an isolated concept and were anchored to
certain texts, being at the same time under the spell of certain
analogies. A few new angles, now perhaps more clearly stated,
were their only useful contributions to science. Their value
was not negligible, but basically they lacked sufficient
strength to provide a good explanation of the origins of
Christianity. Against just such Unilateralism, P. Lagrange
was happily protected by the authority of the Church, whose
success in interpreting Scripture represents "the advantage
of a tested tradition over the impulses, be they ever so
vigorous, of individual minds."[15]

An undesirable counterpart of such an advantage might
occur in the excessive timidity of exegetes who are avowedly
submissive to the doctrinal authority of the Church and to
tradition. A man might confound opinions with ecclesiastical
tradition in its proper sense, and consequently canonize them,

although they have no right to be called truly traditional. Appeal is thus made to theology for a resolution of historical or literary problems, which really do not concern Catholic doctrine, since they clearly lie within the domain of criticism. An exaggerated attachment to the definitive expressions of theology might readily lead to a neglect of the shades of thought and expression often encountered in different parts of the New Testament which deal with the same truth of faith, nuances upon which the critical historian justly insists. This might likewise lead one to underestimate the results achieved in the past fifty years by many historical studies and critical works dealing with the New Testament and with the history of Christianity. P. Lagrange was outspokenly impatient of such timidity, and for his part was confident in genuine criticism and in truly scientific history; for if these avoid with care all *a priori* negations, they cannot contradict Catholic dogma in the certain results they often obtain. He frequently recalled with pleasure the famous letter of Pius X to Msgr. Le Camus (Jan. 11, 1906), in which the Pope first blamed those who accepted suspicious novelties without question, and then condemned those who refused to admit the possibility of a true progress in the understanding of the Scriptures, and preferred to hold strictly to the classical opinions. Moreover, no one has done more than P. Lagrange to prove that a believer, wholeheartedly devoted to Catholic tradition, can handle with fairness and competence a rigorously scientific method in scriptural exegesis and in the study of Christian origins, and can in this field reach results commanding the attention of a science which is independent of all authority.

II. THE CANON AND TEXT OF THE
NEW TESTAMENT

A good example of his principles and methods may be found in the manner in which P. Lagrange studied and resolved the problem of the *New Testament Canon*.[16] The problem is to determine the manner in which the official collection of the twenty-seven so-called canonical writings, which constitute the New Testament received by the Church, was formed. As the word *canon* indicates, these books are *norms,* containing the rule of faith and life which the disciples of Christ ought to follow. The list of these books was fixed by the Council of Trent, and they were solemnly defined as sacred and canonical by the Vatican Council, which stated that they have God for their author, since they were inspired by Him. This is a dogmatic definition, fixing a doctrine from which a Catholic historian may not swerve; but he is free to determine from his study of the documents just how the supernatural fact of the divine inspiration of the whole New Testament was revealed; to point out the principles guiding the Church which welcomed these books but rejected many others; and, finally, to indicate the reasons for the fluctuation of opinion in regard to a few of these books during the first four centuries.

If a scholar were to begin his attempt to determine the criteria used in the formation of the New Testament Canon from the notion of biblical inspiration as it has been elaborated by the theologians, he would have to postulate, for each of these books, a special revelation testifying to the fact that God granted this special charism to the author. Of such a revelation history bears no trace. The Council distinguished between canonicity and inspiration: inspiration is the *intrinsic* cause of canonicity, which is an *extrinsic* trait; and this relationship appears to be a legitimate, dogmatic development. However, from an historian's point of view, it was from the fact of canonicity that the Church moved on to the idea and declaration of inspiration which was already implicit there. On the other hand, since canonicity consists in recognizing an authority similar to that accorded to the Old Testament books, it was applied only to those writings which had an apostolic origin or an apostolic guarantee, for, after all, it was the Apostles who had received the divine light and mission to transmit the gospel, the Word of the Lord, the supreme rule of faith. Such is, in brief, the opinion of

P. Lagrange concerning the origin and character of the Canon of the New Testament.

It is generally admitted that around A.D. 170 there existed in the Church, if not a canon in the strict sense (for the word used in the sense of a "list of sacred books" did not appear until the fourth century), at least a collection of writings which enjoyed a divine authority equal to that of the Old Testament books.[17] That this collection was formed over a period of time is also admitted. It is disputed however whether a New Testament parallel to the Old, and boasting equal authority with it, can be traced to the origin of Christianity. Protestant critics generally deny the fact, and describe the fixation and delimitation of the New Testament in the second century as something new. According to Harnack, for example,[18] the first Christian communities were flooded with edifying writings; these eventually were read in religious reunions as being the work of the Spirit poured out so generously in the New Alliance. But for all of that, these writings were not on a par with the Jewish bible. The present New Testament represents the remains of this primitive literature, drawn up by the Church as a written rule to offset heresy. The make-up of the New Testament, consequently, is the result of the Church's struggle against the Gnostics, and in particular is a reaction against Marcion, whose collection of the sacred books was purged of all that did not fit in with his own doctrine.

In opposing this theory, P. Lagrange maintained as an historical fact that

as soon as the Church became conscious of her existence as the society of the faithful believing in Jesus Christ, she was confident that she possessed within herself sufficient authority to produce — not by human but by divine power — books equal to, and in authority even superior to, the books of the Old Testament; and the Church had received such books.

It was not much before the middle of the second century that men recognized the complete assimilation of the New Testament to the Old by the technical formula: "It is written.''[19] But it is clear that from the start, the gospel, i.e., the teaching of Christ as transmitted by the Apostles, was considered of an authority superior to that of the Old Testament writings.

Commissioned to teach the truth in the name of Jesus Christ, the Apostles preached or communicated this word by writing. Epistles which pronounced judgment on the value of the Old Testament were accepted.[20] This is clear enough and, after all, was there anything in the work of an Apostle which made it less sacred than that of a prophet?

The divine authority which accompanied the person and teaching of Christ was extended to the gospels containing His words and deeds. It is true that the gospels written by Mark and Luke were not, properly speaking, apostolic writings; but they had an apostolic guarantee. Mark was considered to be "Peter's interpreter"; in Luke's work, Paul's good tidings may be discerned. Lacking a direct apostolic origin, no writing could be ranked with the normative writings as possessing divine authority, unless it had at least some apostolic guarantee. This is clear enough from the fact that the *Prima Clementis,* written by St. Clement to the Corinthians in A.D. 95 in the name of the Roman church, was not received into the Canon (except, at first, in a few churches), despite the great dignity of its author, and the assurance with which he spoke in God's name. Yet the epistle frankly affirms the exceptional authority of the apostles and their especially approved collaborators.

The first principle of discrimination in the formation of the Canon, viz.: apostolic origin or, at least, guarantee, is complemented by another, viz.: the manifestation of apostolic origin by common usage in the churches. It is not for Harnack to say that the use of apostolic books in liturgical functions, along with the books of the Old Testament, ended in attributing to the apostolic writings the same dignity as that enjoyed by those of the Jewish bible. Better the other way around: they were read in the Church because of their recognized and exceptional authority. At a later date, when the question was raised concerning the sacredness of the book, the argument was based on the fact that it had been read in liturgical reunions. "Such a reading conferred no value upon the book, but was nonetheless an indication of its intrinsic value; its value was already recognized, since the book either came from the Apostles or was recommended by them."[21]

Once the Church possessed writings whose authority was based on apostolic guarantee, the next step was to codify the collection. The formation of a homogeneous and unchangeable body of sacred writings was possibly hastened by Marcionism and Montanism, to name but two of the heresies. Yet even these were a mere contributing cause, according to P. Lagrange, for the essential thing was the *principle of apostolicity*, which on the one hand maintained the authority of the writings against Marcion, who rejected some of them simply because they were so favorable to the Old Testament, and, on the other hand, gave the lie to the oracles of the Montanist prophets, oracles proposed as a revelation supplementing the gospels and as equally to be venerated, since they were supposed to come from the Holy Spirit.

This principle was admitted everywhere, apparently, at the close of the second century. It did not, however, lead immediately to a universal and final canon of the New Testament. In some churches and among the ecclesiastical writers, over a period of three centuries, there was hesitation and doubt about some books which in the end were universally admitted: Hebrews, James, Jude, 2 and 3 John, 2 Peter, and especially the Apocalypse.[22]

Some of these books do not begin with the name of an Apostle; as, for example, Hebrews and the short Johannine epistles. It is possible that, elsewhere, this name was an artifice. Furthermore, it was possible to cast doubt upon the apostolic origin of writings whose doctrine did not seem to be in harmony with that of the Church. This happened in the case of the Apocalypse of St. John, in which some authors thought they found a dangerous millenarianism. In this brief exposition it is impossible to enter into a discussion of all the details of these arguments, but P. Lagrange has done so in his painstaking study of the pertinent ancient documents. Emerging from that study is the principle which allayed passing or local doubts concerning the canonicity of some of the books, namely, the Church's resolve to conserve without addition everything marked with apostolic guarantee.

The problem raised by the constitution of the New Testament is not, as some Protestant critics put it: How did the New Testament books become Holy Scripture? Rather it is: How did the Church resolve her doubts concerning some points in the writings (superior to the Old Testament from the beginning) of the Apostles or of those guaranteed by them. The answer is: by her tradition. And modern critics have yet to prove that she was wrong.

The first principle formulated by P. Lagrange, in his article (already cited, *RB*, 1900) announcing a vast commentary on the Bible, was that the commentary be based, of necessity, not on the Latin Vulgate of St. Jerome, but on the original texts. The Vulgate has been established as the official ecclesiastical text and was declared authentic by conciliar decree. Because of its recognized substantial conformity with the original texts, and because of its use by the Church, which guarantees the exactness of its doctrinal affirmations, the Vulgate remains a secure foundation for the essential study of Scripture, i.e., the study of religious truth; it should hold first place in all theological and liturgical usages of the Bible. But when the Scriptures must be studied historically and critically, there is need to take hold of them in the original texts. To look at these texts only through the Vulgate would not be to know them as they should be known, "in all their concrete reality, in the nuances contained in their own language, in the genius of their tongues, and in the secret of their literary composition."

To get back to the primitive Greek text of the New Testament, it is necessary to consult the host of witnesses that have come down to us: Greek manuscripts of parchment or papyrus, old versions which are represented by a considerable number of manuscripts, and citations by ancient authors. The innumerable variant readings found here are of little exegetical importance; but it is by using the materials furnished by these manuscripts that textual criticism attempts to establish, as nearly as possible, the original text. The task has not yet been completed in a manner satisfactory to all, and a lack of harmony centers about both conclusions and method.

When P. Lagrange began his labors, Protestant and Catholic Greek editions of the New Testament both reproduced the *textus receptus*. This text, edited by Elzevir (1633) and Robert Estienne (1546–1551), traces its lineage to that of Erasmus; it was nothing more than the text current in the Eastern churches in the fifteenth century.[23] New discoveries of old manuscripts, along with critical progress in the eighteenth and nineteenth centuries, proved this text to be without scientific value. Since then Lachmann (1831–1850), Tischendorf (1841–1872), and Westcott and Hort (1881), have published critical editions fortified with important critical apparatus, and all of them have proposed texts much closer to the original than the "received text." Westcott and Hort's edition met with great acclaim, and the text established by these two learned Englishmen was widely sold and popularized in pocket-sized editions, such as that of Nestle.

In undertaking his commentaries on the New Testament, P. Lagrange did not feel himself obliged to establish his basic text by personal research. For scientific and practical reasons he chose the Westcott and Hort text; where necessary, he pointed out less happy "readings," and was content to modify the places where the English editors were clearly influenced by their personal religious convictions. But as time went on, he was led to occupy himself in increasing measure with this problem, because of the new systems of textual criticism proposed, for instance, by H. von Soden or Kirsopp Lake, or because of the new witness of the papyri, of which that of Chester Beatty is a remarkable example. He finally published the conclusions of his own personal research.[24] We know his principles and method from several articles in the *Revue*, particularly that of October, 1933: "Projet de critique textuelle rationnelle du Nouveau Testament."

The edition of Westcott and Hort exerted a profound influence on the direction of later research because of its classification and evaluation of the manuscripts published by Tischendorf. The Greek manuscripts were first classified and then arranged in families. Since the received text, the official Vulgate of the Greek church, was derived from the recension of the New Testament made by Lucian of Antioch toward the end of the third century, this type of text is called the *Syrian*. The *Western* type is an older form of the text, so named because along with codex *D* it is represented by the old Latin versions. This text was thought to be the result of an intentional revision, and consequently was to be considered suspect. The *Neutral* text, so called because it manifests no particular tendency and because it does not derive from a version but from the original, was represented by the codexes Vaticanus and Sinaiticus. An Egyptian revision of the neutral text gave rise, in the third century, to the *Alexandrian* type. Later critical texts, like that of von Soden, which was based on a new and very extensive arrangement of the witnesses in a system quite different from that of Westcott and Hort, have not lessened the value of the text they established; that is why P. Lagrange adopted it as a basis for his commentaries. Later criticism, however, has shaken one of the essential bases of their theory in establishing that the *Neutral* text is itself the result of an Egyptian revision, perhaps that of Hesychius.[25] The antiquity and value of certain variants of their *Western* text[26] which might well antedate the systematic revisions[27] have also been brought out.

How shall new progress be made in the fixing of the text of the New Testament? Almost all agree upon the fundamental critical principle: "The establishment of the text is a function of the history of the text."[28] P. Lagrange plainly stated that the hypothesis of three or four revisions should always be the starting point. Then comes the task of classifying the manuscripts into families, investigating their genealogy, and determining their origin and worth. Dom Quentin, the learned Benedictine in charge of the work on the Latin Vulgate text, recommended a wholly objective, almost mechanical, method. After the family division, he held, would come the reconstruction of the archetype of each family, which would be as close to the original as we can get while using the present manuscripts. The result "will be infinitely more authentic and justifiable than all the more or less arbitrary choices of unrestrained internal criticism."

To this method of Dom Quentin, P. Lagrange opposed what he liked to call a "rational textual criticism." There is the preliminary business of grouping the manuscripts into families and of passing judgment on the relative value of each family. Then, there is a choice made of the variants in each particular case; and the choice is based upon such rational criteria as the exegetical quality of the variants and considerations of the motives which influenced textual revisions to such an extent that they led to a type of witnesses. The method is of necessity eclectic to some degree.[29]

The best type of text invariably is type *B,* as P. Lagrange calls it, of which the principal witness is codex Vaticanus. This is not a neutral text, as Hort maintained, but a revision, inspired less than the others by the desire to present the text in its clearest and most attractive form, and more careful to obtain the most authentic text. The so-called Caesarean text is still of uncertain origin. P. Lagrange believed he had found its prototype (at least for St. Mark) in the Chester Beatty papyrus; at any rate, it was a revision much influenced by the needs of Christian preaching, depending apparently upon the traditions of *B* and *D.* The latter (*D*) appears to be made up of witnesses of the so-called Western type, and preserves a very ancient tradition; but it is characterized by a tendency to touch up the primitive text in the interests of harmony and amplification.

Whatever importance or interest may attach to these problems, P. Lagrange consistently held for the marvelous integrity of the books of the New Testament, which have come down to us with but slight changes and are substantially the same as when they were first written. More recent works of textual criticism and new discoveries like that of the Beatty papyrus (certainly previous to A.D. 250) bear out this fact.

The liberties taken by the ancients, and which we can recognize by their daring, bear unimpeachable witness to the limits to which their authors were held, and testify against the pretended origin of the sacred books by successive fragments, by alterations, and by editorial handling.

Thus does textual criticism join up again with literary criticism, and lead it away from those radical theories which are, unfortunately, too much in favor among the "liberal" exegetes.

III. THE NEW TESTAMENT AND LITERARY CRITICISM

In her ancient tradition (Fathers and ecclesiastical writers of the first centuries), the Catholic Church possesses information concerning the origin, date, and author of every book in the New Testament. Only recently was the worth of such testimony called into doubt; the break with the past was undertaken by non-Catholic scholars who, by preference, sought for the answer to the origin and composition of the New Testament by internal criticism. As some conclusions were reached which were incompatible with the traditional position, Catholic exegetes for a long time looked upon the workings of internal criticism with undisguised suspicion, detecting within it the lurking menace of subjectivism. At the same time, the preference of ecclesiastical authority was generally given, in cases under dispute, to the conclusions of external criticism.[30]

P. Lagrange was one of the Catholic pioneers who boldly applied the methods of internal criticism to the study of the New Testament, without, however, scorning external criticism. In literary questions, he pointed out, the old traditions were not equivalent to a dogmatic tradition; and yet a very minute study of tradition serves as introduction in all his commentaries. In these careful studies he attempted to distinguish what pertained to the genuine primitive tradition from secondary and later elements, which were naturally of lesser authority.[31] He was convinced that Catholics would have to follow the critics on to their own field of literary criticism in order to defend the tradition efficaciously; one of his greatest services was to show in his own works on the New Testament that internal criticism, if properly exercised, does not lead to conclusions contrary to the essential points of authentic ecclesiastical tradition. Apologetical needs are not the only ones which demand internal criticism of the sources; this is a necessary condition of progress in the historical understanding of the texts also.

The history of theology itself (even if dogmatic theology shows little interest in the matter), and all history in general, depends upon the relationship of parallel works, dates of documents, determination of literary genus, and often even on the distinction of sources.[32]

Literary criticism of the texts is, as such, independent of their dogmatic or historical interpretation. It would seem, then, that believing and non-Catholic critics would meet upon common ground, that is, agree at least upon the essential points of the problems raised by the editing of the New Testament, in spite of their different beliefs. Such agreement is rarely realized, and the solutions reached by P. Lagrange at the conclusion of his research differed very much from the solutions given by non-Catholic critics.[33] The reason for this — and we wish to emphasize the point before going any further — is to be sought in the principles or suppositions, either expressly or implicitly stated, which govern literary criticism, and whose harmful influence and questionable value P. Lagrange frequently denounced. Many critics, in their hunt for "sources," explained the use made of written documents in much too mechanical a way; as if various editors, who were little more than compilers, servilely reproduced the teaching found in their sources. P. Lagrange stoutly maintained, especially in connection with the gospels, that we are treating with *real authors,* who, even when they followed their sources closely, made free use of them and adapted them to suit the purpose they had in mind. Sometimes for purely literary reasons they even modified their form. He pointed out the obstinate prejudice of many radical critics, so quick to discover contradictions and incoherence in the texts and then classify them as interpolations, suppressions, or transpositions. Conservative exegetes may perhaps be overready to harmonize and reconcile everything and to de-emphasize what might be difficult; but the other method provides an easy road to subjectivism and leads to wholly arbitrary mutilation of the text.[34]

Such divergence among the authors is also due to the fact that literary criticism can hardly be separated from historical criticism, where strict objectivity can be maintained only with difficulty. The solution of a literary problem may entail historical consequences which may favor, or oppose, this or that system or theory; on the other hand, conjectures concerning the origin and evolution of Christianity will unfailingly influence the determination of the date, author, or character of the various books in the New Testament. In this connection P. Lagrange never tired of pointing out how the common postulate of all rationalist exegetes, the *a priori* denial of the supernatural (although they would resent the charge), continually crops up in discussions of problems of a literary order. Thus, for example, the accounts of miracles are of necessity to be considered as legends; consequently they are attributed to a rather late editor, for legends simply must have time to take form.[35]

P. Lagrange likewise denounced another vice of reasoning frequently encountered in liberal circles. It is that peculiar *petitio principii,* discernible whenever authors separate and date the documents by comparing them with the successive steps of the evolution of Christianity, according as they conceive it; but this conception is itself based on their literary analysis of the texts of the New Testament.[36] For his part, P. Lagrange tried, wherever possible, to distinguish between problems of a literary and historical order. The processes of composition, use of sources, etc. (the literary problem), were tested by application of literary criteria, i.e., analysis and comparison of the texts, comparative studies of language and style, etc. Appeal was made to history only to check the findings of the literary analysis, and especially in order to furnish chronological information which might permit the approximate dating of the composition of the books. This is the method which he pursued in his commentaries on the first three gospels, and in particular in his study of the relationship of these gospels to one another, commonly known as the Synoptic problem.

A. *The Synoptic Problem*

Catholic commentators were, for a long time, more interested in trying to harmonize the parallel passages of the first three gospels in an historical way than to explain their literary similarities and differences. It was generally admitted that each evangelist had in his own way made use of elements furnished by the common oral tradition, or primitive catechesis, in which the memory of Christ's deeds and words were enshrined. At the same time, it was conceded that each evangelist might possibly have made use of the work of his predecessor, holding to the traditional order of Matthew, Mark, Luke, and John. On the other hand, independent critics interpreted the mutual dependence of the synoptics as a necessary basis for any explanation of their mutual relations, but parted company with the tradition of the Church by maintaining the priority of Mark over Matthew and Luke, which they consider to be proved, (*a*) by the more primitive tone of his theology, marking an early stage in the divinization of Christ, and (*b*) by the use made of Mark by the editors of Matthew and Luke. Moreover, the postulate of another written source is required to explain the similarities of Matthew and Luke in passages not contained in Mark. This second source many critics hold to be a Greek translation from the Aramaic, and is designated either as *Logia* or simply *Q*.[37]

This theory, called the *two source* theory, allows for some of the divergences which have to do either with the unity of the second gospel, or with the nature of the second source. Since one part of our actual Mark finds no parallels in either Matthew or Luke, some critics postulated a *Proto-Mark*, a first draft less complete than our present gospel, which served as source for Matthew and Luke. As for the nature of this second source, some hold that it was made up exclusively of discourses; others, that it contained narrative portions as well, and was thus used by St. Mark.

One of the principal reasons why P. Lagrange began his commentaries on the Synoptics with the *second* gospel, was the need of following the critics onto their own ground, and of taking as a working hypothesis (without thereby prejudicing the solution) the theory of two sources so commonly held by them.[38] What he really tried to do was not to solve the Synoptic problem (for this supposes a profound study of Matthew and Luke also), but to determine Mark's characteristics, and to verify the tradition which makes of him the disciple of Peter, whose preaching Mark's work does little more than reproduce. The *unity* of the work is affirmed after a very minute study of Mark's style (vocabulary, syntax, and especially his manner of composition).[39]

These studies led P. Lagrange to reject the theory of a Proto-Mark, as well as the more recent theory (especially Loisy's) of various strata of documents which were eventually united in a single work. Judging from a close examination of its Semitic expressions, it would appear that Mark is not a translation of an Aramaic text (it is not that full of indications; and yet the unmistakably Semitic tone of the Greek supposes that the author at least reproduced an Aramaic catechesis. The few Latinisms in Mark are no difficulty if, as tradition holds, the author wrote at Rome for Latin readers. Further, he seems to have only oral sources.[40] The accounts are precise and full of picturesque details; if their author was not an eyewitness himself, he was a good echo of one. His purpose was not dogmatic, as St. Paul's was;[41] neither was it directly apologetical nor strictly historical. His gospel was that of the primitive Christian catechesis. In the first edition of his commentary, P. Lagrange held that Mark wrote after the deaths of Peter and Paul, relying on the text of St. Irenaeus.[42] While studying the third gospel, however, he became convinced that St. Luke knew and used the second gospel as we now have it; and this led him to conclude that the third gospel and Acts were written before Paul's death. In the second edition (1920) of Mark, he modified his position, abandoning Irenaeus' testimony as being more the result of a conjecture than the authentic echo of tradition.

1. MARK AND LUKE

The Synoptic problem received direct treatment in P. Lagrange's commentary on St. Luke. In the searching introductory chapter he deals with Lucan sources and takes up the relation of Luke to Mark. The existence of Markan sections[43] constituting a large part of the third gospel cannot be adequately explained by the hypothesis of a common oral tradition common to the two evangelists, but rather indicate a close literary dependence of Luke on Mark. In these sections Luke follows Mark's order exactly, without omitting a single passage or important idea; whereas, in the parallel passages of Matthew, the order is altogether different. Moreover, these sections have their own peculiar stamp, and are clearly distinct from other parts of Luke. Of course, even in these sections there are omissions, additions, or transpositions;[44] nowhere does he reproduce the text of Mark with a copyist's slavishness.

All of this may be readily explained if Luke is looked upon as an author and not as a compiler; as one who used sources without being their slave, and who adapted his borrowed material to the plan he had in mind, or even to his literary tastes.[45] One whole part of the third gospel is without parallel in Mark. In sections common to the first three gospels, those consecrated to the baptism, Passion, and Resurrection of Christ, Luke frequently departs from Mark. But this proves only that he used other sources to complete what he had borrowed from Mark, and sometimes preferred these other sources (for reasons which can often be discovered by a careful examination of detail) to his principal source. This independence of Luke with regard to Mark in certain sections serves to bring out more clearly the phenomenon of his borrowing, but does not rule out his dependence in other places.

2. MATTHEW AND LUKE

The relationship of the first and third gospels is a much more delicate problem, and P. Lagrange did not advance a very positive solution for it.[46] The almost unanimous opinion of the critics is that the resemblance between these two gospels is due to the fact that Luke and Matthew both followed a common source; both, then, were a combination of information drawn from this source and of material taken from the second gospel (Mark). This theory goes contrary to the traditional thesis that the first gospel has its own unity and is anterior to that of St. Mark.[47]

P. Lagrange held that, if by itself criticism cannot positively establish the traditional thesis, neither can it oppose any decisive argument against it; it can even be used to maintain it. He admitted, then, the existence of an Aramaic work of St. Matthew, substantially identical with our first gospel, which existed before the second gospel was published. Did Luke know and use this document? The question cannot be answered absolutely or in a very affirmative way. Here is what P. Lagrange has to say:

> We can see no decisive argument against Luke's dependence on Matthew; but in any case such a dependence has been subordinated to his preference for Mark, wherever he could use him. All in all, the best answer is perhaps to suppose that Luke did not have our canonical Matthew before his eyes, but knew at least some extracts of it in Greek, composed of the discourses in their actual order and such as they are (except for a few retouches) in the text of Matthew.[48]

3. MATTHEW ARAMAIC

In the commentary on Matthew, especially in the important introductory chapter three (XXXII–CXLIX), P. Lagrange takes up the question which dominates the whole Synoptic problem: the existence of an Aramaic gospel of Matthew, its precedence over our second gospel, and the relationship of our Greek Matthew to this primitive gospel.

The first postulate of the critical theory is the existence of an Aramaic writing called Q, supposed to be the common source of Matthew and Luke in the parallel parts of their gospels. However, P. Lagrange pointed out that if this Q was made up only of the parallel passages of the first and third gospels, i.e., many discourses, and a few stories without any bond connecting them,[49] the result would be a *"non-sens, une non-chose,"* or again, a torso, and however beautiful the torso, it would not have been composed in such a mutilated condition. A text obtained by such manipulation must necessarily be completed; and no one can fix the limits of this hypothetical source for, "by the law of good sense and good taste, it annexes to itself the whole of St. Matthew.[50] In other words, it is transformed into Matthew Aramaic."

The critics argue that the Greek original of the first gospel cannot be a translation from an Aramaic gospel, and their first argument is based upon the factor of style: Matthew's Greek is not that of a translator. . . . It is not always easy to distinguish, P. Lagrange replied, between a Greek text translated from a Semitic one, and an original Greek text written by a Semite. But in order to answer the objection, he undertook a thorough study of the Semitisms contained in our first gospel. His conclusion — and it has probability in its favor — was that our Matthew Greek text gives the impression of a translation, rather free, it is true, of an original Aramaic text. It must be admitted that the Greek translator knew Mark's gospel and attempted to follow his text; which explains why the Old Testament in parallel passages is usually cited according to the Septuagint, but elsewhere according to the Hebrew text. This likewise explains the many cases where the choice of words or expression indicates a literary dependence on Mark.[51]

Another and more specious argument is drawn from the diverse character and aspect of the first two gospels. Matthew's accounts are colorless and lack that touch of reality which makes Mark so vivid. Some take this to mean that the author of the first gospel composed a doctrinal work, utilizing the previously published gospel of Mark, and that the author was not himself an apostle or an eyewitness. To this P. Lagrange replied: If Matthew was an historical work composed on the same plan as Mark, it would seem that it was later than, and a development of, Mark. But his purpose was didactic and apologetical, and not historical, properly speaking. His intention was to sustain Christ's disciples in their faith, by defending it against Jewish attacks, and by clarifying the teaching of Jesus. He brings in the facts only to help manifest the doctrine. . . . The first gospel, being the work of a man with a speculative mind, has little in it that would reveal its author to us as an eyewitness; but he was one, just the same, as tradition has always claimed him to be. There are some eyewitnesses who, though they are very serious, cannot see or express all the details of the facts.

The critics find it most unlikely that the first Christian scripture should have been a systematic and doctrinal work. They prefer to look upon Mark's gospel, so direct and concrete, as the first biographical sketch of Jesus. To this objection also P. Lagrange had a very interesting answer. Taking a leaf from the latest development of criticism — the *Formgeschichtliche Schule* — he inquires what the evolution of the Christian tradition and gospel doctrine should have been, judging from the probabilities of general literature, and from the conditions of the primitive Church. The answer: Such an evolution moved steadily forward in the direction of positive history.[52] Controversial writings, therefore, and apologetics, founded on the Scriptures, would have been the first need of the Christian community, for the disciples had to have answers for the Jews; the history could wait. It was to fill this need that the gospel of Matthew was written. It contains the literary genera found in Jewish and even contemporary Greek literature: collections of sayings, apothegms, controversies, parables. Mark's accounts belong rather to the category of news. Both Matthew and Mark used the same oral catechesis, which was by then, surely, already partly fixed in writing; but each used it in keeping with his own plan and temperament. After them came Luke, whose gospel marked a new step toward history in the Greek mode, combining a preoccupation for chronological and geographical outline with a harmonious grouping of the facts and with a psychological historical development.[53]

Another indication of the priority of the first gospel is the doctrine it contains. Many critics claim that it is characteristically Judaeo-Christian, but P. Lagrange preferred to say that the author was a pre-Judaeo-Christian, or one who lived before Judaeo-Christianity became a theory. He admits that Matthew is less markedly universalist than Mark concerning the call of all men to Christianity; but, although some critics maintain that it does, his gospel does not mark a regression toward a position which the Church had outgrown; rather it corresponds with a previous situation in which no pronouncement was necessary. "He is certainly not Pauline, but neither is he a reactionary against Paul. He is pre-Pauline, free of the preoccupations to which Mark bears witness." P. Lagrange did not try to fix the exact date of composition of Matthew's gospel; but he says it can be affirmed that the first gospel, in its Greek dress, is prior to the destruction of Jerusalem in A.D. 70.[54]

B. *The Johannine Question*

With almost unanimous voice, modern criticism rejects the tradition which attributes the fourth gospel, the Apocalypse, and the three Johannine epistles to St. John the Apostle. The oneness of authorship in these works is contested by the greater number of the critics, and some of them look upon the fourth gospel as a patchwork of fragments having neither the same author nor the same date. Most critics agree that the fourth gospel has little or no historical value in reconstructing the life and doctrines of Christ. Renan ridiculed the historicity of the discourses it contains, and set them apart from the accounts; these latter were so full of Semitic coloring and knowledge of the Palestinian milieu that they appeared worthy of credence. The extreme radical critics, however, look upon the entire fourth gospel as a purely symbolic work which contains an elaborately worked-out theology; as such it is pronounced worthless for the historian of Jesus.

In order to answer the critics, P. Lagrange ventured upon their field to study the fourth gospel as an historian would. For a beginning he chose the tradition. Two undeniable facts stand out. On the one hand, the fourth gospel was universally received in the Church as a sacred writing;[55] on the other, it appeared to be the work of an Apostle, of a specially privileged Apostle, although the author does not name himself. It would have been impossible for an anonymous editor to have his work universally accepted as the work of John the Apostle; new works, lacking guarantees, were not received as apostolic.[56] To attribute this work to St. John, therefore, seems justified by authentic tradition.[57]

Now to apply this information to the gospel itself. Vocabulary[58] and the manner of exposition and development, led P. Lagrange to conclude that the gospel had only one and probably a Jewish author;[59] more precisely, a Palestinian author, for the accuracy of the numerous topographical indications of the fourth gospel could have been borrowed from no one, surely not from the Synoptics. Moreover the author has an exact knowledge of Jewish doctrines and customs.[60] To offset these arguments, so favorable to the Johannine authenticity of the fourth gospel, there is one notable difficulty upon which many critics base their arguments: the startling difference between John and the Synoptics in dealing with facts or doctrine. The Synoptics record many incidents but relatively little doctrine, and the doctrine is usually expressed in concrete fashion by parables or comparisons; but in John there are a few facts almost completely ignored by the Synoptics, and these are developed at length with a clearly symbolical intention, together with numerous discourses which present profound doctrines in abstract, theological language.

P. Lagrange does not dispute the symbolical character John gives to his accounts, but he insists on their probability. "Solidly fixed on the ground," anchored in a geographical, historical, well-determined chronological framework which can be checked, they are anything but transpositions of an idea under the guise of history.[61] Neither St. John nor the Synoptics attempted to report, *textually*, the words used by Jesus; it should be recognized that, in the Johannine discourses, there is much that is personal to John. This will appear from a comparison of the style of Jesus' words, and that of John's, in his first epistle; the resemblance necessarily supposes that St. John entered actively into the form of the style of his gospel. P. Lagrange, at any rate, thought that a literary analysis could lead to a clear distinction between Christ's teaching and the theology of the Apostle, and this, even in some of the doctrinal pages of the fourth gospel. He thought, for example, that John spoke in his own name, and not for the Baptist or Christ, in chapter 3:15b–21; 31–36, and 12:44–50; that these sections are actually John's commentary, although they seem to be a development of the discourses in which they appear. Aside from the theology developed in the prologue and these few passages, the teaching of the discourses placed on the lips of Jesus is not much different from that of the Synoptics, making due allowances, of course, for the differences in discourses of controversy and those of intimacy with the disciples, for naturally these would not be the same. The theologian, then, meaning by this the author of the fourth gospel, has not swallowed up the witness, either in the discourses he records, or in the facts which he relates.[62]

IV. THE NEW TESTAMENT AND HISTORICAL CRITICISM

In the field of literary criticism, the efforts of P. Lagrange had chiefly centered on the problem of the origin and composition of the gospels; in the field of historical criticism, it was the value of the gospels, considered as manuscript sources of the life and person of Jesus, to which he gave his full attention. Here there is no problem for the theologian and believer, who look upon the gospels as inspired; they would profit much, however, by determining through critical examination the exact kind of history the authors intended to write. Application of the general rules of criticism, in such a way as to place beyond all doubt the value of these manuscripts — at least as regards their essential message — is also of great importance for the apologete, who has to use the gospels as ordinary human documents, in order to establish the historical basis of the Catholic argumentation.

For the past hundred years, critics have been influenced by the persistent rationalistic prejudice against the possibility of miracles.[63] They have generally belittled the historical value of the gospels, denying that they are the work of eyewitnesses, or denouncing the influence of the faith on them;

the faith, whenever it did not create the facts out of nothing, is supposed to have transfigured their reality.[64] Liberal interpretation, however, conceded that St. Mark's gospel had some serious historical value. Of course, they said, Mark wrote according to the beliefs of the primitive community, and was influenced by its faith and interpretation of the data, but less so than the other evangelists. In his story, they say, Christ is still so human a figure that he can be recognized as a pure human being (Mark relates a few incidents which do not harmonize well with the divinity of Christ); on the other hand, the general lines of his story are set forth with undeniable probability, and can be considered as historical enough. Succeeding critics, following Wrede, found Mark to be almost as dogmatic in tendency as the author of the fourth gospel is supposed to be; his so-called historical document would actually be a legendary record of the dogma of Jesus the Messias. The most recent criticism has emphasized this skepticism concerning the historical value of Mark. It is a dogma of the new school that the early Christian community created the gospel story under pressure of apologetic or religious needs; as a result, the gospels are echoes of tradition, and teach only the faith and life of this community; but they provide no certain historical information concerning Jesus, his works, or his teachings.[65]

Again and again, P. Lagrange was obliged to discuss the principal argument of negative criticism. He does not stop to argue the *terminus a quo,* for all admit that the gospels are an echo of the faith of the evangelists and their readers. "The evangelists are not ordinary writers of history; they suppose belief and wish to awaken it," he says; and this is far from admitting that the whole content of the gospels is a creation of faith. What should be explained is how faith in the divinity of a man, about whom (thus the theory) hardly anything was known, ever came into being at all; then, by what means the community fabricated a human history for this Jesus whom it worshiped; then, how to determine the origin of the elements which entered into this history.[66] There have been many attempts to explain how this could come about, but thus far none has been satisfying or acceptable, as, indeed, the defenders of the system are willing to admit. "There is no reason to be surprised at this, and still less is there any hope of drawing anything favorable to tradition out of it,"[87] for if the theory has not given a definitive explanation of the formation of the gospel tradition, it has at least established the fact that the gospel texts are "improbable and contradictory."

To meet the new argument, the basis of all critical attacks on the historical value of the gospels, P. Lagrange proceeded to a minute examination of each supposed improbability and contradiction. We cannot, obviously, reproduce his conclusions here (they are not all of the same value), but what he has to say, in his commentaries, springs from an exceptional knowledge of the gospel background and of general history, and is of great value for exegesis and apologetics. The discussion of the contradictions, however, brings up the question of the harmony of the gospels, and we can at least indicate his general working principles.

The difficulty is a serious one for those Catholics whose understanding of the dogma of inspiration leads them to far-fetched conclusions concerning the exactitude expected from sacred writers in their accounts of the words and deeds of Christ.

If we were obliged to look upon the joining together of different teachings of Christ in such a manner as to form one great sermon, or even the words "after that," as formal affirmations of the real order, . . . or if the different places assigned to certain facts and nuances in the parables or incidents were to impel us to "double" both discourses and facts,[68] it would be impossible to write a life of Christ which would stand up against the objections of critics.[69]

It is a fact that some of our Lord's most important words, such as these of the institution of the Eucharist, are recorded by the different Synoptics with notable variations; this indicates that rigorous harmony is not to be looked for in all cases. Moreover, remarks P. Lagrange,

St. Augustine, thoroughly convinced of the inerrancy of the

sacred writers, himself laid down this principle, that one author could have described as an early event, what another author would describe as a later happening. Augustine also set up the principle of a reasonable harmonization, in the sense that one gospel might pass over something contained in another, or even could record it differently, but in such a way that the reader would grasp the fact by comparing these different manners of narration.[70]

A less mechanical concept of inspiration helps one to resolve the theological difficulty. From the viewpoint of historical criticism, the question is somewhat different. Yet divergences of details found in various expressions of the tradition of a fact prove nothing against the substantial reality of the fact itself. The so-called contradictions are not a serious argument against the historicity of the gospels unless they can be shown to be fundamental; as, for example, if there were violent opposition, instead of agreement, in the picture of Christ found in the gospels. The prejudices of the radical critics are so deeply rooted that they force every appearance of contradiction, and make no attempt to see whether the traditions, which are divergent as to the order of the facts or as to some details, cannot be gathered into vital unity. P. Lagrange reminded them of the principle of Heraclitus: *Tacit agreement is of greater value than explicit agreement.*

What precisely did he mean? The philosopher was accustomed to express his thought with extreme brevity, but that brevity conceals ideas of a most profound character. Without any doubt, he intends to say that the hidden harmony of the universe, which Universal Reason produces in the midst of the apparent disorder of the world, is of greater power and beauty than such manifest harmony as each man thinks he can perceive for himself in the external things of the world. But if this is true of the external world, how much more true is it in the sphere of ideas! Two manuscripts have no more than the value of one, if one of them is merely a copy of the other. Two authors serve only as a single witness, if one follows the other slavishly. But two manuscripts that sometimes differ imply two different sources, and their agreement then becomes significant. Every author who has his own sources of information, and disposes it according to his own peculiar method, is a witness who has a claim to be heard;

and if two witnesses, after apparently contradicting one another in their way of relating an event, are found finally to be in substantial agreement, then that agreement is more impressive than if they had first come to an arrangement as to what they should both say. This agreement is in itself an added proof that the texts are a true image of reality.[71]

The agreement of the gospels was not the exclusive pre-occupation of P. Lagrange in his great commentaries, where his method was rather to study each gospel separately in order to ascertain its own peculiar characteristics and the author's purpose in writing it, and then to trace out in each the broad outline of the life of Christ and the high lights of his teaching. As far as Mark was concerned, he concluded, "his history of Jesus is completely probable, both as to his preaching, his relations with his enemies, with the disciples, and with the crowd. Burkitt put it clearly when he said that Mark was 'self-consistent.' "[72] The same favorable judgment awaits St. Luke, who even more than St. Mark aimed at the production — after thorough investigation — of an historical work; and as much may be said of St. Matthew who, with his didactic penchant for grouping the words of Christ, was not greatly concerned with the time they were first uttered. In general, the life of Jesus as told by the Synoptics holds together very well, and there is an undeniable likeness in their picture of Christ.[73] When these gospels are compared with the fourth, it becomes evident that they have supplied the groundwork for John's developments.

The gospels are, in a certain manner, the organs of the Church. And it is in the life of the Church that the strongest confirmation of their message is to be found, if it can be shown that the faith and practices of early Christianity harmonize with the gospel story,[74] and yet find in Jesus' life and teaching their only adequate explanation. To illustrate: Faith in Christ's resurrection is inexplicable without the appearances of Christ, as recorded in the gospels, and on this score their historical reality is vindicated by an extrinsic confirmation. The belief in and cult of the Eucharist are likewise inexplicable, if Christ had never instituted and wished it; an echo of his words reaches down to us through the gospel accounts of the Last Supper. In these and similar cases, "the ecclesiastical fact and the gospels mutually support one another and, when united, constitute an unimpeachable testimony."[75]

Can we conclude, then, that the gospels, because they harmonize with one another and with the testimony of the early Church (thus they have historical value), will enable us to write a true biography, a history — in the modern sense of the word — of Jesus? Quite clearly not. That is why P. Lagrange never attempted to write the life of Christ which everyone expected him to write.

I have given up all idea of presenting a "Life of Jesus" of the usual kind, preferring to give to the gospels an opportunity to speak for themselves. They are inadequate as historical documents for writing a history of Jesus in the way in which a modern author would write the history of Caesar Augustus or Cardinal Richelieu; but such is their value as a reflection of Jesus' life and teaching, such is their sincerity and beauty, that in the presence of their inspired words one despairs of any other attempt to reproduce the life of Christ. The gospels themselves are the only life of Jesus Christ that can be written. Nothing remains for us but to understand them as well as we can.[76]

But he did write The Gospel of Jesus Christ, which makes no claim to be anything more than a commentary on the gospel story.

The chief obstacle awaiting the man who tries to reconstruct the life of Jesus is the lack of a detailed chronology in the gospels. To be sure, they contain the general order of facts, which has to correspond to reality and to history. But Mark gives no precise dates; nor does Luke, the very one who was so careful to indicate the temporal setting of the facts. His general plan was apparently predetermined by his geographical plan, and this had repercussions on the chronology. Strangely enough, as P. Lagrange points out, it is in the fourth gospel, the one most distrusted by the critics, that the most exact chronology is to be found. To judge from this gospel, the public ministry of Christ extended over two and one half years, whereas the picture painted by the Synoptics would seem to suppose only one year of the public life (the

Galilean ministry was followed by a single trip to Jerusalem, which terminated with the Passion).[77] Their arrangement can be harmonized with John's without too much difficulty, although the matter would be quite scanty for certain periods. The gospels are of greater assistance in determining the general course of events than a series of facts given in detail would be. With his great knowledge of the Jewish milieu, an historian like P. Lagrange could easily reconstruct the varying attitudes of the various classes who listened to Christ's words, and he could likewise trace the development of our Lord's teaching and His progressive revelations to His disciples. This provides the thread which can be followed as a guide to the facts, even when the sequence of the facts is only more or less certain, or at times merely conjectural.

This method is sure, in contrast to the critical method which consists in casting discredit on the historical value of the whole gospel tradition, and then proceeds to tell the life of Christ in a most arbitrary fashion. On the other hand, the critical method sometimes begins by laying down certain basic facts chosen with the utmost exclusivism, and then proceeds under the guidance of a psychology[78] which presupposes what is to be proved, viz., the purely human character of the religion of Christ, both in its origin and in its development.[79]

V. THE BEGINNINGS OF CHRISTIANITY

Interesting as the literary and historical criticisms of the New Testament are in themselves, they are but preliminary steps toward a scientific history of the beginnings of Christianity. For this, the gospels and writings of the apostolic age are the indispensable documentary basis. While in his commentaries P. Lagrange proceeded to the thorough study of pertinent questions concerning the gospels and some of the epistles, he was gathering materials for just this history. He never found time, however, to synthesize all his data, to trace out a general picture of early Christianity, or to show the establishment and development of the Church together with its dogmas and institutions.[80] He did begin the study of problems which confront a student of the beginnings of Christianity; these studies are scattered throughout the *Revue,* and in works of a more directly polemical nature.[81] The most important problem of all, that of Jesus Himself, and the various systems which independent criticism has put forth in the past half century in the effort to solve it, received much attention.

At the end of the past century, Protestantism had embraced the theories of the liberal school, best represented by Harnack's *Essence of Christianity.* Christ was held up as the greatest religious genius in the history of mankind; but He was not divine, nor the Son of God, except in the sense that His realization of the fatherhood of God far outstripped that of any other man. If He were the Messias — and this is questioned — He was a wholly spiritual Messias, preacher of the kingdom of God and the religion of the heavenly Father. Paul had come to exalt Christ above the rest of mankind and to make of Him a supernatural being existing in heaven before becoming Son of David. But not until the theological fourth gospel was written was His divinization achieved and His divine Sonship, in the metaphysical sense, fully proclaimed.

In answer to this, P. Lagrange wrote: "Exegesis has benefited by this great insistence upon the moral and religious character of Christ's teachings: He was thereby established in a sphere where He towered over the prejudices of His times; and from this vantage point He prepared a veritable regeneration of man, one that in the future would always be at the disposal of men." But, he asks at once, "Is this professor of morals, this respected president of a group of ministers, this useful aide of the State in the formation of virtue in German youth — is He the Jesus of the gospel?"[82]

Liberal theology claimed to find all this in St. Mark, who indeed does accentuate the human nature of Christ; but his is also the gospel of the Son of God. By attributing to Himself miraculous powers and unheard-of authority, Jesus claimed to be as much, without dispelling the mystery which surrounded His divine personality. Our Lord did not hold Himself up as a *moralist;* although St. Mark devotes a large portion of his gospel to His moral teachings. The kingdom

Père Marie-Joseph Lagrange, O.P.

of God which He announced was not simply a renewal, or an expansion, of the inner dispositions of the believer; it was the longed-for object of Jewish hopes and expectation — the messianic kingdom.[83]

A new school of exegesis sprang up to insist upon this particular point. Reacting violently against liberal Protestantism, it attempted to reduce the gospel to what we may call an essentially eschatological messianism.[84] Briefly, the whole gospel announces the imminent coming of the Kingdom of God, i.e., of the end of time, and of the inauguration of a new world, a supernatural one. Christ thought He was the Messias and said so. Just as the Kingdom of God was destined for the future, so Christ was the Messias of the future. He was the mysterious Son of man portrayed in the vision of Daniel; He would descend from the clouds to preside over the judgment of mankind. But He could have had no intention of founding a new religion, for His moral teachings were only provisional, temporary, a simple outline of what had to be done in preparation for this future and imminent kingdom of God. . . .

P. Lagrange realized that the new exegesis had done a great service in divesting Christ of His role of mere moralist, and plunging Him without any reserve into the realm of the supernatural:

Many Catholics applauded heartily when *L'Evangile et l'Eglise* opposed the Jesus of the new school to the liberal Jesus of Harnack's for in the new system there appeared to be a just understanding of Jesus' elevation in a heavenly sphere, along with a very plausible intention of restoring Him to His historical setting.[85] A closer inspection, however, quickly revealed that there would be little profit in the change.[86]

Is it likely that the morality of the gospels and the morality of the beatitudes — pure enough to renew the life of the spirit, and so enduring that even those who are unwilling to accept our dogma wish to retain it at all costs — was only, in Christ's mind, a means of hastening the coming of the Kingdom of God? . . . If Christ had been only a fanatic, a visionary whose dream was suddenly and brutally shattered, then it is difficult to explain how this dream revived so vigorously in His discouraged disciples that it became the foundation of Christianity.[87]

But it was not enough to point out the ultimate absurdities of the eschatological theory. Going deeper into the problem, P. Lagrange attacked the very foundations of the system by an examination of the messianic ideas of contemporary Judaism. He wanted to see if they actually did influence the thought of Christ.

On the part of the eschatologists, there was a sophistical attenuation of the divergences between the Jewish ideas and those of Christ. It would have been remarkable if there had been any perfect agreement on such a subject as an absolute, supernatural, and imminent kingdom of God, whose head would be the Messias whose kingdom would mark the end of history and usher in the end of mankind.[88]

The messianic aspirations of the Jews implied above all a certain nationalism, and included the triumph of Israel. It would be the task of the Messias to assure this. But in the gospels there is not a trace of such nationalism. The expectation of the final coming of the heavenly kingdom (which is said to have been the common opinion) was in reality only the opinion of some groups. In order to prove that Christ shared this opinion and thought the end of the world imminent, and to show that He thought that God had resolved not to better but to replace the world with a kingdom of absolute justice, which He Himself would inaugurate on earth as Messias, the eschatologists call attention to Christ's discourse on the end of the world.

P. Lagrange concluded, after a lengthy study of these passages that the *synoptic apocalypse,* as it is called, was made up of two sets of instructions: one dealing with the ruin of Jerusalem, the other with the end of the world. They have been woven together into one discourse because both stressed the idea of the judgment of God. The idea fits, in varying degree, the catastrophe of the fall of Jerusalem in A.D. 70 and the final upheaval which will spell the end of man's life on earth. Christ taught only that the *present* generation would witness the fall of Jerusalem; but in the first three gospels the two events are cast in the same perspective.[89] He did indeed foretell the imminent coming of God's kingdom on earth, but stopped short of saying that it would be concomitant with the end of the world. "He did not determine the date of His new coming. The nature of this coming is not very clear, but it could be a successive thing, previous to its supreme manifestation."[90]

In the past few years, independent criticism has continued in the ever deepening rut of the eschatological theory, and has become increasingly radical. It has drastically minimized the solid historical core of the gospels, and has cut our knowledge of Christ down to almost nothing. Christ's picture has consequently become more and more indistinct, and His part in the birth of Christianity increasingly insignificant.[91] The next problem is to explain the divinization of Christ and the role of Saviour which Christianity acknowledges to Him. First of all, they say, the idea of a Messias was exploited in Jewish circles, where the so-called messianic texts of the Old Testament were applied to Jesus. But such an explanation is worthless when applied to pagan circles outside of Judaism; and so the influence of the pagan mystery religions is invoked. Paul is said to have taken the essential notes of his theology from them, and was thus able to adapt the gospel to the piety of the Eastern world (which had become Greco-Roman), for by his manipulation the national messianic hopes of Judaism were transformed into the mystery of universal salvation.

The following chapter will deal with P. Lagrange's studies of the pagan mysteries. He concluded that the similarities between the mysteries and Christianity in matters of concepts and rites were entirely superficial. Furthermore, there is so much confusion and uncertainty about the origin and development of the oriental religions, that we might well ask if it were not Christianity that influenced them, rather than the other way around. It is moreover quite unnecessary to look for the sources of Paul's teachings in pagan mysticism, for he himself lets it be understood that he received his faith by divine revelation, and that he took the trouble to be sure that it was the same as that of the Christian Church, of which he had recently become a member. There is nothing in his theology that cannot be traced to the teachings of Christ and the theology of Judaism. He simply did not have to change the gospel into a mystery of salvation; it was already that. There was no need for him to seek out in the pretended myth of dead and risen gods, the quite different idea of the salvation of mankind by the death of a divine Person,[92] for in Judea men well knew that a martyr could offer his sufferings and death to God in order to obtain pardon for the sins of the people. Where there is question of the rites of the Christians, P. Lagrange held that they had no common ground with the pagan mystery rites, beyond a vague desire on the part of the initiated pagan to unite himself to the god he had chosen for the purpose of obtaining salvation; they differ radically from the pagan rites as far as moral requirements are concerned, and are thus quite free of any magical character.[93] From this position of the critics, traditional Catholic interpretation can retain the very definite affirmation of the realistic character of St. Paul's sacramental doctrine. Liberal criticism had interpreted it in a purely symbolical manner.

While he criticized the various systems which undertook to explain the origins of Christianity without supernatural intervention, P. Lagrange stressed any new conclusions which were in harmony with the traditional doctrine. However, he wrote, "Far be it from me to try to group, in an eclectic fashion, all that is best in these critical systems, so as to render homage to the Church for having always taught so; but it is quite permissible to show that the magisterium of the Church already contained many of the attractive features of these theories." Looked at this way, the attempts of negative criticism have not been without profit:

Logically, it ought to lead minds fed up with ceaseless uncertitude back to Catholicism. It is granted that, in the beginning, the lot of the Church and of the Scriptures was closely bound together. It is admitted that the Church is more ancient than the New Testament, and that she is the faithful custodian of this treasure which, she holds, is from God, and which would not dare present itself without the guarantee of her testimony. . . . We now see more clearly than heretofore that the rejection of Catholic dogma means separation from the faith of the first believers; to reject the supernatural is to refuse the testimony of the Apostles. Why should men not come back to this doctrine which is so closely knit to history? Once admit the intervention of God into the world, and even the insertion of God into humanity, and it can be excellently explained.[94]

Such is the conclusion we would expect of a believing historian, as P. Lagrange always wished to be. He never found it necessary to abstract from his beliefs while deep in research. As a true scholar, he tried not to overestimate the manuscript witnesses in favor of the faith. It was enough for him to be able to affirm as an indisputable fact, at the end of his studies, that no textual criticism, no elimination of the manuscript witnesses, no denial of the authenticity of the gospels or epistles could deprive Christ of His supernatural character.

If you do not reject absolutely everything (as do the mythists), if you retain only a tiny residue of the historical tradition about Jesus [then it is clear that] He conceived and manifested His claims to a supernatural role, and died for maintaining them. Independent criticism itself always leads you back, albeit by many detours, to the presence of Jesus, the object of contradiction. If you are not ready to adore Him, you will have to confine yourself to insults.[95]

As for P. Lagrange, we catch glimpses of his piety and devotion toward our Lord even in his strictly scientific works. He was forever trying to know Christ better, to bring out His humanity, so that His divinity might be glimpsed through the details of His historical picture. To nonexperts, P. Lagrange was an example of a life dedicated to the rigorously scientific study of all the difficult problems of the New Testament. His studies involved the utilization of ancient documents and the examination of all modern critical theories; yet his immense labors ended in a firm, and thoroughly enlightened profession of faith in the divinity of Christ, the Saviour of mankind. This is not the least valuable aspect of his work.

L. Vénard
Ecole S. Maurice
Vienne (Isère), France

CHAPTER III

THE HELLENISTIC MILIEU

I N THE first part of the preface which he wrote for Père
Festugière's *L'idéal religieux des grecs et l'Evangile,*
Père Lagrange said:

The history of Judaism shows that the chief enemy of the
worship of the one true God, as practiced by the Jews, was the
culture of Greece. The hostility became an open war of exter-
mination with the coming of Antiochus Epiphanes; but monotheism emerged victorious and was once more established in
Judea. This led the Jews to hope that they would conquer the
world with their faith, especially after the coming of the Messias,
who would assure the triumph of the God of Israel and the Law.

Jesus Christ appeared, and it was the Gentiles who recognized
Him as *Saviour,* a title borrowed from Jewish expectations; but
the Jews turned their backs upon Him. Beyond any doubt this
is the most amazing fact in the history of all religions. We have
tried to show, in our study of her history before the coming of
Christ, how Judaism was to some degree disposed to reject her
Messias. How did it happen that the Gentiles were more docile?
That problem is not less difficult to solve.[1]

The problem of the relationship of Christian beginnings
with Hellenism is an absorbing one, but apparently P. Lagrange had no idea of solving or even taking it up when he
first came into contact with Greece and began to write about
it. Yet no believer, however little he may reflect upon his
faith, can contemplate the masterpieces of Greek art or read
the Grecian poets, philosophers, and orators, without being
moved to think of Christianity. Whether we wish it or not,
we cannot but be struck by the absolute opposition between
Greek idealism and Christian realism. There is at first, perhaps, a temptation to exaggerate this opposition, but careful
study helps to keep it within proper bounds. If the comparison must be made, it is not hard to understand how a priest
and a religious should have taken it to heart to plumb the
depths of the questions it will evoke.

How can we escape such questions, for we are at one and the same time the heirs of both Judea and Greece? From the Jews we have received our sacred books, our faith in one God, and our manner of looking at moral problems; the foundations of our religious faith rest upon the Jews. But to the Greeks we owe our confidence in human reason, our love of order and equilibrium and symmetry, our taste for clear ideas, and our instinctive repugnance for disorder and obscurity. We are not disposed to sacrifice one part of our heritage at the expense of the other. If we love the prophets, who were inspired by God to announce the coming of the Messias to an old world, we do not on that account love less the philosophers who constructed the edifice of human wisdom and proved the validity of its arguments. Here, with full approval, we may quote St. Justin, who said proudly:

> I am a Christian and I am proud of it. I admit that my ambition is to live as one. That is not to say that Plato's doctrines are different from Christ's, but they are not entirely similar, no more than are those of the Stoics, poets, or historians. Each of these saw something noble in the divine seminal Word (Jas. 1:21), and expressed it well; but since they contradict themselves on the most important points, it is clear that they do not possess heavenly wisdom and irrefutable knowledge. Whatever they have taught that is good belongs to us Christians.[2]

Few men were more anxious than P. Lagrange to preserve whatever belonged to Greek culture. He was not afraid that he would fall a victim to the charms of Hellas. Understand us well — we neither have to, nor can we look, in his case, for blind enthusiasm or unrestrained admiration. Did not the Greeks themselves look with suspicion upon an enthusiasm which would deprive a man of his self-mastery, which would make him a kind of plaything of the superior beings? To know P. Lagrange and his interest in everything human is to understand that he looked upon Greece as a spiritual fatherland, where he rejoiced to discover his ancestors.

His personal labors, however, did not seem to orientate him toward Greece. He was known to the educated public only for his Old Testament studies, and others on certain topographical or archaeological problems of Palestine, and for his research work on Semitic religions. Then, without warning, there appeared in the *Revue Biblique* under his signature the first of three articles on *La Crète ancienne*.[3]

I. ANCIENT CRETE

This can be described as a sort of revelation, for hardly a person in France, outside of the specialists, was at that time interested in Crete. Yet in 1907 this Dominican, a biblical and Semitic scholar, called his compatriots' attention to the coast of the island of Minos, where for a number of years the English, Italians, and Americans were multiplying, without anyone suspecting it, the most sensational discoveries. Arthur Evans had discovered, in 1900, the ruins of the palace of Cnossos. In the years following, his further excavations maintained the brilliant standard of his discoveries. Then the members of the English school at Athens explored Zakro and the grotto of Dikte, Praesos, Palaekastro; the Italian mission carried on excavations in the grand palace of Phaestos and at Hagia Triada; an American mission was busy at Gournia. But the French had not found time to turn toward Crete.

When he heard of these discoveries, P. Lagrange went to see for himself,[4] and after one look, wrote as follows in justification:

Surely there is no need to apologize, in a review consecrated to the Bible (studied according to the historical and comparative method), for mentioning discoveries which shed new light upon the history of the ancient East. After Egypt and Chaldea, comes the splendid appearance of Japhet, brother of Sem and Cham. From now on we shall be permitted to recognize the traces of his presence under the tents of Sem. Moreover, nothing that concerns the Greeks can remain irrelevant to men who study the origins of Christianity. Renan used to like to contrast the Greek miracle with that of the Semites. The Greek miracle will now perhaps, while still arousing admiration, appear more natural. Things being such, no pretext is necessary; and it should be quite unnecessary to recall that Crete is the Caphtor, whence came the Philistines and the mercenaries of David.[5]

Are not these lines revealing? Of course, P. Lagrange remembered that the essential theme of his labors was the

Bible; but, almost in spite of himself, he had been won by the splendors his eyes drank in and he could not break away. Crete won him because of what she was, and because of the beauty which she had once again revealed to him. One should not be surprised, then, to read what he has to say about Cretan art:

The Cretans never looked at the human body except in that state of extraordinary tension which clothed it, in their eyes, with greater beauty. In this they are indeed the ancestors of the Greeks, who were so fond of the games. The games were never a mere matter of an exhibition of strength, but rather the occasion to dispose the body nobly, just as, according to Plato, the dance allowed one to contemplate the beauty of the body.[6]

Why this discursus, which we might easily have omitted, if not that P. Lagrange, like the Greeks, had himself been seduced by beauty? He was a man, and nothing human was foreign to him.[7] But while others stopped at the surface and saw no more than the happy rhythm of the body, he did not fail to peer more deeply in his search for souls.

After describing the gigantic ruins of the palace at Cnossos (now identified as the labyrinth of Minos), and after drawing attention to the art objects which once adorned these vast residences and are now the treasure and ornament of the museum of Candia, he was held for a long time to the study of the Cretan religion, as revealed to us in its monuments. The following are the modest conclusions he reached after descriptions of the holy places, the sacrifice, the idols, the symbols (double or double-bitted ax, busts of bulls, and horns of consecration, crosses, sphinx, sacred stones and trees), the divinities and burial places:

The worship of the divinity under a human form, male and female, the cult of animals, or at least the mixture, in the idols, of man and animal; the cult of trees, and to a certain degree, of stones; the sacrifice, altars, open holy places, sacred caves, these are phenomena which are found in almost all the ancient religions.[8]

Shall we stop here? It would be an admission of our deep ignorance of the ancient Cretan religion, if we did not go on to distinguish it from other ancient religions by its particular notes; or if we did not at least bring out its ties with this or that other cult which is well known to us. The immense erudition of P. Lagrange enabled him to formulate hypotheses in this field; it is not surprising that this historian of Semitic religions should turn first of all toward the Semites:

Here is something still more extraordinary: while Assyria or Babylon, which are thought to be representative of Semitic culture, have had as yet less influence in ancient Crete than Phenicia or the land of Canaan in general, we have been able to point out many striking points of contact between Crete and Elam; Elam, that is, Susiana, the meeting place of the Semites and the peoples which the Bible ranges with the sons of Japhet. Recall to mind the cross, the double-bitted ax, the swastika, the three tree trunks bound together in the place of cult, the prominent role of the bull, and the minotaur himself.[9]

Now we have started. P. Lagrange put his questions to anthropology, archaeology, and prehistory, in turn. His pages are of absorbing interest, full of suggestive flashes of insight and unexpected problems. With such a master one hardly knows where he will stop, and it is this that gives so much charm to the journey, for we are sure to learn something wherever we are led. Other guides might perhaps be less ambitious, more prudent. Knowing less, having fewer windows open on all horizons, they would not dream of orientating us in so many different directions. But would they be such an inspiration as P. Lagrange?

It is true that when one believes he is on the point of reaching a conclusion he is a bit disappointed. The work itself closes in almost the same way as the third article in the *Revue Biblique,* with no word to suggest that the author has nothing more to say, and so the problem of origins remains unsolved. After having discussed so many hypotheses and recalled so many systems, P. Lagrange dwells upon a question of undeniable importance for a biblical scholar like himself, but quite secondary as far as general history is concerned: namely, who are the Cretans of whom the Bible speaks? We know that a part of David's Guard were Cretans, but they did not come from the great isle of Crete. They were merely natives of the land of the Philistines. Were not the Cretans of Crete of the same race as these? The Bible, on the other hand, knows of a country which is named Caphtor, whose inhabitants were the Caphtorim; this land would be none other than Crete itself, and not Cappadocia, as the Septuagint has it.

II. THE LOGOS OF ST. JOHN

Writing on Crete, P. Lagrange wished only to jot down his impressions and recollections. But his works on the Greek philosophers were prompted by the desire to clear up as far as possible the problem of Christian beginnings. Contemporary critics stress the elements Christianity is supposed to have borrowed from Greece; how far their interpretation of the facts is just, remains a question.

In preparing his commentary on St. John, P. Lagrange could not overlook the problem raised over the origin of the idea and of the word *logos*. It is an old question, often discussed, and answered in many ways. Some might have thought it a waste of time to take it up again seriously, and would be content to draw their conclusions after having summarized previous works. One would betray how little he knew P. Lagrange and his methods of work to imagine him doing this. First of all, there was for him the matter of loyalty and intellectual honesty: a man is sure only of the things he has studied personally; if interpretation is in order, texts must be read. Besides, we may add, this was a problem which attracted his personal interest. How? There was question of the Greek philosophers, a chance to read some fragments of Heraclitus, to renew contact with what remains of the writings of the Stoics — would anyone allow such an opportunity to slip by his fingers? Impossible!

Naturally, he leads us first of all to Heraclitus.[10] Justly, he remarks:

All studies on the Logos begin with Heraclitus. St. Justin attributed to him the honor of having been the first to proclaim the existence of the Logos, and more than that, of having lived according to the Logos, so that he merited in a way the name of Christian, just as Socrates did.[11]

But even in antiquity Heraclitus was dubbed "The Obscure One," and all his readers agreed that his *De Natura* was hard to understand. What, then, are we moderns to say, who have at our command only a hundred and twenty-five fragments of his work, without context, and often hard to decipher? Our uncertainty is so great that we may ask if Heraclitus ever spoke of the Logos at all, and if the current interpretation given to the passages in which the word occurs is quite justified.

P. Lagrange wished to get to the bottom of this; one after another he studied all the texts, even the most insignificant, which might enlighten him. After he had put to one side all those in which the word *logos* had simply the sense of word, maxim, doctrinal opinion, of nature, constitution, or reason, two aphorisms remained. Everything seemed to conspire against the understanding of these fragments, but he examined them closely with patience and shrewdness. When he had weighed all the evidence, he took up the position, along with the traditional interpretation, which recognizes the Logos here as the universal law and reason of all things. He adds, however,

Although criticism does not succeed in eliminating the *logos* from the teaching of Heraclitus, it certainly does limit its extent. To be sure, there was in his teaching a germ which the Stoics turned to account. But surely it is not this rudimentary and very material logos which could have urged John to set forth the theology of the Word, in order to substitute a supernatural revelation for the gropings of naturalism.[12]

From Heraclitus we pass directly to the Stoics who were inspired more or less by his thought.[13] A few lines of introduction point out the significance of Stoicism in the history of Greek thought, and we reproduce them here because they give us what is practically the definitive judgment of P. Lagrange on a system whose failings he was the first to admit, but whose moral grandeur did not fail to impress him:

After the prodigious intellectual effort of Plato and Aristotle, Stoicism appeared to be a collapse of Greek thought. But what a passion for a moral life animated it; what an ardent, if not always efficacious, desire to practice virtue, to attain to the Sovereign Good, not by contemplation of an ever more perfect beauty, but by the exercise of virtue which placed man on the same footing as the gods! What care also to maintain and defend religious sentiment! The first Greek thinkers had openly attacked religion. The tragic fate of Socrates made the others cautious, but it was common knowledge that the worship of the gods and of the city was no longer anything but a manifestation of natural sentiment as far as the philosophers were concerned. Once the acute crisis of pure rationalism had passed, reason considered itself sufficiently strong to take the gods under its protection, in order to provide a solid basis for worship without deserting the ancient tradition. As a matter of fact, reason soon had to limit its pretentions; and it was the religious sentiment that emerged triumphant. . . .

The Portico acquired an influence which was incomparably superior to that of the Academy or the Lyceum. Its teaching spread over the whole Greco-Roman world as a philosophy which, if not popular, was at least accessible to all cultivated minds. Who can measure the effect of this belief, at once rational and religious, in the moral formation of the people to whom Christianity was proposed, before, and even after their conversion?[14]

In these lines one feels something of the soul of P. La-grange. Certainly this historian understood the incurable weaknesses of Stoicism, the gaps, the errors in its make-up, the frightful pride which the wise man assumes in the very face of nature. When he came to analyze the texts, he pointed out plainly all these insufficiencies. But the seriousness of the Stoics as they posed the problem of life stirred him, as did the religious tone of their attempts to solve it. In that Greek world where so many and such great minds had, as it were, bungled their life by receiving it with mocking smiles, the philosophers of the Portico held a place apart. They were Greeks to the core, no doubt; and it would be wrong to look upon their teachings as Semitic importations; but Greece in them was again invested with grave charm, the tragic charm she once possessed in Aeschylus.

Because they were Greeks, the Stoics were rationalists. We generally contrast rationalism with religion, as if we had of necessity to choose between them; it is not easy for us to see how a man can be at one and the same time a believer and a rationalist. True, the old Greek philosophers themselves helped dig the moat which we have since imprudently widened; but there can be a religion of reason itself, and that was the Stoic doctrine. Cleanthus thought nothing more divine than reason. The world is ruled by it, develops by it, and is maintained by it; it is what it is, being eternal, by the action of the reasonable principle. Man, in his turn the most noble thing in the world, is man only by reason; it is his duty to follow right reason, and only in so doing will he find happiness.

Yet, whatever the role they assigned to reason or, to employ the Greek term, to the *Logos,* we need not believe that the Stoics were the first to tread the path leading to the Word in the prologue of St. John.

Stoicism must be taken for what it is: a pure pantheism which makes it impossible to attribute to the Logos either the role of a creator, or that of an intermediary in creation, or even that of exemplar of the world, or yet of a divine supernatural force which communicates special enlightenment to man, making him capable of practicing virtue, or helping him in the way of the perfection which the Stoic proposes for himself.[15]

III. EPICTETUS AND MARCUS AURELIUS

Among the Stoics there were two, Epictetus and Marcus Aurelius, who held the attention of P. Lagrange.[16] This is not hard to understand. Both of them lived after Christianity had been preached in the Roman world; it was not a question, then, of knowing whether they personally exercised an influence upon the doctrine or the life of the Church. The opposite would more likely be the case. Considering the seriousness of their outlook on life, their gravity in the accomplishment of their duty, and the submission to God's will which they preach, one is tempted to ask if they do not owe what is best in them to Christianity.

At any rate, neither was an original thinker. The works which we hold as theirs are not at all scholarly. Epictetus did no writing himself; his disciple Arrian edited the *Discourses* he had with his master. A résumé of his teaching is found in the short *Manual* which, for a long time even among Christians, was the breviary of ordinary folk.[17] Marcus Aurelius kept a diary of his interior life, and his *Meditations,* scrupulously recorded day by day, reveal his philosophy to us. It is precisely because the *Discourses* and *Meditations* are primarily the expression of personal sentiments and serious lives that we prefer them to any systematic exposition. They reveal the souls of the authors. By such examples we can judge the hold Stoicism had on serious minds. We might hesitate if we found ourselves in the presence of trained thinkers; but Epictetus was a slave, and only after gaining his freedom did he become a teacher of philosophy and a director of consciences. Marcus Aurelius, son of a noble family, was destined at an early age to become emperor, although in discharging his difficult duties he remained a philosopher. We have only to see how these men lived to understand that they looked upon Stoicism somewhat as a religion.

Neither the freed slave nor the emperor was able to appreciate the grandeur and novelty of the Christian preaching. They knew of it, however; both of them expressed their contempt for the martyrs. Speaking of the scorn of death and the fearlessness of the wise man in the presence of the tyrant, Epictetus reproaches his own followers for not acquiring, by reason, those dispositions which others have by aberration of the mind, and the Galileans by a kind of traditional instinct.[18] Marcus Aurelius in his turn wrote: "What can be compared to the soul which at the moment of separation from the body, is ready either for annihilation or transmigration, or future life! Such a disposition must be the result of its own judgment, and not of plain stubbornness as found among Christians. It must be formed after reflection, gravely, in a way that can persuade others, and without tragic ostentation."[19]

This is indeed true misery, and helps us judge the two philosophers. For one of them, Christians called upon to bear the supreme testimony to their faith made a routine gesture; for the other, the gesture was tragic. Are the lives of the martyrs no more than that? Yet Epictetus was a contemporary of St. Ignatius of Antioch; he could have read that incomparable letter the old bishop wrote to the Romans, asking permission to become the prey of the beasts, and not to be prevented from joining Jesus Christ. Marcus Aurelius was a contemporary of St. Justin, who addressed to him a petition on behalf of the unjustly persecuted Christians. Among the men of old whom the apologist declared partially enlightened by the Word figured such wise men as Heraclitus and Musonius, both of whom should have been dear to the heart of the emperor himself. Moreover, St. Justin proclaimed himself a philosopher, and undertook to bring out the resemblances between Christianity and Stoicism. But Epictetus and Marcus Aurelius did not will to see. They did not take the trouble to consider the light which was offered to them. What a pity that was!

The *Discourses* of Epictetus contain a number of excellent prayers: "Lift up thy head, thou art delivered from slavery. Dare to look to God and say: From this moment use me as Thou wilt. I unite myself to Thy thought; I am Thine. I refuse nothing Thou wilt judge fitting."[20] Elsewhere he wrote: "I have submitted my will to God. If He wills that I fall sick with the fever, so do I. Does He will that I undertake a task? So do I. Will He have me aspire to something? So do I will it. Does He wish me to obtain something? I wish it also. Does He not wish it? Neither do I. I consent therefore to die; I consent to be tortured."[21]

Yet a forced note creeps into these formulae. At first glance one does not grasp the shocking implications, for they seem to be expressions of a will wholly submissive to God. But upon reflection we see that this total renunciation is a lie. A Christian is more humble, knowing that the ideal for him is to conform himself to God's plans, but also that the realization of this ideal is the work of grace. The Stoic is self-satisfied in his pride: "Have I broken any of Thy commandments?" he asks God. "Have I abused the faculties Thou didst give me? Have I otherwise used my feelings or ideas? Have I ever reproached Thee? or blamed Thy government? I was sick when Thou didst wish it; others were also, but I accepted the illness willingly. I was at Thy command poor, and poor with joy."[22]

This is decidedly not a Christian way of praying. His docility to the commands of God is not a matter for proud display. One cannot help thinking of the Pharisee in the gospel. The Stoic thanks God for all that He has given him; but deep down in his heart he feels no need for Him. In vain did P. Lagrange attempt to discover in Epictetus anything like a tendency toward humility or some indication of a turning to God; the results were meager.[23]

Much closer to us than Epictetus is Marcus Aurelius, for he was much more conscious of his impotency and weakness. He gives the impression of being a poor soul anxiously debating with himself, clutching at philosophy as the last resort against despair:

With each step there is no footing. As in the marshes of Cades, each day he tests the route he must travel. Against temptations of vainglory he was long accustomed to oppose the specter of death, the vanity of praise, and the oblivion which awaits the famous. He opposed the pardon of a wise man to the banality, the profane coarseness, the often wicked intrigues of his associates, who were unaware of the things of the soul and knew not what they did. He was caught up in this moral struggle from the time he had learned to think. His school sustained him. But his school hoped for a reward in the next life; Marcus could not believe in it. After he dies he will no longer exist, but still he wants to have been something — a man who followed reason in conformity with his nature for the good of the universe. If this was placing a heavy burden upon himself, and if he felt his knees buckling, he then had to remind himself frequently of the consequences of his principles, and urge himself to translate them into action. It was with this in mind that he wrote his *Meditations,* as a consolation for hours of sadness and as a supreme bulwark against the dizziness of the void.[24]

There are many such attractive pages in the fine study of P. Lagrange on Marcus Aurelius. As an historian he felt a lively sympathy for the philosopher-emperor, and he communicates his enthusiasm to the reader. We must admit, however, that the Stoicism of Marcus is far removed from that of Chrysippus and Zeno. It is much more than a physical doctrine, or a system of morality; it is a religion. A man must follow reason; this rule is the object of an act of faith. He does not demonstrate, but believes in, the goodness of reason. Neither does he demonstrate the existence of the gods; he feels them pass by in daily life, or, we might almost say, they are mystically experienced.

To those who still ask: "Where hast thou seen the gods, how do you prove the existence of those whom you honor?" he would reply: First, they are invisible to our eyes. Moreover, is it not true that I have not seen my own soul either, and yet I respect it. The same holds true for the gods. I ascertain their existence by the signs of their power which they make me experience in all circumstances, and I revere them.[25]

Is this not enough? I am not convinced; but Marcus Aurelius was satisfied with the argument. Distasteful as it may be, we must note that he did not reject the hypothesis of the nonexistence of God. "If there is a god, all is well; if there is nothing but chance, take care not to abandon thyself to chance."[26]

Can Stoicism, so proud of itself, so triumphant, offer no more than this? We would like to find more there than this, but it is quite difficult to do so. P. Lagrange attributes to Christian influence some of the ideas of Epictetus, such as monotheism, or more precisely, the personal character of God in the *Discourses,* the duty of the apostolate and of bearing witness to God if called upon to do so, and the praise of celibacy for preachers. He even thinks that Epictetus must have read St. Paul and culled several happy phrases from his epistles.[27] I would like to believe this, but I do not think that the pride of the freed slave would have allowed him to turn his attention to the letters of Paul who, by contrasting human wisdom with divine foolishness, condemned human wisdom.

Following our character or our dispositions, we may prefer Epictetus to Marcus Aurelius, or the other way around. Epictetus enjoys his appointed task, he is confident in the mission he is charged to fulfill; but again I would hesitate to affirm that his mission was not entirely a lay mission.[28] Marcus Aurelius is somber, restless, disillusioned; he performs his duty with courage, but without hope.

The glimmers of light which enlighten Stoicism in the writings of Epictetus are but reflections of a more ardent flame; they may be compared to brightness which sometimes colors the west at sunrise. He chanted the hymn of a false dawn. The *Meditations* of Marcus Aurelius are the sorrowful elegy of a desperate and dying philosophy.[29]

It should be pointed out that this philosophy, before it disappeared, spilled the blood of Christians.

Marcus Aurelius, serious about everything, was very serious about the official religion. Here, perhaps, we must make great allowances for his pride in himself as a thinker. He flattered himself that his morality was not less pure than that of the Christians, and that, quite as well as they, he safeguarded the sanctity of the divine idea. And since the emperor was capable of reconciling rational philosophy with the Roman religion by attributing to himself the wisdom proper to a sage, he would be expected to take it ill that others should attack his gods.[30]

From the beginning of his reign, he made martyrs of the Christians; toward the end of his life he became more severe, and issued, it seems, a general edict of persecution. It was his great misfortune to be responsible for the deaths of Justin the philosopher and the martyrs of Lyon.

IV. ST. JUSTIN

In dealing with Marcus Aurelius, P. Lagrange had frequently come across the name of St. Justin. It is not surprising that he should be so captivated by this Christian apologete as to become his biographer. In our turn, we must salute the name of Justin whenever we meet it and recall to mind that work of P. Lagrange.[31] Was not Justin the philosopher a true Greek? Differently, of course, from Clement of Alexandria, but no less than he. What charms and wins us is Justin's clarity of mind, his honesty of spirit, and the unequaled confidence with which he greets men of good will.

Was it because P. Lagrange recognized in this ancient apologete a kindred spirit, that he could write so sympathetically about him? Himself a modern apologete, he was interested in everything, sought to understand and love all things, was ready to undertake all types of research, and at the end of his labors was content to see his Master, Jesus Christ, to whom he had consecrated his life, better known. St. Justin wrote to kings, to the senate, and to the Roman people. He did not hide his faith or dissimulate the Christian mysteries; it is to him we owe our oldest description of Baptism and the Eucharist. P. Lagrange likewise wrote for all men of good will. He fought against errors without impatience or anger. He denounced prejudice and hatred (for the race of Crescens is immortal); but he was so sure of the triumph of truth that he demanded victory only on the strength of his arguments. Not without great emotion do we read again the last lines of his *St. Justin:*

Marcus Aurelius did not understand. Caligula was a fool, and Nero a degenerate. But Marcus Aurelius! His blindness makes one shudder. Daily he examined his conscience and reproached himself for slight imperfections; but never did he seriously ask what this new sect was which won men over to virtue, and which united into one fraternity slaves and freemen who were enlightened and, as it were, drunk with the light, who were animated by divine strength and desirous of lifting up the world; for their own part they desired only God. Nor did it occur to him that in condemning these men to death he was acting as a tyrant.

Justin had not hesitated to tell him this. In the face of philosophers who were too proud of their wisdom, his efforts were fruitless; but his appeal was listened to by others who were better disposed. It may be that during the course of centuries some of his arguments have lost their value; but we are still moved by his frankness, his consuming zeal, his confidence in the truth, and his sympathy for any generous effort, and finally by his heroism and death for Jesus Christ. . . . Let him be the patron of upright men, sincere men, valiant men.[32]

V. THE RELIGIOUS TEACHINGS OF THE GREEK PHILOSOPHERS

Perhaps we have dwelt too long on Epictetus and Marcus Aurelius; now we must go back beyond them. P. Lagrange provides the opportunity by his series of studies on the religious doctrines of the Greek philosophers. Once again we shall meet the Stoics, but we shall take care not to linger with them here.

Most of these articles appeared in the *Revue Thomiste,*[33] often with an apology from P. Lagrange, as if he needed any justification![34] Actually the only question we might ask on this score is: Were they written according to a preconceived plan, like different chapters of a book, or rather drawn up one after the other, almost haphazardly, the last of them being prompted by the desire to bring out the continuity and to round off the whole? However this may be, they are extremely interesting and provide new proof of the author's insatiable intellectual curiosity.[35]

First, there is Plato, "the greatest name in the religious philosophy of antiquity."[36] Like all who have undertaken this study, P. Lagrange was not insensible to the spell of the *Dialogues.* Their winged style, the matchless ease with which Plato moves about in the most abstract theories, the wonderful flights which instantly transport the reader far from this transient world, the myths whereby we escape for a moment those subtile discussions, and whose meaning in amazement we next ask ourselves, wondering if they are anything more than childish fables — it is difficult to decide just what it is that charms us most in these books, in which the most beautiful tongue in the world serves as a garment for the noblest of ideas.

These ideas are often obscure, but, of course, they developed or changed during Plato's own lifetime. In his study, P. Lagrange first recalls the rational theology, if we may call it that, of Plato, and then examines his mystical theology. This, too, is still enshrouded in many obscurities. It is known that out of condescension for the incurable infirmity of human nature, Plato sometimes felt obliged to make unfortunate concessions.

As director of souls, keen as he was for the correctness of ideas, Plato was not so interested in determining the being of the divine nature and in isolating it from the world; but he did wish to inspire a high idea of the moral value of the divinity, meaning by that either God or the gods; and he was quite sure that the commoners would understand "the gods." Whatever being answers to this conception — which is very fixed in itself — I can do no better than to reproduce the characteristic touches which Zeller has grouped and carefully fortified with texts: After extolling divine goodness and veracity, Plato praises divine perfection which lacks no beauty or excellence; he lauds divine power which embraces all things and can effect all things that are possible; he praises divine wisdom which has ordered all things for a single purpose, as well as omniscience which nothing escapes, justice which leaves no crime unpunished, no virtue unrewarded, and goodness which is solicitous for all men and for their higher good.[37]

Although he had some harsh things to say about Plato's rational theology, and did not scruple to note its deficiencies in comparison with Christian teachings, P. Lagrange, like so many others, felt the irresistible charm of his mysticism. After citing a page of the *Banquet*,[38] which treats of the love of God and the contemplation of it, he wrote:

Without any doubt, the love of the Beautiful never inspired in an ancient artisan a more beautiful page than this. . . . Incomparably charming as these words may be, however, they should not escape analysis. The philosopher realizes very well that, though he be borne upon the wings of desire, he remains a philosopher, that is, he can only use his reason. . . . We, too, stand enraptured at the sight of this philosophical beauty, but we are the more astonished at the mixture of the sublime with such inferior ingredients. This would not justify us in being unappreciative of something truly unheard of in the bosom of the ancient world, in this intuition that the supreme good of man is to see God. But, choked in the chaos of polytheism, this mysticism awaited the hand which would disengage it and make place for it in a religious conception that was completely sound.[39]

There is something else. Plato envisaged only a dialectical exercise in the soul's loving ascent toward God: "The initiation is described as a true method, i.e., a method whose steps are determined in advance upon a road which mounts to a desired summit. It is a technical discipline in which the apprenticeship should be begun very early under the guidance of a master capable of directing it in a suitable manner."[40] Here once again appears that thoroughly Greek idea of the primacy of the intellect — as if moral perfection were nothing more than a gnosis; as if it were enough to know God to unite oneself to Him and resemble Him. Many have been the errors and faults committed in every age in the name of this principle. Plato himself too often felt his own wings break. He never succeeded in drawing men of his own time after him to heights which were not made for them.

Aristotle is not nearly as fascinating as Plato. We might even say it takes some courage to read his writings. Plato charms men into following him, but it takes an effort to study Aristotle. Yet the examination of his religious thought is a veritable duty for a Dominican, for a Thomist, or, more simply, for a Catholic. It is true that the first centuries of Christianity lent a more ready ear to Plato; but from the thirteenth century onward, thanks to the great influence of St. Thomas Aquinas, Aristotle became the master, and we are all to some degree his disciples. Though we might prefer the supple, flowing dialectic of Plato, we have no right to deny audience to the rigid logic of Aristotle.

P. Lagrange was led to study Aristotle by a work of Jaeger,[41] and his study reflects this somewhat fortuitous origin. To be sure, the great historian had not waited this long to meditate upon the religious thought of the Stagyrite, but he was fortunate to find in Jaeger a key to many closed doors. One of the greatest difficulties in interpreting the works of Aristotle arises from the condition in which they have come down to us. In many instances we have before us only notebooks, sketches which appear to be incomplete, editings by his students. Into this chaos Jaeger attempted to instill some order, showing that the thought of Aristotle did not always remain absolutely the same. It had been transformed, developed, corrected in the course of years, and so it is not surprising to find, often even in one and the same book, unmistakable traces of revision.

The proof of the existence of the first mover (God) is a classic which constitutes Aristotle's fundamental contribution to theodicy. "This first mover is unique, eternal, incorporeal, indivisible, most pure act, that is, not simply intelligence but the thought which thinks itself and in this thought finds its beatitude."[42] When he had pointed out these formulas in the *Metaphysics,* P. Lagrange added:

Human reasoning had never before attained to such a lofty idea of God: pure spirit, entirely distinct from the world, the supreme intelligence, thought which was constantly occupied with the only object worthy of it, perfectly happy, sovereignly perfect, embracing in its absolute unity all perfections. It is idle to insist upon this and to cite the texts; these points are perfectly clear in Aristotle, and no one disputes them. This is his greatest glory.[43]

It is precisely this transcendence of Pure Act, this thought of the Thought, that is disturbing and frightening. For Aristotle, God was so distant that for all practical purposes He was inaccessible. No prayer could reach up to Him, and He was uninterested in a world He had not created. He ignored mankind. Men could only pass close to Him, without raising their eyes and without praying to Him. It is true that after proclaiming the absolute unity of the first mover, Aristotle proceeded to either forty-seven or fifty-five other unmoved movers which presided over the movement of the stars. He was at one time charged with contradiction, but Jaeger and P. Lagrange call it development. Toward the end of his life Aristotle devoted more and more of his time to astronomy and the positive sciences. He tried to harmonize his philosophy with the discoveries of Eudoxius and Calippus, and from this came his doctrine of subordinated movers, which appears so strange and profoundly illogical to us.

At bottom it does not matter too much. Aristotle did not succeed any better than Plato in introducing his philosophy into practical life. Both men were strict observers of the traditional cults and official religions. Was it out of a spirit of conformity, or fear, or deep faith that they so acted? Perhaps all of these causes concurred in influencing them. Their incomparable glory for having resolutely distinguished things of the spirit from corporeal things remains undiminished. They both quite plainly affirmed the existence of one transcendent God, even if they did introduce alongside of Him other corporeal or incorporeal gods who were demanded by the apparent logic of a system, or by the religious exigencies of social life.

Reason, having reached this high point, could not maintain it, and the rational structure remained incompleted. The Academicians took refuge in scepticism, and the Peripatetics devoted themselves to the sciences, without concern for the First transcendent Mover. Both the Stoics and the Epicureans were astonished that a man as intelligent as Plato could believe in a bodiless god.[44]

Briefly, now, a word about P. Lagrange's studies on the Stoics, Cynics, and the Masters of the New Academy. Neither the Stoics, nor the Cynics, nor the Sceptics of the New Academy marked any genuine progress of religious thought.

Stoicism did bring out the idea of Providence, and proclaimed the fraternity of men; it also affirmed that the blessed city of Zeus was worth more than the city of Cecrops. These were not small victories; but the materialistic pantheism which underlay all the religious speculations of the Portico spoiled everything, and it seems that the later Stoics never repudiated it. Some years ago an attempt was made to popularize Posidonius, to make of him "the great intermediary between East and West, the heir of two worlds in whom the spirit of exact research was fused with ecstatic abandon, the peacemaker between Zeno, Plato, and Aristotle, the road from Hellenistic philosophy to neoplatonism."[45] He was also said "to have the signal merit of having done more than anyone else to restore Pythagoras to honor in the Roman school."[46] This is just so much rhetoric. Once the craze had worn thin, it should have been admitted that we know nothing certain about Posidonius, and that the lovely constructions designed to give us his doctrine are built upon the clouds. In company with K. Reinhardt, P. Lagrange makes him out to be a genuine Stoic, and reduces his real influence almost to nothing.[47]

Before this, Seneca had been the man of the hour. For how long a time was the authenticity of his supposed correspondence with St. Paul admitted? When these letters were proved to be gross apocrypha, there were those who made of him a "Christian before Christianity," because his writings revealed a religious soul alive with pity for the miseries of mankind.

It is not our business to detract from Seneca, but how can we forget that this man

. . . who possessed immense riches and led an ostentatious kind of life (which he abandoned only out of prudence), accustomed to dealing with all that Rome held to be most cultured and elegant, admitted very early into the intimacy of Caligula's sisters, this minister of an immense empire was unable to put his philosophy into practice with the intransigence of the little Greek who, draped only in his mantle, was always ready for a dispute, and firmly resolved to crush his adversary.[48]

Not to forget what is essential, there are contradictions in the doctrine preached by Seneca. Time and again he speaks of God and of the gods; but at the very moment he seems on the point of bringing forward the transcendent God, he dreams only of reason, the interior master. He tries to console himself and others, but philosophy is the only remedy he has for all ills. He recommends the practice of a daily examination of conscience and brings this examination to a close with a pharisaic acknowledgment of his own excellence. He declares that he is the brother of his slaves, their companion in slavery, but never dreams of sharing his luxurious life with them. How sad it is to see a man, otherwise noble and generous, ending up in such a condition; and what a condemnation of the doctrine responsible for it.

Yet, for all of that, we prefer the Stoics to the Cynics; although P. Lagrange strove to justify them in some points. He writes:

Of all the ancient sects, even including Stoicism, Cynicism was the one which most brazenly fostered pride, and openly preached a morality most candidly destitute of all religious motivation. Minds such as these were ill-disposed for Christian living. But against the general lack of manliness and headlong search for well-being, and against the craze for literary fame and the ticklish vanity of the philosophers, Cynicism raised a fierce protest which would not displease even Christian ascetics. The Cynics clamorously held themselves up as examples, and to some extent this was an example which Christians were bound in honor to surpass. The struggle of Cynicism against a society without ideals, where men were the slaves of pleasures and prejudices, a struggle for freedom and haughty independence — this was taken up by Christianity, but against sin and the flesh, and for the purpose of enthroning charity.[49]

VI. PHILO OF ALEXANDRIA

With Philo of Alexandria we do not quit the Hellenic world, but cross the border into a new domain, that of Judaism.

There are two men in Philo. He was philosopher enough to find a place, in the collection of d'Arnim, among the sources of the Stoics. M. Bréhier found it possible to write a whole book about him considering only his relations with the Greco-Roman world. But he was also a rabbi to the fingertips, and M. Ritter saw no difference between his *Halakah* and that of Palestine, for the interpretation of the precepts of the Law; nor does Akibah manifest a more fertile imagination in extracting endless consider-ations from the least words of the context. Yet one wonders, especially after reading the *Poimandres* of M. Reitzenstein, whether he did not also borrow some things from mythology.[50]

No one, surely, has studied the history of Christian origins and come into contact with Philo without pausing over him. We might almost say that this salute to the Jewish philoso-pher of Alexandria is a kind of ritual consecrated by usage, and one that cannot be neglected with propriety. Over a long period, the immediate origin of the doctrine of the Word (taught so clearly in the prologue of St. John) was sought for in the works of Philo. This doctrine clothes the entire teach-ing of the fourth gospel with a bright light. It appears among the first words with such sharpness that it is difficult to be-lieve that John did not find it somewhere ready made, that he was not simply content to adapt it to the primitive teach-ings of Christianity. As, evidently, Philo often speaks of the Logos, explaining by it many things both in the order of cre-ation and in that of revelation, the question naturally arises: Was St. John a disciple of Philo, after first being a disciple of Christ?

This particular question has been broached in different ways. Besides the disciple who carefully gathers up the words of the master, there is the disciple who is unconsciously subjected to the influences of a school. Few critics dared to suggest that St. John purloined the fundamental theses of Philo directly; but many have held that he could have lived in an environment which was impregnated with Philonian ideas, and that, although he himself was unaware of it, he owed the best of his theology to the Alexandrian Jew.

Today scholars are much less inclined to be influenced by the apparent resemblances between the teachings of Philo and St. John for, after all, these resemblances resolve themselves into a common use of the word *logos*. We are more inclined to compare the teaching of the Apostle to that of the sapiential books and to St. Paul. It remains that the person and work of Philo are worthy of examination in themselves. The problems they raise have lost none of their interest.

This Jewish philosopher is the only known representative of a mentality he must have shared with some of his compatriots. Philo was certainly not the only one who effected the fusion of the Jewish and Greek spirit, but he is the only one whose works we possess; and, as he wrote a great deal, we may in our leisure examine in his works the result of this intimate commingling of the two mentalities. On the other hand, Divine Providence brought him into the world before Christ, and took him from it after Christ; thus he was a contemporary of the Saviour and of the first Christian preaching. He might have heard of Jesus, might even have been present in Alexandria when trouble reared its head at the teaching of the gospel.[51] It was long believed on the authority of Eusebius and Jerome that the Therapeuti, so carefully described in Philo's *De Vita Contemplativa*, were Christian ascetics; but, regretfully, this identification has been rejected as unfounded.[52] However he is regarded, Philo attracts attention; it is natural that P. Lagrange had frequent occasion to speak of him.[53]

The first interesting thing about Philo is that he was a religious thinker. The theory of the Word provides a kind of privileged ground for beginning a study of his philosophy, because in it there are currents which issue from the most diverse sources: inspired writings of the Old Testament, doctrines of the different philosophical schools of Greece, especially of Stoicism, and religious beliefs of Egypt. Philo borrowed from each of these sources in turn; it is not surprising that the first impression made by his books is somewhat disconcerting.

Nowhere does he propose a systematic and definitive exposition of this doctrine of the Word. He is both commentator and exegete, and he speaks of the Logos apropos of this or that biblical passage. P. Lagrange puts it nicely when he writes:

He did not dream of refusing to believe the revealed teaching of the Scripture, nor was he at liberty to set aside the traditional interpretation of that Scripture. Nevertheless he was resolved to find in it the main points which he admitted as a philosopher. At times docile to the text, at other times he bent it to his fancy, and, divided as he was between the teachings of the synagogue and the disputes of the Greek schools, how could he fail to have produced a confused work? If one hesitates about his thought, and that is frequently the case, the best chance of discovering it is to consult his secret preferences: his whole heart belonged to Israel.[54]

Many commentators, however, have been deceived and see in Philo a renegade to paternal traditions. They would not have committed this blunder if they had remembered that the philosopher was once commissioned by his fellow religionists of Alexandria to head an embassy to Rome to plead in their favor, a fact which is sufficiently indicative of his loyalty as a Jew. One should always bear this in mind when reading a random passage in his works in which Greek thought seems triumphant. That is an illusion, for beneath the Hellenist, the Jew continued to live and keep his faith.

The all-important question for us in this matter is: Was the Logos of Philo a person? Did Philo conceive it as a person distinct from God, or only as a divine attribute? By reason of contradictory texts, this question is almost insoluble. Philo taught that the supreme God must not come into contact with what was finite, and so the Logos was necessary; it ought, then, to be distinct from God. On the other hand, it was identical with the objects it was obliged to unite, and consequently it was a property of God as well as a force acting in the world. This contradiction was called forth by the logic of the system. It is not certain what we are obliged to choose. Depending on the case, the Logos of Philo is or is not a person.

If a choice simply had to be made, then P. Lagrange was in favor of the personality of Philo's Logos, for he wrote:

At any rate, Philo clung closer to the biblical truth than he did to the theorems of the Stoics, whose terminology he used pretty much as he liked. The Bible gave him a glimpse of this great angel who spoke in the name of God, acted as God, and to whom men spoke as to God. The angel of the Lord was a reality for Philo; when he names it Logos, he does not wish to say that it represents the Logos, but that it performs the precise functions of the Logos, i.e., that it is to Israel what right reason was for the Stoics. To liken them was only following the principle of his whole work. But the angel was manifestly an individual distinct from God, and only appeared in God's place in order to elevate men to Him. . . . [55]

The studies which P. Lagrange devoted to the sanctifying role of the Logos set off some of Philo's mystical tendencies and reveal him as a loyal worshiper of Yahweh. Here the rift grew between his pagan wisdom and the Jewish religion, and a good judge could write of him: "Philo completely dehumanized ancient morality."[56] With reason, though, P. Lagrange protested against such a drastic judgment. The great novelty which Philo introduced into the Stoics' set of rules consisted in making the Logos not just right reason which counsels a man, but the divine reason and the divine active word as well, the minister of God's gifts. This divine word in a positive way gives strength to the soul by offering itself as spiritual food and drink; it also inspires sorrow for sin by procuring a cure for it.[57]

Some very penetrating studies on the mysticism of Philo appear in *Le judaisme avant Jésus-Christ*. Citing a passage of Philo's *De Abrahamo* (112), P. Lagrange remarked:

While the movement of the soul is analogous to that of the *Banquet,* there is this difference: the beauty of Plato is only an immovable object which awaits its admirers, whereas the God of Philo makes all the advances and comes to illumine man with its own proper light. On the other hand, Philo differs from the Christian mystics, for they, admitting a passivity of soul in certain divine operations, had in mind a passivity which did not prevent the intellect from acting, without knowing how it did; whereas Philo looked on contemplation as an ecstasy which drove out a man's intelligence and replaced it with the light of God.[58]

The fate of the Jewish philosopher of Alexandria remains shrouded in darkness, in spite of all the studies dedicated to him. Philo was at the crossroads, and apparently did not succeed in making up his mind to take one road or the other. Greek by education and surrounded by Greek influences, he was a Jew by religion — in a word, by whatever there was in him of depth and vitality. In reality he did not know how to be either a Greek or a Jew; and that makes him appear a rather tragic figure. It does not seem to have bothered him. Tirelessly he gave the best years of his life to commenting on the sacred books of the Jews — his own people — in a language calculated to make their acceptance palatable to the Greeks. In his exegesis he exercised all the most ingenious and subtle resources of allegory. Yet he failed to convert the Greeks, and in the Jewish world his name was quickly forgotten. After the fall of the Holy City, Jewish thought centered upon itself and crystallized in the Talmuds, from which all foreign influence was sedulously excluded. Philo was saved from oblivion by the Christians. He was probably ignorant of their teachings, and would have despised them if he knew them. Eusebius cites him with approval, and St. Jerome goes so far as to list him as an ecclesiastical writer. He exercised a great influence — not always of the best — upon Clement and Origen. Today it has to be admitted that his immense effort, as well as that of his Alexandrian predecessors,[59] taken as a whole, was a failure.

VII. THE HERMETIC BOOKS

While pursuing his studies on the fourth gospel, P. Lagrange came upon Hermeticism as well as Philo; but he certainly would have discovered it somehow even if he had not been directed to it by St. John. He had long been familiar with the works of Reitzenstein on the *Poimandres* when he finally took up the question seriously.[60] He himself admitted that, when he began the commentary on the fourth gospel, he found it impossible to evade this obscure study; and, as the commentary on St. John did not contain his findings, he decided to publish them in the *Revue Biblique*.[61]

The subject is obscure. We might add that the method followed by P. Lagrange was not to clarify it very much. A general introduction was meant to show the theological interest of Hermeticism and to introduce its principal characters: Thot, Hermes, and Hermes Trismegistus. Then P. Lagrange simply analyzed and translated as need arose from the various works which make up the *Corpus Hermeticum*, accompanying this with clarifications of details in the text, criticisms of previous interpretations, or comparisons with parallels in Greek, Jewish, or Christian writings. His only conclusion was chiefly unfavorable:

Are there any good reasons for believing in Hermetic influence upon the first Christians and their writings? No, we reply. In the first place, none of the Hermetic writings in our possession go back beyond the second century, or rather beyond the third century A.D.

Between Hermeticism, i.e., a doctrine of (even revealed) understanding, and the Christianity of St. John, which is an object of our faith, there is absolute opposition. As a matter of fact, regeneration cannot have been a primitive theory of the sect, for it is found in only one Hermetic treatise, the thirteenth. It is unquestionably a doctrine of light, as all Platonism is, but like Platonism, it is not a doctrine of an interior life communicated by grace. . . .

To conclude, then: in regard to Hermeticism there has been much ado about nothing. We have indeed taken great pains to arrive at such a sorry result, but it is always seasonable to free the gospel from compromising comparisons.[62]

We must look to Egypt for the birthplace of Hermetic literature. The Egyptians adored Thot, the god of speech and writing, at Hermopolis. The Greeks who settled in Egypt likened their Hermes to Thot, for he was the messenger of the gods and their interpreter. Thot-Hermes was called Trismegistus, or "three times very great," and in the syncretism which around the Christian era tended pretty much to confuse the gods, he was supposed to be the great revealer.

Gradually a literature arose in praise of Hermes Trismegistus, comprising as we now have it, seventeen *libelli,* written over the period of a hundred years, and bound together only by an artificial unity; the collection may be dated about the fourth century A.D.[63] There are also the *Asclepius,* an important work often cited by Lactantius, and wrongly listed among the books of Apuleius; four large fragments cited by Stobeius of a sacred book called *La pupille,* or *The Virgin of the World* (Kore Kosmou); a few fragments of a collection of fifteen books known to Clement of Alexandria and assembled at Athens;[64] the *Strasbourg Cosmogony,* a papyrus fragment, so called by its discoverer, R. Reitzenstein; and a few other fragments or treatises on medicine and astronomy edited by W. Kroll. Of course, the list is incomplete, and the papyri ought certainly to swell this already complex ensemble.

With such literature, we might expect that the members of the Hermetic religion would have left many traces of their piety. Actually we know nothing historical about the fate of Hermeticism. We are told of those who were ignorant and needed enlightenment;[65] there are hints that the disciples of Hermes were persecuted;[66] but this is all very vague. Were there ever any Hermetic communities anywhere? A mosaic inscription, found in 1921 at Lambridi, appears up to the present to be the principal argument in favor of their existence. The most important inscription of this monument bears the name of a woman, Cornelia Urbanilla, who was saved (masculine) from a great danger and lived (masculine again) twenty-eight years, ten months, twelve days, and nine hours. The mosaic itself explains the inscription, for it represents a hermaphroditic personage — the dead woman, probably — stretching out a hand to another hermaphrodite who was probably a god (masculine), if not the supreme God. Genii, a mixing bowl, and a deep cup complete the tableau. J. Carpopino recognized in these the characteristic traits of

Hermeticism, and concluded to the existence of groups of initiates in Africa toward the last third of the third century.[67] His arguments have been generally admitted,[68] but we submit that we should like to have more precise information about the life of these Hermetic communities.

The Hermetic books are themselves far from being clear. P. Lagrange analyzed them at length, and in his articles gave a translation and commentary of the most important ones.

Side by side with beautiful passages on the union of the soul with God, there are frequent masses of meaningless verbiage. Chances are that this literature would have interested no one in our day if someone had not thought of comparing it with the gospel according to St. John and the epistles of St. Paul. The Hermetic books as we know them were written after the New Testament, however, and it may be affirmed that the ideas they express and even the words employed in them were sufficiently current in the first century of our era for the two saints, John and Paul, to use them.

To illustrate: In the fourth gospel, light and life play a large part. Christ is represented as life and light; He came both to vivify and to enlighten. He cured the man born blind, and raised up Lazarus to prove that He had this double mission. The Hermetic books often speak of light and life; hence, some conclude that St. John borrowed both words from the piety of which they are the expression.[69] P. Lagrange has an entirely different explanation:

The supreme *nous* is light (in the Hermetic writings); but that does not explain the couplet. The two concepts are proposed as a translation of the male and female elements of the supreme *nous,* which were handed down to the heavenly man, his son, and then to those born of him; finally to all men, even of a different sex. Then, how explain the duality of the *nous,* which is masculine, and the soul, which is feminine? That is something very arbitrary, a gloss from the bisexual faculty, traced back to a twofold intellectual faculty. . . . This aspect of the divine nature in man is found nowhere else in Hermetism. But it could be the author's attempt at adaptation. Actually the two words life and light are oftenest found in passages which could be detached. Since the Logos had been added, by, it seems, Christian copyists, to our text of the Poimandres, and in some others known to Lactantius and St. Cyril, we are inclined to say as much of life and light.[70]

This hypothesis of an interpolation is certainly not imperative. The association of life and light is so natural that it would occur to anyone; but by itself it does not suffice to establish a relationship of dependence between the writings in which it appears. We are sure, at least, that all the arguments by which men have attempted to prove that the New Testament theology was borrowed from Hermetism crumble as soon as they are subjected to close scrutiny. P. Lagrange never overlooked contemporary works; he resolved to examine the value of these arguments, to test them patiently, without trying to avoid that often distasteful task of reading all the extant Hermetic works or fragments. His conclusion, after an honest examination, was that the pretended similarities have no serious foundation. "As for the influence of a spiritual and monotheistic teaching upon the development of Christianity, that is quite another and a much larger question. In that case we should have to speak of Platonism or neo-Platonism; for ordinary Hermeticism, with its avowed pantheism, was still farther removed from the religion of the gospel."[71]

CONCLUSION

With Hermeticism we have come to and even gone beyond the time when God, who at sundry times and in divers manners spoke to our fathers by the prophets, manifested Himself to the world by His Son, by whom He made the world (Hebr. 1:1-2). The golden age of Hellenism had gone forever, and so its mission was at an end. P. Lagrange followed its course with interest from those far-off beginnings. He watched the Greek miracle manifest itself for the first time in ancient Crete and followed it up to the day it wore itself out in vain appeals to the mysterious divinities found in the Hermetic books. Eagerly he delved into the most insignificant nooks where the thought of her philosophers and poets was expressed, where the genius of her artists was given free sway, and where the ardor of that piety, so often enthusiastic and mystical, was developed.[72] We may truly say that there are not many men of our time who have shown so much interest in the various aspects of Hellenism.

There is a human quality to this curiosity which appeals to us. How, when he had thought it all over, could he have remained untouched by the charm of Hellas? Everything about Greece was made to captivate and bewitch us. One of the frescoes of Cnossos so vividly recalls the silhouette of the Parisienne of our day that it is called by that name; and are not the interlocutors assigned to Socrates by Plato in his Dialogues our own contemporaries?

P. Lagrange, however, was too priestly a man to allow himself to be bewitched by the miracle of Greece. While he studied the divers aspects of Hellenism, he never lost sight of the fact that his life was dedicated to the service of the living God, and that the gods of Greece were dead gods, no matter how beautiful the verses composed for them or the temples raised in their honor. He was ready to believe, like Justin or Clement of Alexandria, that all minds of good will, including those which lived before the fullness of time and the giving of the supreme gift of God to humanity, were partially enlightened by the Word, the true light "which enlighteneth every man coming into the world"; but he was not blind to the feebleness, the shortcomings, and the wickedness of Greece. With patience he lent an ear to the indistinct voices which rose upward, calling — though they did not know it — for a liberator, addressing their prayers to an unknown god. He saw the philosophers bring forward, one by one, those stones which one day would be built into a temple by the preachers of the gospel. His heart stirred at the anxiety which led men to look for a much-needed salvation in the mystery religions. As he pursued his patient task with all his strength, from within and all around him, came a host of arguments which demonstrated the divine transcendence of Christianity.

P. Lagrange did not really have to look for these arguments. Nowhere did he set up a thesis or present himself as an apologist. But the facts were so striking as to appear invincible. Is it not true that the theology of Plato won no disciples, that the distant god of Aristotle drew none to love him, that Stoicism came to an end in the pride of Epictetus and the incurable pessimism of Marcus Aurelius?

Such a heap of ruins! Men would have despaired if it were not for the fact that, when the ancient wisdom failed, the best of them knew enough to raise their arms to the Saviour whose birth in Bethlehem of Juda was brought about by God. P. Lagrange leads us back to this Saviour and, for that reason especially, the lesson he gives us is profoundly salutary.

GUSTAVE BARDY
Grand séminaire de Dijon, France

CHAPTER IV

THE COMPARATIVE HISTORY OF RELIGIONS AND THE REVEALED RELIGION

I. GENERAL REMARKS

THE comparative history of religions is not a thing of yesterday, although it still bears about it some characteristic marks of the daring and the energetic power of youth. Continually taking over new fields, it unceasingly multiplies comparisons of doctrines and rites which are not only most diverse but also widely separated in time and space. Since the beginning of this century it has tried especially to find analogies between Old and New Testament on the one hand, and pagan religions and philosophies on the other. The initial motion came from the Germans. French, English, American, and Italian scholars have followed their lead.

P. Lagrange was one of the first to insist that the parallels flooding in from all sides were important for the study of revealed religion. He set out in this branch of research to sift comparisons which were simply ingenious from those which were truly scientific statements of fact. In the work of discrimination he took great pains to be impartial, even to those who offended his scholarly exactness, his priestly convictions, and his piety. His was a middle position between a fatuous state of illusion and an uncompromisingly hostile attitude.

To begin with, he did not anathematize comparative history of religions; if such a science did not exist it would have to be invented, for the relations and analogies between diverse religions cannot be denied. No matter how far back we go in history, we never find different human groups living shut up in sealed compartments; the more we learn about the past, the more we discover about the influences and crossings of tribes, peoples, and races. Early in this century, in a monumental and otherwise remarkable history of the peoples of the Orient, Maspero described the earliest Egyptian and Chaldean civilizations (almost) as if each had developed in splendid isolation; hence he was led to date his second volume, *Premières mêlées des peuples,* from the 18th Egyptian dynasty (fourteenth century B.C.). It is now recognized that from the third millennium B.C., Egyptian, Semitic, and even Indo-European influences met and met again in anterior Asia, growing on to an old autochthonous stock which for lack of a better name is called Asianic.

We may go even further. The human amalgam reaches far back into prehistory, for it is proved that in the upper paleolithic age there were, in France, black, white, and yellow men (men of Grimaldi, Cro-Magnon, and Chamcelade types).

On the other hand, even the rites of such advanced religions as that of the Greeks can only be explained by customs and ideas no longer to be found except among the primitive peoples of our own day. Old agrarian cults still survive, in which men try to act on nature by sympathetic magic, pouring out water, for example, so as to bring rain. Here the dead, the very ancient dead, speak; and they closely resemble our present-day savages.

Comparative history of religions can have its word to say even when revealed religion is being discussed. As P. Lagrange wrote in 1904:

The world is invincibly preoccupied with the religious problem. That Christianity or the first writers of Christianity borrowed something from man's previous attempts to draw near to the divinity or to assimilate it to oneself, that even myths entered into it's symbols, has nothing astonishing or shocking in it. (Cf. Calmes' study, "Les symboles de l'Apocalypse," *RB,* [1903], 52, 59.)[1]

It was quite necessary that a new religion, even Christianity, speak the language of the times in which it appeared, and that it make reference to conceptions which this language supposed, even when it was going beyond them. P. Lagrange congratulated Deissmann for having studied the New Testament vocabulary with this thought in mind, and for not denying, for all of that, the transcendence of the faith which was there expressed.

Deissmann has brought out the real, living, simple, even every-day aspect of the New Testament writings. Certainly he did not intend to conclude from this that the content also was borrowed from the surrounding atmosphere, for he points out more than once how the spirit appeared more powerful in this common clothing. This reflection is imperative, when there is question of cult and religion. It is a fact that a great number of terms passed over from the cult of the Caesars to that of Jesus Christ. The sovereign was God, Son of God, Saviour, and men spoke of His parousia.[2]

Recognition should also be made of progress in the exegesis of the New Testament, a progress effected by this method of the history of religions.

The method of the history of religions is leaning far toward the right. M. Clemen is less refractory than before. In proportion as it so leans, however, it loses entirely its character as a school, and becomes a movement which carries the German critics toward new regions — new often in reality, following upon discoveries which are likewise new, because they have been too much shut up in literary criticism and in protestant opinions. The dogmatic conceptions are far removed from ours, or rather they no longer count, which permits us — this supreme reserve being well under-stood — to agree on many points. If documentary research and research according to monuments are pushed to their fullest extent, we will have no complaint.[3]

P. Lagrange was careful to extend to scholars the same justice he rendered to science. He did not issue a blanket condemnation of them because they based their work on the method of the history of religions. M. Clemen often opposed the conclusions of this school which the Germans called *religions-geschichtliche;* he is described as "well-informed and prudent, and (P. Lagrange continues) if I am any judge, a Catholic critic could subscribe to many of his judgments."[4]

In Gunkel, Lagrange detected a certain adherence to a very broad and watered-down variety of Christianity.[5]

Loisy's *Essence of Christianity* was still more reduced than that of Gunkel; yet he recognized the fact of a difference between it and the mystery religions (cults of Isis, Demeter, Attis, Mithra, Dionysus). For this P. Lagrange gives him credit, stating that, in his study of the mystery religions, Loisy "more than once did justice to the superiority of Christianity."[6]

Even yet the old professor of the *Collège de France* refuses to break away completely from Christianity. He protests against the accusers who call him the "gravedigger" of Christianity. "We only aspire to be the precursors of its renovation."[7]

In the case of Solomon Reinach, things were different. The Master of Jerusalem declared with some sadness:

It is very easy to perceive that, according to Reinach, the Catholic Church is a world calamity, and so he hates it. This disposition does not rule out his scientific honesty (Jesus said that persecutors of His disciples would think they were rendering God a service), but his attitude reflects passion, even blind passion.[8]

Finally, and in the last place, come the authors of the collection *Christianisme* (with the exception of M. André Boulanger, author of *Orphée*). After some sharp criticism directed at M. Stahl, author of *Les Mandéens et les origines chrétiennes*, and fully deserved from a scientific point of view, P. Lagrange wrote:

I cannot conceal the impression made on me by some of the works in this collection which is directed by M. Couchoud. It seems indeed that these men are amusing themselves at the credulity of the public, just as in the times of Diana Vaughran. In discussing it, therefore, we have the feeling of falling into a trap, even while pointing it out.[9]

Whatever their intentions and dispositions may be, authors who attempt to explain the very origin of Christianity by the theory of a union of the Jewish faith with aspirations of the pagan soul (Clemen is not of this number), fall into grave errors of method which may be summarized as a lack of critical exactitude, and arbitrariness.

Homo loquax — M. Bergson warns not to confuse him with *homo sapiens* — readily believes that he possesses an inexhaustible stock of words and gestures with which he can express his thoughts and feelings. Actually the stock is quite limited, as is the sensible experience from which it is borrowed. At any rate, it is clearly inadequate to translate the richness of our interior life. Witness as proof the many meanings words have when taken in conjunction with their verbal or psychological context; even then they cannot remotely equal this inner richness. Consequently, especially where religious ideas and sentiments are concerned, widely divergent spiritual attitudes and beliefs may creep in under the same symbols and the same rites. Further, just as sensible experience provides men with many common images, no matter how widely separated they may be in actual life, religions may present similarities of language or of externals; but these will not necessarily indicate any common origin, or the borrowing of one from the other.

Hence the great danger of exaggerating the importance of analogies between doctrines and especially religious rites, and of concluding to a dependence in cases where a merely distant resemblance can be traceable to the general laws of language and the common basis of human nature.

With this in mind, P. Lagrange congratulated M. Clemen for distinguishing language from thought:

He does not make the common mistake of confounding the expression with the thought. He shows how an expression, even a technical pagan one, could in the New Testament take on a new meaning, e.g., τροχὸς τῆς γενέσεως, the wheel of life in the epistle of St. James (3:6). All the more reason for admitting some contact of thought which will not prevent originality of conceptions.[10]

For these reasons, prefacing the statement by saying that he does not dream of scolding him for being an ardent devotee of the comparative method, he says of Reinach:

Theologians (for whom Reinach has little use) pride themselves on the precision of their reasoning. . . . Certainly there will be subtleties. Listen, then, to a specialist as foreign to our faith as Reinach: "Progress in a science, so speaks M. Van Gennep, depends upon the ever greater precision of its terms."

Again: "Every scholar in the field of ethnography knows that, with a bit of luck, he will find half-civilized modern parallels for any ancient custom or belief. What is important is that the parallel be borrowed from a modern form of civilization which is really comparable to the ancient civilization, and that the fact to be explained be an actual element of that ancient civilization." These are rules of elementary logic.[11]

The abuse of words reaches its climax when vocabularies are deliberately befogged. P. Lagrange judiciously draws attention to this in an article in *Le Correspondant*, July 25, 1910:

There is a continuous affectation on the part of our historians of religions to use words having a definite Christian meaning when they speak of pagan religions.

In a scientific work, this is a dangerous game and a source of grave confusion. It is not unusual to read of "the Mithraic communion"; and yet M. Cumont informs us that "the supper of Mithra and his companions" ought to be understood in the same way as "the socialism of Diocletian."[12]

. . . We accuse no historian of religions of deliberately making use of equivocal terms; we simply point out that they prejudge without seeming to do so the syncretism they should demonstrate. Nowhere but in the science of religions would such a faulty method be permitted.[13]

Besides superficial comparisons, another lack of rigorous method is to block together texts of vastly different dates, a process which permits one, for example, to guess at the meaning of the rites of mystery religions of the time of St. Paul, according to Apuleius, who was born *c*. A.D. 124, or Prudentius, who lived around the end of the fourth or the beginning of the fifth century A.D.

The trouble with men who study the history of religions is that they see resemblances everywhere, and consequently — much more grave — dependences everywhere; and with these they establish a relationship without taking *dates* and *values* sufficiently into consideration. The ascendancy of Christianity toward the middle of the fourth century was such that "the pagan reform attempted by Julian the emperor was clearly inspired by the institutions of the Church."[14] No one denies that. It would be most surprising if this official attempt which emanated from the emperor himself had not been preceded by like attempts on the part of the priests or philosophers, who had from the second century onward understood the triumphant upward surge of Christianity.[15] Thus it was not from the taurobolium that the idea of redemption arose; on the contrary, this idea was borrowed from Christianity.[16]

Still another justifiable reproach against historians of religions, who try to explain Christianity as a Judaeo-Christian syncretism, is the arbitrariness and spirit of their system — a result of rationalistic prejudice. P. Lagrange brought this out by showing what part they played in the series of different schools in Germany, where every effort was made to explain the origin of Christianity by purely natural factors.[17] The liberal school had detached Christ entirely from His background; the eschatological school had so identified Him with it that one wonders how the disciples of such an exclusively Jewish master succeeded in conquering the Greco-Roman world.[18]

Next came the syncretist school with a new but, again, a strictly naturalistic explanation.

In 1917, M. Windisch could say: "After more than ten years, the New Testament again finds itself under the aegis of the history of religions."[19]

Christianity was said to have invaded the Greco-Roman world because it was a synthesis of Jewish and pagan elements. What is always taken for granted is that the only valid causes are the purely natural ones.

Criticism of Christian origins, resolved as it is, especially in Germany, to pay no attention to tradition and to eliminate the supernatural, is constantly searching for purely human antecedents which would have produced the most extraordinary religious fact of history. The history of religions, and of philosophies, has been examined with a curiosity that is quickly satisfied with the most elusive comparisons. First came the "mysteries," then Hermetism. Today it is the Mandeans who lead the parade.[20]

II. OBJECT OF THE PRESENT STUDY

In order to explain Christianity, at whatever cost, in a purely natural way, i.e., to reduce it to the plane of other religions, the vast field of the world and of universal history has been explored. Men have looked successively and sometimes simultaneously to India, Babylon, to all forms of Greek thought and piety, and to the numerous manifestations of oriental syncretism in which Semites, Iranians, Egyptians, and Greeks have collaborated.

Here I will consider only the mystery religions, the religions of Iran and Mandeism. Of the latter two I will speak much more briefly. M. Bardy has made a study of Hermetism and M. Chaine of everything that concerns the Semitic world. The mystery religions which are Iranian in their oldest form and Mandaean have this in common, that they stressed salvation in a life beyond the grave; while the national cults of the Greek and Roman cities concentrated especially on the temporal prosperity of the state and of the individual.

It is thirty years since P. Lagrange became interested in the question of mystery religions. In order to follow step by step a considerable movement of research and of hypotheses, he wrote digests of systems, made profound studies of particular points, wrote reviews of books which dealt with it, and made notes on any archaeological discoveries with a bearing on the subject. In France he had many imitators: Mangenot, Vénard, Jacquier, P. de Grandmaison, P. Allo, P. Pinard de la Boullaye, and others; but I believe that, from the point of view of the technical discussion of such studies, the most important and remarkable contributions came from P. Lagrange.

We are indebted to him, first of all, for four synthetic expositions of the theories concerning the relation of Christianity to the mystery religions: (1) An article first published in *Le Correspondant,* July 25, 1910, on "Les religions orientales et les origines du christianisme à propos de livres récents," and reprinted in *Mélanges d'histoire religieuse* (Paris, 1915), 69–130; (2) the chapter in *Le sens du christianisme d'après l'exégèse allemande* (Paris, 1918), entitled: "L'ecole du syncrétisme judéo-païen"; it is limited to German scholars, whereas the preceding study included French authors, or those writing in that language; (3) a long review in the *Revue*

Biblique, XXIX (1920), 420–446, of Loisy's *Les Mystères païens et le Mystère chretien* (1919); and (4) a brief résumé of the origin and evolution of Loisy's ideas, in *M. Loisy et le modernisme* (Juvisy, 1932), 200–217.

Also to be found in the *Revue Biblique* are P. Lagrange's careful, critical studies of the mysteries of Eleusis and of Attis: "Les mystères d'Eleusis et le christianisme," *RB,* XXVIII (1919), 157–217; "La régénération et la filiation divine dans les mystères d'Eleusis," *ibid.,* 63–81; 201–204; "Attis et le christianisme," *ibid.,* 419–480; "Attis ressuscité," *RB,* XXXVI (1927), 561–566.

From 1904 to 1934, beginning with a review of the first number of the *Forschungen* (Studies) of Gunkel and Bousset, the two best known proponents of the German school of the history of religions, the founder of the *École* at Jerusalem faithfully published, in his *Revue,* book reviews and simple notices which constitute a daily record of the latest developments of the Judaeo-pagan syncretists, together with the criticisms and objections which met them on the road.

Since the publication of a work by Reitzenstein,[21] rational criticism has chosen, out of all the different pagan influences which would have contributed to the formation of Christianity, especially that of the mystery religions; with these we shall soon deal. Bousset in his turn took up the ideas of Reitzenstein.[22] From 1911 on, Loisy interested himself in Reitzenstein's theories,[23] and, in 1919, published his synthesis of the question;[24] it was brilliant, but it differed from the stand taken by Bousset.

Since P. Lagrange aimed his own studies on the mystery religions principally at Loisy, we shall present a résumé of the opinions of the professor of the *Collège de France.* We have done this elsewhere under the pseudonym of Philonous.[25]

"Marshaling into a single vast synthesis all the gifts of his great erudition, Loisy reduced Christianity to the status of 'a particular case' (though both typical and eminent) of that whole movement which, impelled by its belief in immortal-

ity, slowly transformed the old national and nature cults of
the Mediterranean world into universal religions.

"The Roman and official Greek religions were only interested in the common, and entirely earthly interests of the city,
kingdom, empire. Individual preoccupation in a moral life,
in one's personal destiny in another world, in the part played
by the gods in both worlds . . . [the gods see to this] either
badly or not at all. They seem to be quite deficient, incapable of satisfying their own followers, who thereupon
turned to the mystery cults and to Christianity, which offered
them what the old religions could not give.

"What these greater forms of piety and belief offered (i.e.,
the mysteries of Dionysus and Orpheus, of Demeter and Kore
at Eleusis, of Cybele and Attis, of Isis and Osiris, and of
Mithra, and finally the Christian mystery) was refuge from
a 'denationalized, universalized, individualized' cult. They
were not limited to assuring prosperity to a human group —
however large it might be — but they gave to initiates of *any*
race an especially efficacious guarantee of blessed immortality
. . . as if by a special and individual privilege, by a veritable
grace which was applied to their person.

"There is no doubt that the mysteries also issued from
national religions, but it was not done by way of direct development. The process may be sketched roughly as follows.
During the course of centuries, a very old rite — usually a
sacrifice, but sometimes a sacred marriage, *hierogamy* — was
thought by primitive man to aid the forces of nature, particularly the vital energies of the plant or of the animal, in their
beneficent work, by his own acts of 'sympathetic' magic. This
old rite was given a mythical explanation, and was thought
to symbolize or, rather, to re-enact a divine happening in the
days of long ago. The hope of a blessed immortality became
for many such an imperious need that it seized upon both the
myth and the rite, and gave them a new meaning, one entirely different from that conferred on them first by the utili-
tarian magic of prehistory, and later by the interests of the
old city. The age-old *sacrifice* by which farmers and shepherds
assisted the rebirth (from spring to spring and from one gen-

eration to another) of the frail spirit of germination or fertility, became the principle and sacrament of immortality when
there was substituted the spirit of a personal god who died
and rose up again as the spirit. Through the *rite*, the initiate
shared in the destiny of a Saviour, i.e., in his death and
resurrection.

"The analogy with Christianity, they say, is evident. The
story of Easter, Baptism, the Last Supper, were all born in
Judaism, i.e., in a narrowly national religion. Stephen, Barna-
bas, Paul, Apollo, the author of the epistle to the Hebrews
and of the Johannine writings, these first Hellenistic
preachers of the gospel, in the enthusiasm of their faith, spon-
taneously constructed a universal religion, which, although
they were not aware of it, was conceived according to the
model of the pagan mysteries, and yet was greatly superior to
them all. Jesus became the Lord and Saviour to whom men
united themselves in the closest of unions through the Sacraments; by sharing in His death, the believer is 'assured of a
share in His resurrection; in a sense, he already had a share
in it here below.' "[26]

III. THE PRINCIPAL MYSTERY RELIGIONS

A. *Preliminary Remarks*

It is evident that the preceding lines are merely a résumé
of Loisy's work, and should not therefore lead us to overlook
his minute studies of the texts. P. Lagrange studied the same
texts without finding in them the system elaborated by the
learned professor of the *Collège de France*. Here obviously
we cannot go into his detailed criticism, but we shall pick
out his most important remarks apropos of the mysteries of
Dionysus and Orpheus, Eleusis, Cybele and Attis, Isis and
Osiris, Mithra; and shall conclude with the results of the
founder of the school at Jerusalem.

There were many other mysteries besides these in Greek
or hellenized lands: the mysteries of Andania, of the more or
less orthodox branches of Eleusis; as, e.g., in Arcadia, at
Phlionte, Megalopolis, Pheneos, those of Cabires on the isle

of Samothrace, those of Apollo at Claros, of Artemis at Ephesus, and others.

We limit ourselves to the afore-mentioned mysteries because it is upon them that the historians of religions insist, and also because at present, at least, they are the best known. Of course, we have no complete and certain knowledge about them — anything but that. The secret imposed upon the adepts and from which they derived their name was well kept, for we have only veiled allusions for even the better known mysteries.

B. *Dionysus and Orphism*

From Thrace, where the god was apparently called Sabazios, came the cult of Dionysus. The primitives strove to exercise dominion over the animal kingdom by immolating an animal of the species they desired to dominate, thus gaining control over its spirit. From this practice arose the principal rite of the old cult, viz., the cutting to pieces of a bull or a kid. That is almost all we know with serious probability about it. We do not know if the votaries desired to unite themselves to the animal "god" by eating its flesh, for one form of the Dionysus myth included no such eating. Among the civilized Greeks, this bull god or kid ceased to be an animal god; instead it became one of the most brilliant creations of their poetic genius, while retaining something of the irrational frenzy of the Thracians. A Greek god cannot die; it is Dionysus who devours the flesh of the bull, and is replaced in his role as victim either by Penthaeus, who was put to death by the Bacchantes, or by Orpheus, who was torn to pieces by the Maenads.

However, there *was*, in the Greek pantheon, a god immolated in connection with Dionysus: Zagreus. He came from Crete, where the story of Osiris, the Egyptian god who was torn to bits, was already known. He was apparently fused with Dionysus when this latter was still looked upon as a sacrificed god, and it was on the authority of that Creto-Egyptian tradition that the Greeks, despite their cult of the immortal gods, welcomed his myth. If we may believe

Pausanius, this myth was fixed by Onomacritus in the time
of Pisistratus, tyrant of Athens from 501–527 B.C. According
to the story, the infant Zagreus was kidnaped by the Titans,
who lured him away with balls and dolls; he was torn apart
and eaten by the Titans, although according to some, he tried
to escape them by assuming the shape of a bull. Athena res-
cued his heart, and Zeus devoured it; thus there was nothing
to prevent his being born anew as Dionysus, son of Zeus and
Semele. Other legends omitted the feast of the Titans, holding that Zagreus was born again each year, just like the vine,
and everyone knows that Dionysus is the god of the vine.

Orphism was grafted on to these mysteries which recalled
the myth of Zagreus-Dionysus, giving them an incomparable
religious value. The significance of Orphism appears more
clearly from a study of the Golden Tablets (found in some
tombs in Crete and southern Italy, and dating from about
200 B.C.) than from the speculations of the Neo-Platonists of
the fifth and sixth centuries of our era.

Orphism taught an original fault, which can only be the
murder of Zagreus at the hands of the Titans. Stricken by light-
ning, they had disappeared, but from them had been born men
who bore the responsibility of the original crime. Reborn by
passing through various forms, according to the teachings of
metempsychosis, men could be delivered from these vicissitudes
by leading the Orphic life. They then hoped to present themselves to Persephone, become gods, and enjoy happiness. The
Orphic life consisted in purifications which were at the same
time their deliverance: no contact with life or death, abstention
from meats, wearing of white clothing to symbolize their purity.[27]

After a careful study of the alleged texts, P. Lagrange concluded that the revealer of the mystery was not Dionysus, but
Orpheus; further, that the "passion" of Dionysus was not the
principle of salvation, but rather the original crime and the
greatest obstacle to it; that the god did not rise from the
dead, and that his followers, like good Greeks, only toyed
with the idea of a resurrection; that the Orphic rites were
only a purification; that the union with the god was realized
in Orphism by a kind of possession *antecedent to* the rite of
dismemberment (which was therefore not a theophagy), or

perhaps also by a sacred marriage. Orphism certainly was able to prepare souls for the idea of the passion, for the dogma of original sin, and for the practices of Christian asceticism. Consequently, some of the Fathers thought that Orpheus had been the disciple of Moses; even Christ is represented in the catacombs under the figure of Orpheus. However, Christianity had no need to go to the mysteries of Dionysus for any of its elements.[28]

C. *The Mysteries of Demeter and Kore, and of Prosperina at Eleusis*

The character of the Greek goddess Demeter is twofold. On the one hand, she was an agrarian goddess, goddess of corn (Ceres), spirit of the fruitful earth and vegetation; her favorite Triptolemus was the first to work the soil with an ox-drawn plow. On the other hand, she is the sorrowful mother who seeks for her daughter Prosperina,[29] who had been kidnaped by Pluto. When during her search she stopped at Eleusis, she struck the earth with sterility and would not lift the curse, except on the condition that Prosperina spend two thirds of the year with her mother in Olympus; the remaining third was given to Aidoneus-Pluto, master of Hades. Demeter, like Zagreus, came from Crete where Egyptian influences were at work.

This second aspect of Demeter probably grew out of the first. One may conjecture that as Prosperina was primitively the spirit of corn — or as folklore would word it: daughter of the corn — she descends into and reappears from the earth after the fashion of seed which falls into the furrow and comes forth as green and then ripe corn. The connections of Demeter and Prosperina with the underworld were stressed by the Egyptian sources. P. Lagrange adopted (as did Loisy) the ideas popularized by Frazer concerning the transformation of agrarian gods and goddesses, by the above-mentioned process, into divinities of the nether regions and of the world beyond.[30]

The mysteries in honor of Demeter and Prosperina were generally celebrated at Eleusis, some ten miles from Athens.

The lesser mysteries took place at Agra, a suburb of Athens, on the banks of the Illisos; there the rites of purification occurred, and the "mystagogues" of the sacred families of Eumolpides and Keryces began their instruction of the candidates. This took place during the month of *Anthesterion* (January–February). The great mysteries lasted for eleven days, beginning with the 15th of *Boedromion* (September–October). First, there was the warning of a secret to be kept, a bath in the sea, different sacrifices; then, after a procession from Athens to Eleusis, the ceremonies of the initiation properly so called took place on the eighth and ninth days. It was carried out in the central part of the sanctuary at Eleusis, in the *telesterion* (initiation hall), a room with seats in tiers, which could accommodate three thousand people. The interior arrangement of this room has been quite accurately reconstructed according to excavations of 1882–1895 and 1920.

So well has the secret imposed during these rites been guarded that we have only crumbs of information concerning the ceremonies which made of the candidate an *epopté,* or seer. Before their entry into the *telesterion,* the candidates consumed the *kykeon,* the drink which had once restored Demeter after her long fast. Then, having performed certain acts about which we know nothing, they pronounced the formula given us by St. Clement of Alexandria, an ex-initiate: "I have fasted, I have drunk the potion (*kykeon*), I have taken [the thing] from the chest, and after using it, I placed it in the basket, and again from the basket into the chest." According to Dietrich, the mysterious object alluded to was a *pudendum.* Loisy thought of a *phallus,* or of serpents, as having the same signification; in this hypothesis, the basket would have had a symbolic meaning.[31]

It may be that the formula cited by Clement was related to the very course of the ceremonies which were celebrated in the *telesterion.*[32]

During the night, according to the expression of Clement, a "mystical drama" was enacted, portraying the descent of Prosperina to the underworld, Demeter searching for her daughter accompanied by the candidates who waved their torches, and finally the return of Prosperina to the light. Coming after the lamentations, this was a moment of joyful expansion; the torches, no longer useful, were extinguished. A text of Plutarch preserved by Stobeus suggests "a [foot-]race of the mystae in the underworld, leading them to a country of light, image of their future destinies."[33] A sacred marriage was mimed, more or less in the nude, by the hierophant and a priestess, and represented the union of Demeter with Zeus, according to Foucart and Loisy, or — and this is P. Lagrange's conjecture — the union of the goddess with a mortal Celeos, father of Triptolemus.[34] After this the hierophant proclaimed:: "The divine Brimo has begotten Brimos," that is, as it is thought, "The strong has begotten the strong."

The sacred marriage promised first of all . . . richness, i.e., good harvests. Originally the sacred marriage had in view only the end of a plague or good results in agriculture.

We have seen that, if the homeric hymn to Demeter presupposed the culture [of fields], from the fifth century on the legend affirmed that Demeter had given, that is, had revealed the cereals. This must have been the last act of the drama; and indeed, in Hippolytus the climax of the vision [epopie] was the showing of an ear of corn which had been harvested in silence. This was done, it seems, in conjunction with the sacred marriage [originally meant to stimulate the fertility of the earth . . .]. The significance of the ear of corn still remains a mystery. Some can see it in a symbol of life transmitted by generation. . . . Others were led to think of the rebirth of which the corn is symbolic. . . . Naturally the ancients could have conceived of another symbolism, one similar to that of the Egyptians who planted corn on sarcophagi so that the sprouts would typify Osiris.[35]

What was the spiritual value of these mysteries? It is now everywhere agreed that they were not invested with any lofty meaning simply because they enshrined an esoteric doctrine whose meaning we have not been able to discover.

The exegesis of the Stoics and Neo-Platonists was "always a superficial thing, a gloss for the curious and argumentative. At any rate, whatever efficacy was attributed to the rites, a distinction must be drawn between the representation of the abduction of Prosperina and the sacred marriage." The myth of Demeter was a divine history which concerned only divine persons; its utility for men was never considered. To see in the "passion" of the goddess a salutary event for the world is "to transport a Christian idea into the mysteries."

On the other hand, the sacred marriage must have been considered as an efficacious symbol. Souls could be inspired by it, perhaps "under the impulse of divine grace," to think of a union of the higher parts of the soul with the divinity. But by itself, the rite did not suggest faith "in a divine power communicated to the initiates to help them practice virtue." The guarantee offered by the mysteries sufficed and occasionally even supplied for the absence of virtue. This point is admitted by the critics. The initiated were certain, with a religious assurance, of their salvation, and no demands were made on them for conversion or a new life.[36]

P. Lagrange clarified and developed his ideas on these points in two articles on the "Régénération et la filiation divine dans les mystères d'Eleusis."[37] The mysteries of Eleusis aroused hopes for the time which followed death, but the promised happiness was supposed to be realized on earth. "One must have entirely lost this point of view — which is essential and absolutely certain — in order to speak of a resurrection at Eleusis." Moreover "the Greeks never took the resurrection of the body seriously."

Elsewhere, among the Pythagoreans and Orphics, men looked forward to a new birth. . . . But the hope of the Orphics was to be delivered from this circle of births, and the Pythagoreans hoped to raise themselves to the starry heavens.

The initiates at Eleusis could no more hope for a rebirth than they could for a divine filiation. The happy life assured them was not

. . . the divine life of Olympus, reserved to the gods; and so we may conclude, inversely, that those who remained in the Elysium were not sons of the gods. . . . Had the initiates become sons of Demeter, even by mere adoption, their place would have been with the gods, just as Christians, sons of God, are admitted to His presence after their death. But they remained in Hades, and they did not have to be adopted by Prosperina to be admitted to her society; at least there was never any question of a kind of rebirth, until the coming of Apuleius, a syncretist, and the Hermetic writings. . . . The rite of initiation suggests nothing similar in favor of the initiate, since it was a rite of sexual union wherein he cannot figure as cause and as result.[38]

D. *The Mysteries of Cybele and Attis*

Cybele was the name bestowed by the Greeks upon the supreme goddess of the Phrygians. Two lions were her constant symbol. She was queen of a mountainous country of luxurious vegetation and infested with savage beasts, especially lions. From her most fervent adorers, especially the priests, she demanded castration, as did the Babylonian goddess and the Syrian goddess of Hierapolis. Such unfortunate mutilated victims, the Galles, could not evidently be considered the spouses of the goddess; they were, rather, her heroic servants who had vowed themselves to her, and who in order to make the dedication complete, had rendered themselves incapable of having a family among men.

Their voluntary mutilation was believed to contribute to fecundity in the interests of the social group. A similar custom existed among primitive peoples as regards restrictions and sacrifices. Some deprived themselves or were so deprived in order that the greater number might enjoy a good they had in mind and desired, without arousing the gods, who had their share, to jealousy.[39]

Grafted on to this barbarous custom of voluntary castration was the myth of Attis, the beautiful shepherd who resisted or was unfaithful to the love of Cybele. The irritated goddess drove him mad, so that, in a paroxysm of fury resembling that of the Galles when they bloodily consecrated themselves to their heavenly queen, he made himself a eunuch. In most of the tales he survived the operation, came to his senses, and joined himself definitively to Cybele. The Greeks were horrified at this rite and myth, and it seems that in olden times "they either did not know the exact cult of Attis or they adopted it, but made of it no more than a doublet of Adonis."[40]

In Rome, on the other hand, the cult of Cybele, the

Phrygian Mother, or the "Great Mother," was solemnly "established in 204 B.C. by the transportation of the black stone of Pessinonte, which was her representation. Still, during more than two centuries, hers was an alien cult served only by Phrygian priests. Only under Claudius, probably, did Roman citizens become affiliated to it."[41]

Cybele and Attis were conjointly honored either in the public feasts or in the mysteries. At Rome a ceremony on March 15 was indicated in the Philocalian calendar (A.D. 354) by the expression *Canna intrat;* this seems to have been a procession of people carrying rods, in memory, no doubt, of the Phrygian river Gallos, whose name brings to mind that of the Galles. On the XI of the Kalends of April (March 22) the calendar reads: *Arbor intrat;* a cut pine, representing Attis, the "cut one," was carried about. A fast, called *castum* or *castus,* was probably related with the severe diet prescribed after castration. The IX of the Kalends of April (March 24) reads: *Sanguen.* It was really a bloody day. "Whipping and gashing themselves, the Galles mixed their shrill cries with the sharp tone of the flutes; and when the neophytes reached the climax of their frenzy, they accomplished the supreme sacrifice, insensible to the pain, with a sharp stone."[42] The debris was thrown against the statue of the goddess, coloring it with blood, and then was buried with honor. The VIII of the Kalends of April (March 25) was consecrated to *Hilaria.* It was the feast of the Mother, when everyone felt free to do anything, and made merry; however, we lack positive information about the accompanying rites.[43] After the repose of the VII of the Kalends of April, *requietio,* came finally the great feast of the *lavatio* or washing.

An image of the goddess (the famous black stone imported from Pessinonte) was placed on a wagon. Before it were displayed precious works of art. The procession wound its way to the Almo, a small tributary of the Tiber, and the nobility thought it a privilege to follow on bare feet. The cart and the goddess were washed, and then came the return to the Palatine. On that day masquerade and disguise were permissible; it was the ancient prototype of the Roman carnival. The Romans thought thus to commemorate the arrival of their Mother, and her bath in the Almo; this bath made her forget the rivers of Phrygia.[44]

Besides the Galles, there were the mystae of Attis who were not held to castration, but who could nevertheless benefit from the protection of the Great Mother and her consort by taking part in certain mysteries. The rites of these mysteries are summed up by the following formula which Clement of Alexandria places on the lips of an initiate: "I have eaten from the kettledrum, drunk from the cymbal, I have carried the *kernos* (a large earthen dish), I have penetrated into the nuptial chamber."[45] The formula tells of a meal of initiation eaten upon the kettledrum (*tympanon*) while drinking of the cymbal which was slightly hollowed out. Then came the *kernophoria;* the *kernos,* whose contents are not indicated, was carried on the head. Finally, the initiate "was introduced into the chamber of the goddess, not to share her couch, but there to play the role of chamber eunuch; he was in a religious sense the master of the chamber, boasting all the privileges that a faithful servant could expect of the goddess."[46] This initiation accompanied the great feast of spring.

Added to these rites, at least in the fourth century, was a means of union quite peculiar to Cybele, the bloody rite of purification called the *taurobolium.* "The person who was to receive the *taurobolium* wore upon his brow a miter and a crown of gold; he wore a silk robe let down to the waist and exposing the whole upper part of his body. He entered a ditch covered with a plank bored with holes. Then a bull was led on to the plank and sacrificed by plunging a long knife of peculiar shape into its breast. The blood spread over the plank and from there into the ditch where it flowed over the devotee who impregnated his whole body with it."[47] The *criobolium* was addressed to Attis himself; it involved the sacrifice of a ram.

What was the meaning of these myths and rites? Loisy unhesitatingly declared that Attis was a god who died and arose; that the public feasts, and still more the mysteries, permitted one to partake in the benefit of his death and resurrection, and find therein a principle of blessed immortality. After a minute study of the texts, P. Lagrange declared: (1) There is never any question of the resurrection of Attis; (2) the *taurobolium* was not a rite whereby men shared in the power of Attis.

There can be no question of the resurrection of the beautiful shepherd in most of the texts, including the most ancient ones, for the simple reason that he does not die as the result of his mutilation. That is reasonable enough, for the myth was ordered to a rite which was not death but castration.[48] Where there *is* question of his death — and that was probably the result of contamination with the legend of Adonis, the Syrian god of springtime vegetation who is born again after being mourned — no mention is made of his resurrection.[49] Neither do the ceremonies of spring in honor of Cybele at Rome suppose his resurrection; the cut pine is the mutilated shepherd but the *Hilaria* commemorate the joy of the goddess who again finds her shepherd. Firmicus Maternus, long after the beginning of our era, was the first to speak of the resurrection in this regard.[50]

The idea of sacramental communion with Cybele or Attis has no more foundation in the texts than the preceding opinion of a risen and resurrected god. The repast taken on the kettledrum and cymbal at the outset of the initiation is never affirmed to be one of bread and wine; we are not dealing here with the consuming of the god in union with his passion.[51]

Prudentius speaks of the remission of sins in connection with the *taurobolium*. But note, first of all, that he is a Christian poet of the fourth–fifth centuries A.D. Moreover, his description clearly indicates that the blood of the bull was supposed to wash away past faults by effusion, but not to regenerate by drinking; and finally, belief in the attribution of efficacy in the sacrifice of the divine power of Attis is nowhere to be found in his verses. There is nothing about a mystical union with the "passion" of Attis. The *taurobolium* originally was a sacrifice offered by the offerer or offerers for another, namely, the Emperor; only in the fourth century do texts appear which attest to its reception as a rite of initiation. If in the fourth century, 376 to be precise, an inscription designates the recipient of the *taurobolium* as *renatus*, we must not forget that at that time and chiefly owing to [the action of] Julian the Apostate, pagan cults formed a bloc against Christianity and attempted to vanquish the religion of Christ by borrowing some of its ideas.[52]

E. *The Mysteries of Isis and Osiris*

The touching, curious legend of Osiris and Isis is a familiar one. Osiris ruled over Egypt and was a progressive, beneficent monarch. Falling into the trap laid for him by his brother, Seth or Typhon, and seventy-two accomplices, he was sealed alive in a coffin and thrown into the Nile. After a complicated series of adventures his body was torn to pieces and scattered. His sister and wife, Isis, buried him with care. Many cities of Egypt claimed to possess his tomb and body. Some versions of the legend portray Isis and her sister Nephtys seated beside the body, singing a funeral lament which became the prototype of all funeral lamentations. Moved by such sorrow, the sun god dispatched from heaven the jackal-headed Anubis who, with the help of Toth and Horus and the two sisters, reassembled the torn body and then embalmed it according to rites observed thereafter in all embalmings. Isis fanned the body with her wings, and it came back to life; but only to rule over the nether regions, while on earth Horus took over the work of his father.

Isis won predominance over her brother when the cult spread from Egypt into the Mediterranean world, and the reason for this was probably the fact that he played a purely passive part in the legend. . . . Statuettes of Isis were found in Etruria and Latium from the seventh or sixth century at the latest, but it was principally after the conquests of Alexander that the Egyptian goddess invaded the ancient world. The countries of Greece and Sicily welcomed her. At Rome she had to struggle against the republican senate of Augustus and Tiberius, but her feasts and mysteries were openly observed even by the elite from the time of Caligula to the Christian emperors.

Both public feasts and mysteries were celebrated in honor of Isis. The feasts took place in spring and autumn. In spring the lying-in of the goddess, mother of Horus, was celebrated, along with the feast of renewed navigation, for she had become goddess of the sea. In autumn the faithful rejoiced with her over the finding of Osiris' body after having lamented with her for his loss. Apuleius, born A.D. 124 at Madaure in Africa, provides us with our very sketchy information concerning the mysteries of Isis. In his "Metamorphosis of an Ass," he recalls his own initiation in these enigmatic words: "You perhaps wonder, curious reader, what was done and said. I would repeat it if I were permitted to speak. You would know it if you had the right to hear it, but for this rash curiosity, both ears and tongue would be guilty of the same offense. But if, nevertheless, your religious desire holds you in suspense, I will not torture you longer. Listen then, and believe, for I speak the truth. I have touched the threshold of death, and having trod upon the threshold of Prosperina, I have come back, carried across all the elements. I have seen the sun shining with pure light in the middle of the night. From close by I have approached and adored some of the gods of the underworld and of heaven. What I have related to you, you have indeed heard, but you cannot understand."[53]

Plutarch (A.D. 46–120), even before Apuleius, had spoken of the mysteries of Isis, but in very general terms, as "very holy initiations, representing by means of images, allegories, and figurative scenes the long past sufferings [of Osiris and Isis], as a lesson of piety and encouragement for men and women who expect those same trials."[54]

What meaning and religious value are to be recognized in the cult of Isis and Osiris?

The myth in its purely Egyptian form must be distinguished from the public feasts in honor of Isis, and from the mysteries of Isis and Osiris.

1. The first point will not detain us long:

Osiris' death and resurrection was the death and rebirth of cereals. Happy symbol, which St. Paul turned to account (1 Cor.

15:35). Dead as a god, Osiris found his life again only to continue it in hell. . . . After the fashion of Dionysus, he was born again, glorious, in Horus, the truly triumphant god. Nowhere in the Egyptian rites is there any evidence that people tried to identify themselves with Osiris while they lived in the hope of participating in his immortal life. This would not have made sense. The dead could be an Osiris only after death. Then he was "an Osiris," and could hope for no more. Even so it was necessary to take good care of his tomb and to give him, at least verbally, food adapted to his new state. We are certainly dispensed from insisting on these old rites.[55]

2. The public feasts were very clearly centered around the *Heuresis,* or finding of the body of Osiris. When this occurred, joy overflowed.

It is not less certain that Isis gave her husband a decent burial after she had found his body [she was his sister as well as wife]. Loisy employed a very equivocal expression when he wrote: "Osiris was definitively buried in immortality by Isis" (p. 129). . . . No, for Osiris was buried in one or fourteen tombs, according to the number of villages which boasted of possessing his remains.[56]

Two days after the *Heuresis,* November 3, named *Hilaria* as in the Attis mysteries, the cycle came to a close. Was this a recollection of his resurrection after burial? Nothing authorizes such a statement, for according to the Philocalian calendar, November 1 was already the feast of the rebirth of the god.[57]

But were these rites supposed to procure immortality? M. Lafaye, a specialist in these matters, believed they were.[58] He remarks, however, that the Latins, who should have been well informed on this subject, did not believe in it. Plutarch, who looked about in all directions, suspected no soteriological import in the rites. If they had any efficacy at all, they were most probably thought to insure a temporal utility. Primitively, no doubt, Osiris was the spirit of the grain which died in the earth and was reborn with the ears of corn. "When the Nile had subsided and the grain was sown, one hoped for the growth which was procured by the magical rite of the water, and hoped to see the sown grain come back to life."[59]

3. As for the mysteries, it is possible that Plutarch had turned rationalist in the above-cited text, yet this Platonist

was in no way hostile to mysticism. It is to be admitted that the faithful saw in the Isis initiation:

A promise of happy immortality, guaranteed by the intimacy acquired with the god. But no one can say that the candidate was associated with the "passion" and resurrection of Osiris. What surpasses all tolerable license is to extract such teachings from Apuleius. Yet Loisy says this clearly, and he says concerning Lucius (Apuleius' hero): "Lucius receives the same assurance, and a moral renovation, thanks to his association with the death, burial, and resurrection of Osiris" (p. 275). Yet it is only at the end that Apuleius mentions the name of Osiris, to tell us, after the complete description of Lucius' initiation to Isis, that he still had to be initiated into the mysteries of Osiris.[60]

On this point Loisy has written a fine page on the Osiris rites; it is a *"tableau tout entier brossé de chic."*[61]

One may object that Apuleius did indeed mention a kind of death, by means of which the initiation was conferred; and it was followed by a return to life.[62]

Assuredly, but it was the death of the initiate himself. He was considered dead because secrets can be confided to one who is on the point of dying. Once dead, he goes to heaven and to hell. . . . Such a death is in no way the union with a salutary death. He must die symbolically in order symbolically to enjoy the happiness of the elect. It is for this reason that the initiate begins in some way a new life. . . . The new birth was not, after all, so rare an idea; it finds a natural place here. But Apuleius lacked what was essential: salvation, i.e., justification by the merits of a suffering god.[63]

The myth concerning Osiris not only does not affirm salvation by his death, it actually excludes it. Isis could grant immortality.

. . . but what did Osiris' death accomplish? He was traitorously assassinated and, though a god, was even denied burial. He owed everything to Isis. In what manner was his death a sacrifice? It is quite plainly not a voluntary sacrifice, as Loisy himself admits. But, then, at this price, what god would have accepted it? Yet without it, what efficacy could it have? Where find in the Greco-Roman mysteries of Isis the slightest indication that the initiate was saved by Isis in behalf of the passion of Osiris? As for the Osiris mysteries, of which Apuleius makes mention, they are absolutely unknown.[64]

The fact that Osiris' death was not voluntary is enough to distinguish it radically from that of Jesus.

F. *The Mysteries of Mithra*

Mithra was a Persian god, a god of light, "invested, like the Babylonian sun, with control over the acts of men. He who sees everything has a good chance of being a good judge. At any rate, he is almost the sun, and most of the time he became the sun."[65]

Passing into Chaldea, Mithra made contact with the *Chamach* of the Chaldeans, and his cult became charged with astrological speculations. He was already known in Asia Minor in the fifteenth century B.C., as we know from a tablet discovered at Boghaz-Köy, on the site of the ancient Hittite capital in the buckle of the Halys River; but the great centers of Hellenic civilization remained closed to him. In the West, he appeared as a Latinized figure around the time of Pompey, and reached his zenith in the time of the Flavians; in the third century his was the most active of the pagan cults. But it is an exaggeration to hold, as Renan does, that his success was a threat to Christianity.

Having no precise dogma, the followers of Mithra put their trust in their legend. Mithra was born from a rock. Together with the sun he had captured the primordial bull, and at the command of his companion he had slain it. The death of the bull gave birth to the world; Mithra, then, was creator. He was the god of truth (the Persians abhor lying) and of justice, and was gracious to his followers during their life on earth and after death. Tertullian maintained that resurrection was a part of this system. Various combinations of texts led to the belief that the bull would be immolated anew to open up the era of salvation. A better explanation was thus at hand to explain the supreme importance of the scene of the slaughter of the bull, which occupied the chief place in all Mithraic sanctuaries.[66]

Many *Mithraea* or sanctuaries of Mithra have been found; they were natural or artificial caves in which the mysteries of the god were celebrated. The initiates were divided into seven classes, only the last four of which were admitted to the mysteries. In succession, they were Crow, Occult, Soldier,

Lion, Persian, Courier of the Sun, and Father, with fitting costumes and the obligation of playing out the role, even to uttering the cries of these animals. Proofs of courage were required; but once admitted, the candidate found himself in a fraternal society, where freedmen rubbed elbows with the highest nobility. Sacred repasts with bread and water were served. Mithra was believed to have eaten this, with the sun as table companion.[67]

P. Lagrange did not think it necessary to treat at length, or often, of the relation of Mithraism with Christianity, because he considered the hypothesis of an influence of the mysteries of Mithra upon our faith and our sacraments as utterly improbable. Yet he did reply briefly on this point to Solomon Reinach and Loisy. Reinach held that Mithra was mediator between God and man, and that he assured the salvation of men by a sacrifice.[68] In reply P. Lagrange pointed out that the word for mediator, *mésités,* as applied to Mithra,

. . . is found only in Plutarch, and with an entirely different meaning [from that of a mediator of salvation]. He was supposed to be mediator because he held *the middle* position between good and evil. None of the many inscriptions in his honor ever call him mediator; for his faithful, he was the supreme god; for personified time was only an abstraction. Nowhere do we find Mithra reconciling the world to God, least of all by the offering of his blood.[69]

Loisy looked upon Mithra as a suffering god for two reasons: Mithra immolates the bull which was originally a divine animal, a god; and its passion was therefore the passion of a god. P. Lagrange replied: "If Mithra was first a bull, and became the god who slays the bull, then there certainly was at least a division into two."[70]

Loisy's second argument is rather startling. The bas-reliefs in the *Mithraea* depict the slaughter of the bull, and show Mithra with a melancholic look about him, for this slaying is the passion of the god himself; he was a suicide![71] Cumont, the great specialist in these matters, provides our answers: After Alexander, the sculptors of Greece liked such sad faces; the group of the bull-slaying Mithra seems to have been conceived in the second century B.C.; and, finally, Mithra seems to have slain the bull unwillingly, at the command of the sun.[72]

On the side of the rites, Loisy saw in the slaying of the bull "the central rite of the religion."[73] Cumont does not agree that the principal scene of the monuments of Mithra portrays a sacrifice, as the bull there has the appearance of an animal at full gallop; he does not believe that the so-called sacrifice was repeated in the cult. "At least," P. Lagrange adds, "this murder of the second century B.C., and after, was not the passion of the god, for according to the authentic explanation of the texts he appears as a creator."[74]

Reinach, in the same place, spoke of a Mithraic baptism and communion; to which P. Lagrange answered: "Mithraic baptism was an ordinary ablution; the 'communion' was nothing but an offering of bread and wine, and no one can say that they represent Mithra."[75]

IV. EVALUATION OF THE MYSTERY RELIGIONS
A. *An Improbable and Useless Hypothesis*

P. Lagrange's evaluation of the hypothesis that "Christianity was a synthesis or syncretism of Jewish messianic hopes with the hopes and salutary rites of the mystery religions," may be expressed as follows: The hypothesis is (1) improbable and (2) useless.

1. *The hypothesis is improbable:* To reach this conclusion one should not remain in the abstract. "The concrete figure of the god together with his special myth," writes Bousset,[76] "is no longer clear. But in all [his myths] there was an idea of such mystical power that it captivated Hellenic piety in the mysteries: the idea of a dying but resurrected deity who brings salvation."

The only difficulty a realistic critic of Bousset's imaginative synthesis might raise is this: Paganism was never aware of the religious essence of the various pagan phenomena found in a book; the mysteries did indeed exist, but not a general theory concerning them which could have influenced St. Paul. He knew them in all their concreteness, and then — ugh! Only in the crucibles of the critics and in virtue of learned abstraction is it true that "the concrete figure of the god together with his special myth is no longer clear."[77]

Truly, in the concrete, the mysteries could only arouse the disgust of the Apostle of the Gentiles.

Let us ask what impression the concept of a suffering, dying, and resuscitated god of the mysteries could make upon his thought, *supposing that this idea had been clearly perceived and insisted upon.* . . . As Paul said elsewhere, he adored Jesus as Son of God because this belief was imposed upon him by direct revelation. Far from facilitating this belief, the ideal of the mysteries would rather have anchored him to his pure monotheism. He was led to believe in the suffering Son of God, not because of, but in spite of, the mysteries.[78]

Eight years before writing the passage just quoted, P. Lagrange had taken up the case of the "adept" of the mysteries, in connection with the *Adonis and Eschmoun* of Count Guillaume de Baudissin, which appeared in 1911 (Leipzig).

Let us for once come to some agreement about this preparation for Christianity. Let the problem be expressed *in concrete terms.* We are not dealing with a pagan who did not believe in myths of resurrection. It is difficult to imagine that some zealous Christian would have first taught him these things, only to destroy them later on. We are dealing with a devotee of the cults of Osiris or of Adonis, *as far as we know them.*

From what we know of Christian polemics, the Christian would either attack the myth by way of euhemerism or by the Stoic method. In other words, he would prove to the pagan that Adonis was never more than a man, that his goddess was an impure courtesan, and that Adonis was never raised up by her. Or, he would show in Adonis the sprout or the grain of corn, and explain that the myth was only the translation of a very common phenomenon, and that consequently there was no resurrection. In other words, the pagan ought first to be convinced that he was wrong in paying homage to Adonis and believing in his resurrection.

Could we say that there would remain an impression upon his spirit, some interior disposition to accept more readily the history of a God-man risen from the dead? And would the stamp of sensuality which had marked his soul incline it also to adhere to a religion of purity and renouncement? Is it not natural that this pagan, if convinced of his error, would try to apply the same penetrating criticism to Jesus? We suppose that he admitted as the first religious principle the cult of a risen god, not determining which one. Many apologists would argue that a shadow of the truth is more harmful to a conversion than absolute ignorance of the proposed truth. At any rate, when dealing with such complex psychological problems, one should express himself with much reserve.[79]

There are more than doctrinal considerations to render highly improbable the fact of borrowing (even unconsciously) from the pagan mysteries by Christian preachers and their converts. Despite progress made toward spirituality and morality — which P. Lagrange recognizes — there was that sensual and barbaric atmosphere which very often accompanied the celebrations. The Fathers of the Church were so explicit in their descriptions that "we can no longer reprint their words." Some, however, question their impartiality. They should not doubt such men as Athenagoras or St. Clement of Alexandria.

They were not fanatics, narrow-minded, as Tatian doubtless was, for he disliked everything the pagans did. They were, on the contrary, painstaking in their search for any traces of truth in paganism, especially in its philosophy, which would help bring about an agreement. They are so explicit about the mysteries that we can no longer reprint their words.[80]

No doubt the desire of a happy immortality, which swept over the Greek world like a wave from the sixth century B.C. onward, did lead some souls to the mysteries, notwithstanding their obsceneness. Quite naturally one addressed himself to the gods of the world beyond. But these gods already had their mysteries, and the concept of mysteries is broader than that of salutary mysteries. Issuing from the crude naturalism of primitive rites, the mysteries represented not the *Passion* but *the passions* of the gods, as Athenagoras points out in a little known passage (chap. xxxii). In other words, their παθή are distinct from their παθήματα or sufferings, which implies both their sufferings and their moral dispositions, adventures, and weaknesses. Hence the secret, or mystery, which would not shock the growing rationalism of the Greeks; hence also their tolerance of flagrant moral turpitude. One is reminded of Fontenelle's cynical remark: God made man to His own image, and since then man has certainly reflected it.

2. *The hypothesis of a Judaeo-pagan syncretism is likewise useless.* There is no reason to deny the originality of Christianity in relation to Judaism, or its breakaway from it. "It [Christianity] is still successor to that religion, but the life of Christianity most certainly does not trace back to a grafting borrowed from paganism."[81]

One can find in Judaism, without having to go elsewhere, aspirations to immortality, and a guarantee of it by an initiation which was open to everyone. It is true the Sadducees did not believe in the resurrection or in the sanctions of the next life, but "actually, most Jews under the influence of the Pharisees, lived in more ardent expectation of a life with God in the next life than the majority of pagans."[82]

The guarantee of this happy immortality was the covenant God had struck with the nation, and also the admission to the nation by the initiation of circumcision. Here the Jewish faith was stronger than all the convictions of the pagans, so strong, in fact, that it survived the political destruction of the nation. One could not be saved without good works; neither could he be saved without initiation in the Jewish religion. The initiation was offered to all, as in the mysteries, for they did make proselytes. This universalism was superior to that of some of the mysteries, e.g., a man had to be able to speak Greek to be initiated into those of Eleusis. Finally, by the Jewish initiation one was united both to the people and to God.

Useless for the most part also because of the existence of Judaism, the mysteries were still more useless in face of a singular fact: *Jesus.*

Christian tradition explains things very simply. Jesus clearly saw His destiny. He could attain to glory only by accepting sufferings and death in expiation for sin. Is He to be denied such a presentiment? Yet He died; and after His resurrection His death could not be explained to the Jews who remained His disciples, except in the sense that it was the plan of God, who accepted that death for the salvation of mankind. This conception was inescapable, if Christ was the Messias who died and rose from the dead. Paul argued from it with greater insight than the other apostles. There is nothing obscure about this reasoning, certainly nothing that surpasses historical probability. The Messias of Israel was to expiate for all Israel. The world? If Paul had to look for the idea of a world-savior outside of Israel, he did not have to seek it from the mysteries. The idea was current, or even official, in Asia.[83]

What could Paul have gotten, even by association and in an unconscious manner, from the mysteries? The only laudable thing about them was their desire for salvation in union with the divinity, and that is the most general of all religious ideas. A desire for purification from personal sin was not at all prominent in the mysteries. It would have been a stroke of genius to purify the idea of [a divine] passion, in the sense of an expiatory suffering, and to transfer this idea, which was incompatible with the divine nature, to the humanity of Jesus. *But antecedently to all comparisons of this kind, there stands the fact of Jesus, and it makes sense all by itself.*[84]

These remarks have to do with the very origin of Christianity. To a certain extent its development could have been favored by the mystery religions.

It is a fact of experience that nothing impeded its progress except an absolute and rarified notion of divine transcendence. Both Jews and Moslems are not ordinarily convertible. But the poor folk who sought with such ardor for intercourse and intimacy with the gods were better prepared to welcome the good news of the Incarnation.[85]

Speaking ten years previously of oriental religions in general, and not exclusively of mystery religions, P. Lagrange had strongly emphasized the providential preparation made for the true faith in the very midst of paganism, where it appeared.

This need for expiation and anxiety of soul which led from one purification to another, satisfied only by the bloody rite of the *taurobolium,* and the desire for union with God — were not all these preparations for faith in Christ?

It may still be so. Anything is preferable to indifference!

Cicero's cynical and sceptical contemporaries would not have been so desirous of receiving the good news as those who hastened to the initiations of Isis and Mithra. . . . During the days of the empire a new phenomenon occurred: religion became at once both individual and universal. To quote St. Paul: There is no more either Greek or barbarian; no more patricians, no *plebs* ignorant of the sacred rites; no more treason in adoring the gods of Véies if one were born at Rome. All, Roman citizens and provincials, master and slave, senator and freedmen, embraced the cult they thought would give them happiness. And at the same moment religions stepped across the city boundaries and became universal religions, superior in this to Judaism, which never would admit that religion goes beyond the race.[86]

At the same time, like most oriental religions and the national religions of Greece and Rome, the mystery religions raised many obstacles to Christianity. The aspiration toward a next life, satisfied cheaply, failed to develop further, and the pride of the initiates repelled them from a good news which was very often preached by simple, uncultivated folk [such as were the Apostles]. The dependence of all pagan cults upon the State inevitably led to a limitation of their universalism. There were gods who fraternized with other gods, but the One who pretended to be the only God was excluded. Finally, the ancient naturist base, which in the mystery religions was too often expressed by obscene or brutal rites — never wholly stamped out — assured to all these cults an alliance with the lower passions against Christianity. Thus, before they disappeared, we see them forming a bloc with official paganism and the old city-religions for the purpose of resisting the progress of the gospel. Under Julian the Apostate, this was the command of authority. Nevertheless the old Greco-Roman pantheon, along with the Eastern "cult of the Emperor," retained numerous worshipers and was protected by the sanction of law.[87]

B. *Confirmation of the Opinions of P. Lagrange —*
The Arbitrariness of the Syncretists, and the Decline of the
School of the History of Religions

The conclusions of P. Lagrange, about the pretended syncretistic origin of Christianity, resemble those of experts in

Hellenism who have no particular religious affiliation. In 1928, M. Aimé Puech, professor at the University of Paris and a Member of the Institute, wrote as follows concerning St. Paul:

Although the expressions borrowed from the language of the mysteries are more and more frequent in his epistles as he advanced in age, and as his preaching among the Gentiles met with growing success, *Paul's work was absolutely original* [italics mine], his doctrine is *entirely new,* and he created it by applying the notions contained in these terms to Jesus who is the Christ.[88]

In 1932, M. Louis Gernet, professor at the University of Alger, and M. André Boulanger, professor at the University of Strasbourg, published a volume entitled *Le Génie grec dans la Religion.*[89] Their general conclusion is as follows:

As opposed to Greek religion of the first century of our era, Christianity remains, as far as we are concerned, *something specific.* It is vain to seek in the Hellenic world any equivalent for the two characteristic doctrines of Pauline Christianity: the expiatory value of Christ's passion, and justification by faith.

Without being a result of it, Christianity did benefit from all the religious evolution of the three centuries immediately preceding our Christian era.[90]

Boulanger had already written in his *Orpheus:*[91]

The Orphic regeneration was the result of a magical action, mechanical in a way, and independent of the dispositions of the initiate; it implied no act of faith on his part. The Christian resurrection is effected in the soul of the believer. . . .

. . . Orphism, despite its tendency toward monotheism, accommodated itself to innumerable Hellenic deities, and must for this reason have aroused an insurmountable disgust in a Christian.

. . . It is extremely exaggerated to maintain that Orphism was the "precursor" of Christianity in the Greco-Roman world, and that it supplied Christianity with her first adepts. But it is true, none the less, that Orphism was a sort of distant preparation for Christianity.[92]

M. Guignebert, fellow professor of M. Puech at the Sorbonne, and like MM. Gernet and Boulanger a contributor to the collection of M. Berr,[93] recognizes neither these reservations nor these nuances; and the contrast is perhaps not to his credit as a scholar.

There is not the shadow of a doubt that Christianity dwelt in the midst of the mysteries, and was nourished by them.[94]

The opinions of these French Hellenists are shared by Protestant and foreign exegetes who are not all conservatives:[95] A. Harnack,[96] A. Schweitzer,[97] G. Kittel.[98]

The very men P. Lagrange criticized strengthened his position by their exaggerations and arbitrariness. Guignebert belongs to this group, as does Solomon Reinach, who made this statement (singled out by the *Revue Biblique*), so frightfully a priori, that if anyone were to make it outside of the field of comparative religions, he would be instantly discredited.

Christianity is connected with this religion of obscure mysteries. Even though we have no indication that the hypothesis is probable, it must be invoked so as to establish the continuity of religious phenomena (*faits*) without any transcendental intervention.[99]

Loisy was incapable of making such brutal statements. Yet from a purely scientific point of view, his own recent theory concerning the syncretistic origin of Christianity is not strengthened by his dissection of the texts. In 1920 P. Lagrange pointed out, at the end of his review of Loisy's *Les Mystères paiens et le Mystère chretien*, that only twenty years elapsed between Jesus and the epistles of St. Paul: not a great deal of time even for the avatars he supposes. Whether or not Loisy read these remarks, he saw the difficulty, and wherever he thought he detected the mystery-influence in certain passages of the epistles (even the most respected ones, such as Romans and Corinthians), he dated those passages as being of the second century A.D. Only vague reasons such as "lack of order in the ideas," unsupported by detailed philological arguments, are given for this radical operation.[100]

For some time now, in Germany, the home of almost all the systems which try to explain Christianity rationalistically, it is becoming apparent that the school of the history of religions has succeeded hardly better than its predecessors. The search is on for something else, thanks to the incurable instability of naturalistic exegesis, and at present a great deal of attention is directed to the study of the *forms* of the gospel tradition.[101]

V. THE RELIGIONS OF IRAN

A. *The Religion of Iran and Judaism*

The religious book of the ancient Persians was the *Avesta,* in which hymns called *Gathas* stand out as expressive of a particular religious system. Concerning the dates of the *Avesta* there is a great divergence of opinion. In 1904, P. Lagrange dated them around A.D. 50–75;[102] but Cernoy and other specialists in the question claimed an earlier date for them. With a modesty that is the mark of a true scholar, P. Lagrange bowed to their verdict. Later this verdict was questioned.[103] The really important issue is rather what influence the reform of Zoroaster, as represented by the *Gathas,* had upon Judaism. As in 1904, the Master of Jerusalem insisted in 1931 upon the improbability of the Persian religion's having influenced Judaism.

Basically this whole question of the influence of the Persian religion upon Judaism does not seem to me to be stated in a very concrete way. While reading the *Avesta* and other books, the critics came across a few lofty passages; these they extract, coordinate methodically, compare with the doctrines of Judaism, and are not surprised at any influence they could have exercised upon it [Judaism]. *It would be necessary to leave the books aside* and to ask how this foreign religion would have appeared to the Jews in its daily life and practice. It was certainly about the same as it was in Christian times, though not so elevated; for the Zoroastrian reform steadily gained ground and triumphed under Sapor. Christians regarded it as a religion of polytheists, or as they thought, of demon worshipers, a potpourri of superstitions, rather than a true religion. Surely the same impression was made upon the Jews by this ancient religion of the Persians, and without the special prestige of science or philosophy. Why should they have been tempted to learn of this school, or to have been won over by a statement of morality much inferior to their own?[104]

P. Lagrange examined four particular points, following Bousset, author of one of the most important works on *Judaism in late Hellenic times,* a work which was re-edited at Tübingen by Gressmann in 1926, after the death of the author.

1. Bousset asserts with other critics that the Jews must have borrowed the idea of a final conflagration of the world from the Persians.

The conflagration of the world is not an Iranian doctrine, nor even common in Judaism, for the Sibyl belongs to Egypt. In ancient Iran the catastrophe was supposed to occur by cold.[105]

2. Judaism is also supposed to have borrowed from the Persians its belief in the punishments of the next world and in the resurrection. However,

. . . belief in retribution is general from the sixth century B.C. onward. According to the Persians, judgment of the just and of the guilty took place in a mechanical fashion, by crossing or not crossing the bridge of separation (*Çinvat*). That is characteristic. There is nothing like that in Judaism, where the end of the world is envisaged; or rather, the transformation of things into a better world, a doctrine which Isaias taught and which is not peculiar to the Persians; there is no specifically common trait. Resurrection from the dead is attested by the Jews [at least in Machabean times], but it is not expressly stated either in the *Gathas,* or in the attestations of ancient Greece.[106]

Leaders in the school of the history of religions, which attacks both Old and New Testament, have insisted much that the doctrine of resurrection is an ancient Persian belief. In 1904, P. Lagrange made a close study of the only two texts advanced as proof; Greeks, not Iranians, wrote them. In the first, Herodotus proposes the resurrection as a fanciful hypothesis. The second text, a fragment of Theopompey, is handed down by three authors: Plutarch, Diogenes-Laerce, and Aeneas of Gaza, in three different forms. Only the last named, who lived in the fifth century A.D., mentions the resurrection explicitly.[107]

3. Dualism is said to have come to Israel from Iran, and to have induced a considerable development of demonology

in Judaism in the two centuries preceding our own era. Dualism is indeed an old Iranian belief. But in the *Gathas,* as in the Bible, there is not a real dualism, for the evil powers are therein constantly subject to the supreme God. The Persian origin of the demon Asmodeus in the book of Tobias ought to be recognized. The demon is *Aeshma,* an Iranian *deva* or demon; but the story of Tobias takes place in Persia, and this detail is part of the local color.[108] Iranian influences perhaps stimulated Jewish thought on the subject of demonology; yet in this regard only apocryphal books, such as Enoch, are adduced.[109]

4. Iranians spoke of their Messias, of Saviours, *Saos-hyant.* But on the one hand, the origin of the Jewish ideas is both ancient and authentic; on the other, the "saviors" of the old Persian texts are nothing more than preachers and reformers, as were Zoroaster and his companions.[110]

P. Lagrange pointed out and criticized still other comparisons in 1904. He particularly contested the parallel drawn by Stave, for example, between the seven angels who stand before the Lord in the Book of Tobias (12:15) and the seven Ameshas-Spentas. They were only six in number, he maintained, and seven could only be obtained by including their father, Ahura Mazda. The Semites, he went on, did not have to be taught how to use the number seven, and "the angels of the Hebrews are great personalities with special missions," while "the Amesha-Spentas were abstractions which became active: good thoughts, docility, immortality."[111]

There is no doubt that the *Avesta* does contain some lofty conceptions, but these were unable to overcome the primitive naturism of the Iranian religion. These ideas could have acted beneficently upon the Jews, under certain conditions. Thus:

. . . the Persian religion of a war between good and evil, which led to the victory of the good only in the next life, did emphasize the supreme importance of the struggle in which every man is engaged. The kingdom of the true God was not expected on earth, for it was Paradise. The accent lay wholly upon the individual destinies after death. Would not such a religion, if it had been clearly conceived, have influenced the thinking of pious men who returned from the Captivity under the protection of Cyrus? It is certainly possible. At any rate, the suggestion could be made only on condition that one admits the one, true God, absolute Master of this world and the next, whose kingdom, commenced here on earth, is consummated in eternity.[112]

B. *The Religion of Iran and Christianity*

The *Avesta* is not the only religious literature of Iran. That land also produced the Manichaean books, at least the better part of them, and other works written in Pahlavic, the literary Persian during the first centuries of our era. Pahlavic literature comprises a translation (very poor) of the *Avesta* and its commentary, the *Zend*. (The first translator of the *Avesta*, Anquetil du Perron, mistakenly gave the name of *Zend* to the Avestic tongue; *Zend*, like the word *Avesta* itself, belongs to the Pahlavic). Vast compilations followed: *Bundahism*, a kind of *Genesis* dating from the sixth century A.D., the *Dinkared*, ninth century, a collection of Mazdean traditions, etc. From these late productions and from various Greek writings which are judged to reflect Iranian influences, Reitzenstein and H. H. Schroeder distilled a doctrine of salvation which (they said) had in pre-Christian times penetrated "into Judea and even Egypt."[113]

In résumé, this is their system: The human soul is a heavenly being come down upon earth; it was imprisoned in matter, it was liberated [redeemed], and it liberates [redeems] individuals. The myth is connected with the end of the world and the final resurrection.[114] We have tried to show, wrote P. Lagrange, referring to the *Revue Biblique* (1922, pp. 282–286),

. . . how fragile a base the Manichaean writings provide for such deductions. Thanks to recent discoveries, these writings are now better known, but a revival of popularity cannot make them old, and there can be no doubt that it was Mani's intention to attach himself to Jesus.[115]

In a note the reader is referred to Prosper Alfaric's *Les Écritures manichéennes,* which are Pahlavic and old Turkish writings coming chiefly from Tourfan or Chinese. Alfaric says:

> Even if they were all [authentic], they would have to be used with great reserve. Most of them are not dated. Most of them have no titles. We do not know either their place of origin, or their nature.[116]

The real Mazdean writings do not provide any surer basis for the hypotheses of Reitzenstein than the works of Mani and his disciples. In his review of Reitzenstein's book, P. Lagrange made a careful criticism of a recently discovered text of this period. The text was written in the northern dialect of the tongue spoken in the kingdom of the Arsacides; the fragment is obscure, its translation uncertain even for Professor Andreas, a specialist in the field, to whom Reitzenstein's work is dedicated.[117]

Bundahism is also invoked by M. Schroeder, for example, who declares in a grand manner that the date means nothing to him (it is the sixth century A.D.), for its tradition reaches back to the fifth century B.C., a tradition that is eleven centuries old. The tradition tells of a Gayomard (the name means "mortal life"), a giant created by Ohrmuzd, who died at the age of thirty from a narcotic administered by Ohrmuzd himself, and from whose seed, forty years later, the first human couple was born. The "glory" conferred from on high upon the first man and woman gave him his freedom. Behold the prototype of Jesus! Moderate as P. Lagrange was in his judgments, and careful as he was in his writing, he could not refrain from crying out: Dreams! Mystification![118]

VI. MANDAEISM

Recourse is now had to the Mandaeans to "explain" Christianity. The Mandaeans were revealed to the scientific world by a work published in Rome in 1652 by Fr. Ignatius of Jesus, a Discalced Carmelite missionary of Bassorah in lower Mesopotamia. He thought that the sect from the region of Shatt-el-Arab was Christian, but in that he was wrong, for the Mandaeans are strongly opposed to Christianity. We know more of their teachings and customs now, thanks to the studies, in the past century, of H. J. Petermann (1860) and Sioufii, the French vice-consul of Mossoul (1880). Some Mandaeans are still to be found, but their number is steadily decreasing, together with their knowledge of the lofty doctrines of their sect. Their sacred books were edited and translated in a masterful way by Lidzbarski: *The Book of John* (Giessen, 1915), *The Liturgies* (1920), and, much the most important, *The Gniza* or *Treasure* (1915). The books were written in a rather peculiar Aramaean dialect; in their actual redaction they date from the period which extends from the fourth century A.D. to the advent of Islam.

In these writings two different doctrines appear. First, the Gnostic mythology, wherein an inferior god named Ptahil (the supreme god was Massa), in collaboration with the power of evil, the Mother-Spirit Raha, executed the work of creation; and second, monotheism, wherein the king of light creates all things by his word. The second doctrine has clearly been superimposed upon the first.[119]

In 1928, P. Lagrange studied the texts in their minute details in order to test the theories of Reitzenstein concerning the influence of Mandaean ideas upon the Synoptic gospels; of Gauer, who affirmed the same influence upon the gospel of John; of Bultmann, who tried to confirm Bauer's thesis by the use of recently edited texts of Lohmeyer, who intimated that there were at least some Mandaean infiltrations to be found in the Apocalypse, whether one considers the Mandaean religion itself or the gnosis from which it sprang. It will be enough to point out some of the general ideas.

The Mandaean writings are very evidently guilty of plagiarism from Christianity. Thus, the miracles of Jesus are attributed to Enoch, or mention is made of John the Baptist. They had a special devotion for John, and hence came to be called, inaccurately, the Christians of St. John. In Mandaeanism the three most undeniable traits of eastern gnosis appear: ". . . a series of emanations from the first principle, a creator who is not the supreme god, and the fall of the soul into an inferior world."[120]

The Mandaeans had no need of a redeemer, since flowing water sufficed for the remission of sins; they therefore did not expect salvation from a human Messias. According to the logic of their very spiritualistic system, the angels, those great creatures they called the Outhras, could do anything. The abyss between matter and the spiritual world obliged them to look upon the descent of souls upon earth as a downfall which only death would repair. The superior beings with whom souls held such touching conversations needed to have only a human appearance for this intimacy. Hence no Incarnation nor Redemption.[121]

The efficacy of Baptism comes from the death of Jesus Christ; for the Mandaeans it came solely from living water. The Spirit, so important in St. John, is for the Mandaeans an evil power. Frequently men range far afield seeking the origin of the New Testament ideas; actually these are visibly connected with the teachings of the Old Testament: Son of God, Son of Man, etc.

VII. GENERAL CONCLUSION

As we follow step by step his research concerning the application of the comparative history of religions to the Bible, we experience a growing admiration for two qualities which P. Lagrange possessed to a remarkable degree: an historical spirit, and priestly charity — which means that his soul and his mind walked in harmony. As an historian he was always careful to interpret and analyze the texts with the greatest possible philological and scientific strictness, realizing at the same time that a text did not have its full significance until it was framed in its literary and its human context. Analysis and synthesis are the two essential and complementary steps of history and of all science.

P. Lagrange had no desire nor capacity to study history, and especially religious history, from a purely "spectacular" point of view, or as a pure intellectual. Souls were involved, and at their approach his priestly heart kindled. If, as in some of the Orphics or in some authors of the *Gathas* of the *Avesta*, he discovered noble aspirations, he rejoiced. When he ascertained among them sad aberrations and the deplorable proximity of sensuality or savagery to mysticism, he experienced feelings of pity rather than hatred; but did not despair of finding again in these lamentable mistakes the more or less conscious appeal of the religious instinct toward the common Father of all men.

Toward critics, whose rationalistic prejudices and obstinate willfullness caused him to explode with anger and indignation, he exercised charity; and there is no doubt that he felt sincere pity for those whose denial of all transcendence condemned them to wander in circles in their vain search for the truth.

Shall I avow this? The Master of Jerusalem, endowed with gifts as a philologist and thinker, did not always possess the gift of clear expression, one free of overlapping ideas. This was almost certainly due to his feverish activity. And yet, though it often takes a little time to condense his learned studies, he creates about him such a salutary intellectual and moral atmosphere that one is well repaid for all the trouble. Let us hope that the efforts of this book to make his work known will give a greater effulgence to this beneficent influence.

His contribution to the history of religions may be stated as follows: P. Lagrange took up an idea dear to his precursor, the Abbe de Broglié. In 1885, some fifty years ago, this priest had exposed the idea in his *Problèmes et conclusions de l'histoire des religions,* and as developed by P. Lagrange it was this: The faith has nothing to fear from comparisons of different beliefs and rites, provided the comparisons are made with the desired critical rigor, and with an appreciation of their spiritual value and hierarchy, without which there simply cannot be any real understanding of religious phenomena. P. Lagrange was of the mind that if comparisons were dealt with under these conditions, they could provide good arguments for honest apologetics. Thanks to his patient and loyal studies, we see that Christianity has about it a specific and undeniable originality. This statement, which the most exacting science cannot really weaken, is the experimental basis of our belief in its supernatural transcendence. It is the diamond steel cannot scratch.

While combating the school of Judaeo-pagan syncretism, P. Lagrange saw that in spite of its fundamental errors, it did bring out one of the essential marks of the *good news*. Jesus preached penance from the beginning to the end of His ministry, thus sealing forever the alliance of religion and morality. Thanks to the immense hope which it ushered in over the whole world, the gospel has given unconquerable strength to the instinctive optimism without which life, thought, and action would be radically impossible for us.

Yet Christianity is not merely a code of morals or a simple eschatology. From the beginning it appeared as a mystery of salvation. Indeed, it is the only salvation-mystery worthy of the name, if we understand by these words a participation in the sufferings and triumph of a Saviour, one brought about by belief and worship, and at the same time by the interior gift of the soul. Essentially, it demands adhesion to defined doctrine, the practice of rites that are really efficacious; it demands a social and hierarchical organization, without which neither dogmas nor rites could exist or persevere as they should. In other words, from the point of view of history and of the faith, Christianity is by her original constitution a Catholicism.

Let us add at once that Christianity is also a contradiction to the syncretists, and a constitution directly due to the will of Christ. After all, such an origin is the simplest and most natural explanation, seeing that any other will be sought in vain. If one should wish to speak of evolution, here is creative evolution in the proper sense of the word.

ÉTIENNE MAGNIN
*Honorary Professor at the
Institut Catholique de Paris*

CHAPTER V

THE INFLUENCE OF P. LAGRANGE

A TESTIMONIAL

SPECIALISTS in exegesis and history have written about the value of the works of P. Lagrange, and have pointed out the horizons they have opened up or the opinions they confirmed, *nova et vetera*. I am going to try to show the *silent* action exercised by these works among people who perhaps could not check their technical worth, but who have at any rate breathed in their salutary influence.

I

First of all, it is eminently just to thank P. Lagrange for the great service he has rendered to many Christian universities, which had been (or could easily have been) led astray from the faith by what is called Biblical Criticism. Thanks to him, sincere belief could become, or at least remain, a "reasonable service," when everything conspired against it.

Many of us recognized some of our own experiences in a recent novel by Malègue, in which we read of the defeats and triumphs of the light in the life of a young modern intellectual. The author will excuse us for borrowing the name of his very typical hero, and will at the same time permit us the liberty of here and there correcting or completing his picture.

Augustine grew up in a university atmosphere. At home and at school, at the *Faculté* as well as at the normal school, in a thousand different ways, there was awakened in him what from his infancy was called the critical spirit. What is this critical spirit? A constant concern never to be duped, a thirst for good proofs, loyalty to self, serene confidence in reason, modesty in research and in the consequent discoveries which spur one on to further discoveries. It was this spirit of work and sincerity that Augustine wished to employ in verifying his faith, his most precious possession.

To hear it whispered that Criticism was dishonest and proud — this shocked him. He knew his masters well and esteemed them highly. Why criticize them for studying the sources of the faith with methods which had brought new life to so many other problems? Why not try in its regard what his masters and their masters, Boissier, Bédier, Lanson, Croiset, Bérard, had tried in profane matters? There was no question of revolt in this; far from that. Augustine was honest, but he wanted to be sure. It was not his fault that God had given him talents that forced him to undertake labors which in the eyes of the simple were just a waste of time. "Unhappy people," said Pascal, "who oblige me to touch upon the proofs of religion." He was surrounded by these unhappy ones: respected professors, comrades, friends; book reviews, conferences, and doubts were confided to him, questions asked. "Be always ready with an answer to everyone who asks a reason for the hope that is in you." What St. Peter advised was what Augustine wanted.

Study this textbook, this catechism, this approved conference, people would advise him. But to answer with respect those independents who questioned him, he could not rush in with an argument from authority, or seek refuge in this or that decree. Such things have great weight with believers, because they engage a part of the authority of the Church, which they hold to be divine. But unbelievers ask if the Church is divine, and want to see its credentials. To "those outside," the magisterium counts little; what counts is the "divine" language of facts, and the universal fact of reason in all men. Then a voice murmurs to Augustine that no one man is equal to such a task, that all signs are ambiguous, that he needs only honesty in his heart in order to transform obscurities into light — let him trust in the experience of so many saints, both men and women. But would this not still be a virtuous defeat? In the unbelieving world in which he lives, silence on his part can be a scandal to his companions, or — what is even worse — a confirmation. When shall his *Credo* likewise be a credit to him? Ah, how he hoped for the appearance in the Church of a man just as critical as his teachers, who at long last would give him a feeling of security!

There is such a man. He knows that *now*. He has heard him cited by his adversaries. Now, when the traditional jibe about the slavery of Catholic criticism is pronounced (quite as necessary, apparently, as the English toast to the king, or the academic compliment to Richelieu), he can fearlessly point out this savant, shorn of all such titles as Révérend Père, and O.P., reduced to the neat scientific bareness of: Lagrange. In libraries where men claim to sift the chaff from the wheat, his books stand, impassive, heavy, fortified with all modern apparatus. They, too, bristle with machine guns, reinforcements, provisions, armament, color; and they are conceded to have a rightful place in the struggle. Now, before he so much as opens a book, Augustine experiences profound relief, seeing that this telling blow has been inflicted upon the enemy in the Voltairean struggles wherein scorn is used as a weapon. After all, he muses, numbers and statistics do not count so much as quality and authority. One aviator only was needed to prove the possibility of transatlantic flight; strictly speaking, only one exegete is needed to prove that the faith can remain in spite of all the criticism in the world. For Augustine it suffices to know that there is someone who reads, weighs, and compares everything independently; he no longer feels abandoned. In this man, and in his equals, he puts a human confidence which prepares for and nourishes the faith. Perseverance and peace are an imperative necessity for conscientious people like Augustine. Blessed are the men, he repeats, whose blessed work sustains so many minds.

But this man does not uphold only the intelligence.

Now that Augustine has more certitude, and can pray with fervor without his cursed doubts, he comes in contact with others who also live in Christ at the university in the midst of so many different creeds. All have not his thirst for reasons and motives, but he knows of some who want sure and critical texts even in their piety. Just as a good carpenter must have a well-squared prie-dieu before he can pray well, so some of them in their spiritual life desire precise texts and exact references. The craft demands it. The huge commentaries of P. Lagrange, those four blocks cut out of rose-colored granite, fulfill this desire.

Alongside this fourfold guard, however, and issuing from its austere splendor, Augustine has frequently noticed another book, rose-colored also, less voluminous but apparently quite worn from use. This book the master wrote with perhaps greater joy, for in it he could rekindle his erudition with his heart. We can understand how the craftsman, who for thirty years had laboriously worked over a stained glass window peopled with prophets, Apostles, and the four animals, would of an evening joyfully contemplate the light whose gentle caress aroused these figures to life. In this same spirit P. Lagrange wrote his *Evangile*. Augustine owned a copy of it and knew of many others, primary teachers, both men and women, living in villages off the beaten path, who had this book among their prized possessions. For these normal school products toward whom so much criticism had been directed, the familiar gospel incidents took on a truer relief because they were recounted by one who had lived amid these very scenes.

Musing over all these benefits, and comparing this Dominican's life with that of other savants of his own country, Augustine now finds it most appealing. Other men had studied all about Christian history; but, out of discretion or method, they had neglected the burning battlefields of "the religion of Israel" and "the origins of Christianity." *He* shut himself up, took up his position on the important field of prehistory, certain that there was always a way to reconcile the independence of a critic with a filial spirit. Others who had begun this task were satisfied after a few preliminary soundings or syntheses; he persevered even during the arduous times. And behold, he leaves us not a few sparse works, *opera,* but a solid structure of ideas and studies, an *opus.* Others had studied the Scriptures in their rooms, and, if they saw the Holy Land at all, it was in a hurry. While still a young man, P. Lagrange had exiled himself in Jerusalem, inspired by the hope that the spirit of the Holy Places would be propitious to him. Some others were rewarded at the end of their lives with great honors, even bishoprics; but he labored unto the end as a simple religious. Others, or rather, *one* other — how can we speak here without sadness of the man whose loyal adversary and living antithesis P. Lagrange was, and will remain? What a contrast between the two! It brings to the mind such names as Renan and Newman; so much study and perseverance on both sides, so much devotion to science, but how different the results!

II

Here, let us leave Augustine, who is too much a part of his times and its crises to be able to see more than a narrow part of it. Let us try to peer behind the veil of time, and ask how a future historian will evaluate this man's work. I suppose an historian would say something like this:

For many centuries the Scriptures had been looked upon as books which had nothing in common with other books, without earthly roots, something truly fallen from the heavens, to such an extent that it seemed wicked to apply to them the same methods of explanation used in dealing with books written by men. Going to the other extreme were men who considered this Book a purely human work, a collection of myths and legends, and the fraudulent product of an eastern civilization. If God, however, is the author of the Scriptures and guarantees their religious truth, why would He not have exercised in their composition that sovereign discretion and respect for secondary causes, which seems to be His method in governing nature and bestowing grace? From the point of view of the faith itself, then, there would already be something of an invitation to approach the study of the sacred writings with literary and historical methods. This would even be the only way to understand the *polytrophy* of prophetical revelation pointed out in the epistle to the Hebrews, the divine "plan" of grace of which the Greek Fathers so often spoke.

Such a theandric consideration of the holy books — human in its procedure, but divine in the concept of revelation which governs its usage — was almost born in the sixteenth century, at the time of the Christian prereformation. If it had succeeded, much of the cleavage would have been avoided. Colet, the teacher of Erasmus, and Cardinal Fisher, the friend of St. Thomas More, had sensed it, and had indicated and applied it at Oxford. The success of Protestantism brought a halt to their efforts. Protestants were less willing than Catholics to see the human element in the Scriptures, now become their only rule of faith; and the spirit of mimicry, not at all unusual in controversies, led Catholic exegetes to follow them in this view. "Truth which has come from God has at the start all of its perfection," wrote Bossuet; but he had borrowed the axiom from the Protestant Jean d'Aillé. Richard Simon was suspect in both camps. What had happened?

When criticism reawakened, it found itself in the camp of the enemies of the faith. These men would no longer admit of any particular revelation, but after the manner of Hegel, saw this very revelation in human history. Confusing critical *method* with critical doctrine, unbelieving exegetes laid down as their first principle and dogma, the denial of all transcendence. The results are known to all the world.

*   *   *

We are now in a position to place the work of P. Lagrange in proper perspective.

Taking advantage of the critical method, and of the light shed on his work by Christian doctrine, he attempted to set up the kind of sacred science which the Fathers and scholastics would have admired and strenuously employed, if they had only known about it. Certainly a biblical science could have been more directly concerned with its own philosophical bases, such as source, influence, filiation, borrowing, development. St. Thomas and Newman would probably have insisted more on the mental bases of the structure. But it was certainly preferable that the new founder of biblical science should be a *humanist,* taking this dubious word in its most diverse and richest sense; I mean, a learned man who joined to a personal knowledge of ancient and oriental languages a delicate appreciation of humanity, manifesting itself in such essential, rare virtues as moderation, discretion, prudence, sympathy, and reserve.

But let us go further in our hasty analysis of a contemporary. As a result of his constant contact with ancient and modern men — the one mutually enlightens the other — he acquired an interior understanding of history which could be divided into a sense of the *development* of historical events, and a sense of the modes of the genera and *languages* in which this development was narrated by different sacred or profane authors. More than any other, P. Lagrange was prepared to exercise this famous comparative method, which appears simple only to the simple. Comparison for him will not be merely an occasional procedure; it will be the very law of his spirit, a law full of life and finesse. It enabled him to lay hold on the transcendent quality of Israelite history, at once so commingled with other histories and yet so diverse. The future historian will write of the originality of his work something like this: "After examining the research work of P. Lagrange and his disciples, we can understand what a new and remarkable support the critical method, sustained by a spiritual philosophy, brought to the ancient faith."

Now is the time to quote the old saying: "If a bit of knowledge leads a man away from God, much of it brings him back to Him," or with Pascal: "Atheism is a display of vigor, but only up to a certain degree." Actually in many points of secondary importance criticism does not bring the student back to the same point as the traditional opinion; but it corrects some of its outlines and childlike notions, fortifies its principal defenses, makes the faith more worthy of our assent, and shows history to be less marvelous but more divine.

III

After indicating the services rendered to modern minds by the work of P. Lagrange, we have tried to mark out his place in the historical development of the sacred sciences. We beg the reader's indulgence for our intrusion upon reserved grounds in attempting to show the example he leaves us in the order of charity.

We have seen that he gave new reasons for belief in orthodoxy by confirming tradition. How, then, did it come about
that he was misunderstood by some of his brethren? Why? I
wonder if those who were astonished and at times scandalized
at him have given enough thought to the conditions under
which the advance guard must fight?

Heroes of the front lines live face to face with the enemy,
watching his movements and his methods, listening while
mines are dug under their own trenches; they are like shock
troops who advance in a "No Man's Land," and who tomorrow may abandon out of prudence an old position whose continued possession might lead to complete defeat. It sometimes
happens that from far-off observatories, perhaps because of a
defaulter from their ranks, the heroes are mistaken and suspected — tragic error — of being the enemy. But incidents
such as these, which are almost fatal in such a gigantic struggle, are accepted with a silent courage truly heroic on the part
of the fighter and thinker. For them, such trials are pressing
invitations to test again their opinions, to correct them if necessary, or to reassert them with unassailable proofs. This is
good for their spirit, and for their souls.

If Christian scholars can attain heroic virtue, it is not by
external zeal or martyrdom, but by perseverance in the midst
of all this. They are never greater than when they recognize
with Pascal that truth without charity is not complete, and
charity is realized only in the bonds of unity: *Veritas in cari-
tate, caritas in unitate.* Naturally this twofold balance is not
to be won without pain. How good it is, then, that in these
troublesome times there are a few real scholars who have
taken such onerous duties upon themselves. I have known
three such men.

The first is P. de Grandmaison, S.J. Still ringing in my
ears is the reply he gave to Paul Bureau, during a *Week
of Catholic Writers.* Pointing out the value of authority and
the duty of intelligence, he said: "What does it matter, if our
reputation is strewn about, along the road where Truth
passes!" The second was an unknown master, remarkable for
his knowledge and competence, the Lazarist priest, P. Pouget.

He was blind during the last thirty years of his life, yet full of light and zeal, and an incomparable scriptural scholar. The third is P. Lagrange, who outlived both the older and the younger man. These three, so different and so completely independent from one another, are three mirrors in which we see how true science, instead of developing selfishness and pride serves instead to sharpen the intellect, strengthen character, fortify the faith, widen hope, and, finally, to discipline and transfigure love.

When P. Lagrange was three years old, he was led to the Curé of Ars and was blessed by him. Symbolic gesture, full of meaning, prophetic of a special destiny. The Curé, exegete of consciences, the sublime ignoramus for whom study had been the harshest penance, blessed in this little one a ministry quite different from his own: blessed also remoteness from sinners and a voluntary solitude. The goal awaiting at the end of the two different careers was the same, however. It may be that the saint had communicated to this child something of his own spirit of penance and innocence, so indispensable for the thinker. For — and this is no common merit — like the works which charity inspires, it disposes at one and the same time to both knowledge and piety; to knowledge first of all, and to piety by a divine gift. Such a spirit leads to the fountains which quench the thirst.

The work of P. Lagrange may be corrected, or taken up and carried further; no matter. More than a method, P. Lagrange gave to the world a spirit which our critical and mystical century has often sought for in vain. If it be not temerarious to try to define what is undefinable, we may formulate this spirit by imitating the psalm, saying, or rather, singing: *Humanitas et veritas obviaverunt sibi, critica et pax osculatae sunt.*

JEAN GUITTON
Agrégé de philosophie de l'Université
Docteur ès lettres

CHAPTER VI

P. LAGRANGE — A MEMORIAL

(MARCH 10, 1938)[1]

THE professorial staff and students of the *École Biblique*
in Jerusalem sat busily at their desks. The convent bell
clanged noisily. Soon after a lay brother mounted the
steps bearing a telegram for the superior. Five minutes later
the whole community was thoroughly aroused, for the news
contained in that telegram was: P. Lagrange anointed. The
older men, PP. Vincent, Abel, and Savignac, stood dazed and
disconsolate; one could see that they were sunk deep in personal thoughts of the past. The noonday mail came. In it was
a letter from P. Lagrange to P. Vincent, brimful of new plans
and projects for future lines of inquiry; it was full also of
questions and comments on the latest archaeological and
anthropological discoveries taking place in Palestine and
elsewhere. So lively were these questions and remarks that the
fine face of P. Vincent relaxed; surely this illness could not be
as serious as was first suspected. The shadow of gloom
lessened perceptibly. Five o'clock came, bringing another
telegram: P. Lagrange died this morning at nine o'clock.

Only one who was at St. Stephen's that fateful day could
appreciate the jarring impact of this news. Once more the
older men were silent; so, too, was the rest of the community.
Everyone moved about as in a dream, each wrapped in the
recollection of his personal associations with P. Lagrange.
Their grief was sincere and apparent, and singularly indicative of the nature and stature of the man whose death moved
them so greatly.

The year 1940 marked the fiftieth anniversary of the founding of the *École Biblique* at Jerusalem. Since April of the preceding year plans had been drawn up for the publication of a
memoir dedicated to the memory of P. Lagrange. The project
was everywhere enthusiastically received, scholars from all

parts of Europe and America had written in to pledge their co-operation, and manuscripts began to pile up on the editorial desk of P. Vincent. The memoir seemed assured. It was to have appeared in November of 1940, but the war which swept over Europe swept away all hopes of its immediate appearance. Rather than permit the golden anniversary of the *École Biblique* to pass by without some notice being taken of it, the following pages present a belated sketch of the extraordinary career of its founder, P. Lagrange.[2]

I

Albert Lagrange was born, as he himself liked to recall, the year following the definition of the Immaculate Conception, on March 7, 1855, in Bourg-en-Bresse. His mother took the sickly child, when he was three years of age, to receive the blessing of the saintly Curé of Ars. After the customary preliminary studies at Autun, and after five years, study of law in Paris, where he obtained the degree of Doctor of Laws, young M. Lagrange spent a year in compulsory military service. This completed he entered the *Grand Séminaire* at Issy, near Paris. There he struck up a lifelong friendship with MM. Batiffol and Hyvernat, but he was not destined to remain long with them, for it was at Issy that Abbé Lagrange decided to become a religious. On October 5, 1879, Frère Marie-Joseph received the Dominican habit in the historic convent of St. Maximin near Marseilles. During the year of novitiate he indulged to the full his "passionate taste" for the written word of God. The day after his profession, religious orders were expelled from France, and Fr. Lagrange found himself at Salamanca, where he was ordained priest on December 22, 1883. There he concluded his four years of theology by obtaining the degree of Lector in Sacred Theology. During this period he had taken a course in Hebrew at the same university. An interval followed during which he taught church history; but eventually, at the end of 1888, P. Lagrange was sent by his superiors to study oriental languages under D. H. Müller and O. Reinisch at the University of Vienna. For three semesters he pursued these studies.

II

Since 1882 the Dominicans in Jerusalem had been in possession of the traditional site of the martyrdom of St. Stephen. It was long debated whether to make of it a hostelry for pilgrims or a resthouse for missionaries. Still, such an ideal location seemed better fitted for an intellectual center devoted to the study of the Scriptures. It was then that the Master General, Fr. Larroca, remembered P. Lagrange and his bent for scriptural studies, and accordingly directed him to proceed to Jerusalem and there establish a school.

On March 10, 1890 (mark the day), P. Lagrange arrived in Palestine. He arrived without great enthusiasm, scarcely knowing what to expect when he got to St. Étienne. When finally he entered its gates he found a tiny community living in what had once been the municipal slaughterhouse; the rings to which the animals had once been attached were still hanging from its walls. The library, he soon discovered, consisted of the two books he brought with him: the Bible and a guidebook of the Holy Land. This was the proverbial beginning on a shoestring.

After a few weeks P. Lagrange set out from Jerusalem on an extended tour of Palestine and Transjordan. Several months later he returned, a changed man, for he had seen the Bible relived under the tents of the Bedouins, and had heard the silent stories spoken to him by the innumerable ruins that dotted the countryside. He was ready to begin.

The new school opened its doors on November 15, 1890. Before an audience dignified by the presence of the French consul and the religious superiors of the various houses in Jerusalem, P. Lagrange delivered a discourse in which he outlined the ambitious program of the school. The faculty: four priests, only one of whom had been trained in biblical lore; the student body: three Dominican novices. But the initial impulse had been given, and he had begun so humbly and so low that the only possible direction to be taken was onward and upward.

Courageous and novel was the work thus set in motion. Beginning around 1850 research and progress in archaeology and philology had, with a speed unparalleled in any other branch of science, been steadily pushing back its horizons. But unfortunately almost all of this work was done by unbelievers and rationalistic critics who employed their new knowledge to attack the Bible and the traditional defenses of Christianity. Catholic exegesis was definitely on the defensive. If some few Catholic scholars availed themselves of the work that was progressing without them, they did so halfheartedly and timidly, uncertain whether "today's theories" would not prove to be "tomorrow's absurdities." P. Lagrange had quite opposite views, for true exegesis based on sound theology had nothing to fear from true science. He was convinced that the time had come for Catholic scholars to put themselves on a par with any other scholar, to use the same weapons but with a truer goal and better logic. He realized the utter futility of attempting to oppose rifles with crossbows. He wanted some of the rifles on his side. For this it was decidedly not enough to utilize the new knowledge; there was pressing need for Catholics to seek for the truth in new sources, to examine excavations and inscriptions at firsthand, to make discoveries. . . .

Never for an instant was it his purpose to devote his energies exclusively to a study of the sciences connected with the Bible; his goal was always single: to make the Bible better understood. He has sometimes been accused of treating it as merely a human work, but this is false. For a keen Thomist like P. Lagrange the Bible was a divinely inspired book containing the word of God, but it was not merely a collection of revelations. It was also a human work, written by human instruments writing freely and without constraint under the constant, efficacious influence of the Holy Ghost. Surely there is no need to place limitations on God's power and to say that He could not move free things freely or necessary things necessarily. He used instruments in the composition of His Book, human instruments which were not mere machines nor yet completely independent agents, but truly authors in the strict sense of the word. They judged with divine and infallible judgment of things known from their own experience or research, and God who inspired them to write and who moved them to make those judgments, willed those same judgments and made them His own. Whatever the hagiographers affirmed, God affirmed; whatever they denied, God denied, because both their affirmations and their denials were freely formulated under the guidance and inspiration of the Holy Ghost. God respected His human instruments; they preserved all their human characteristics, and left their impress upon the Word of God. Without, therefore, minimizing the divine element in the Scriptures, exegesis must penetrate the thought and intention of the human authors, for we know what God wishes to say through what the sacred writers really mean to say. To discover this one must take into consideration a surprising number of factors.

Of first importance is the establishment of the original text as far as is possible. Second, the Bible has always been the treasure of the Church, which jealously guarded the monumental commentaries written by the Fathers on the Scriptures. The history of exegesis, then, was to have its proper place. Third, half of the Bible is composed of historical books. The authors, including here the prophets and didactic writers as well, were children of their times. They lived and labored in definite historical circumstances, faced with crises as grave to them as our own are to us. All these things are reflected in their works. Consequently it is necessary to examine with painstaking care the circumstances of time and of place in which they were written. This demands competency in ancient history both political and religious, a thorough knowledge of the customs and geography of the biblical countries, and more than a passing acquaintance with the latest archaeological investigations. Fourth, exegesis, which is a work of reconstruction, will strive to penetrate the thought of the sacred writer guided and aided by theology. Along with the courses of exegesis the *École* pursued its courses of theology. Finally, since the Church is the sole authentic interpreter of both Tradition and the Scriptures, the Catholic exegete must always submit the results of his research to this supreme arbiter.

With this immense program — often imitated since, but then quite new — the *École pratique d'études bibliques* was now established. It needed a voice, and in January, 1892, the *Revue Biblique* made its first appearance. P. Lagrange was its most faithful contributor. His first article on the proper location of the City of David was judged by some to be so "radical" that there was talk of citing him before a Roman Congregation for it. *Un son de cloche?* He was too busy to notice. The infant foundation was that same year encouraged by a Brief of Pope Leo XIII approving its plans and program. With such high approbation the *Revue Biblique* received promises of collaboration from men like Vigouroux, Corluy, Cornely, Knabenbauer, van Kasteren, and others. For various reasons some of these shortly withdrew their promises of assistance.

The school was called the *École pratique*. An essential part of its program required that the professors spend some of their time revisiting with their students the biblical sites. In 1893, P. Lagrange and the school made a trip to Mt. Sinai, returning from Sinai to Cades in eleven days as did the Hebrews under Moses. In 1897 Petra was the goal of another expedition. Egypt, Transjordan, Samaria, Galilee, Baalbek, Palmyra, and the rest of Syria were in turn visited and explored whenever conditions permitted of travel. Accounts of these voyages were faithfully recorded in the *Revue*.

The *Revue* of 1900 published a "Project for a complete commentary on the Scriptures." The *Études bibliques* were to be scientific works based upon good translations of sound critical texts; they were to be model treatments of the various books by Catholic scholars, containing the best conclusions of historical, geographical, archaeological, and theological studies. In 1903 the first book of the series, *Le Livre des Juges*, appeared from the pen of P. Lagrange. The same year he published the *Études sur les Religions Sémitiques,* a work that is still highly regarded by authors of our own day. To these technical works there was now added another which was to cause a veritable tempest: *La Méthode Historique,* dealing principally with the exegesis of the Old Testament.

But, to fill in the lacunae. The Catholic Congress of Fribourg (1897) chose P. Lagrange as president of the exegetical section. It will be remembered that his conferences at this congress dealt with the Mosaic authenticity of the Pentateuch. His own order conferred on him the degree of Master in Sacred Theology, September 29, 1901. In 1902 he delivered a series of lectures at Toulouse on the Historical Method. Returning to Palestine by way of Syria, he found at Beyrouth a copy of the Apostolic Letter, *Vigilantiae,* establishing the Biblical Commission. To this he unhesitatingly gave his wholehearted adherence. That it was accepted at Rome without misgivings is evidenced by the fact that he was called to Rome early in the next year, where Cardinal Rampolla informed him that Leo XIII had it in mind, if it were agreeable to those most concerned, to make the *Revue Biblique* the official organ of the newly established Biblical Commission, to which P. Lagrange had been named consultor on January 26. Moreover, in the Institutum Biblicum, soon to be set up in Rome, P. Lagrange was to have a place.

It was finally decided that P. Lagrange should return to Jerusalem and his work and that the *Revue Biblique* should publish the official communications of the Biblical Commission. The "New Series" began, therefore, in 1904, and the *Revue* continued as official organ until the institution of the *Acta Apostolicae Sedis* in 1909.

In February, 1904, Fr. Frühwirth, Master General of the Order, authorized the second edition of the *Méthode Historique.* Shortly thereafter the dark clouds which had been gathering since 1892 broke forth in full-throated thunder. An eminent Catholic scholar launched a violent attack upon the *Méthode,* and this led P. Lagrange to write his *Éclaircissement.* The storm was now raging in full fury. Modernism in all forms, principally in those sketched in the works of Loisy, was fiercely assailed, and many of the attacks were directed at P. Lagrange as well. The tempest was to continue until 1912.

During this time, as his superiors had counseled, P. Lagrange serenely pursued his work, taking no direct part in the controversies. What this must have cost him may be gathered from some of the attacks: some critics claimed him as their own champion; some Catholic writers declared roundly that he was worse than the rationalists, for *they* at least came out clearly and said what they really believed. But P. Lagrange aimed not at destroying; he lived to build. That is why he promptly and sincerely signified his submission, when in 1907 Pius X issued the *Lamentabili* and the *Pascendi*. It was suggested then that he turn his inquiries to the New Testament for the time being, which he did immediately and without murmuring. The first of his great commentaries appeared in 1910 with the publication of *Saint Marc*.

But the Modernist crisis was not yet over; it continued to wreak havoc in the fold of the Church. No one was too sure just where the border line lay between what was orthodox or unorthodox, and finally the Church spoke. A decree of the Consistorial Congregation forbade the use in Catholic seminaries of two books named expressly, and of others unnamed, such as "certain works of P. Lagrange." Perhaps it was thought that the keen, searching analyses and discussions of dangerous modern theories found in his *Saint Marc* should wisely be kept from the hands of unformed seminarians, but condemnation it assuredly was not. There never has been a formal condemnation of any work or proposition of P. Lagrange.[3] This decree was dated June 29, 1912; on the following day P. Lagrange drew up a declaration of his submission "of mind and heart, without reserve, to the commands of the Vicar of Christ" which was joyfully received by Pius X. Then, as he had asked to be removed temporarily from the School, P. Lagrange was recalled to France. Less than a year later he was again at Jerusalem with orders to carry on his exegetical work.

No sooner was one war over than another began. World War I seemed destined to ruin completely the work of the *École Biblique*. The younger men were all in active service with the French armies; Kemal Pasha and his staff occupied the cells of *St. Étienne,* and Palestine was again the battle ground as it had been so frequently in history. P. Lagrange attempted to remain at the School, but he was arrested by the Turks and was released only after Pope Benedict XV had personally interceded in his behalf with the Emperor Franz Josef, who in turn brought pressure to bear upon the Turkish authorities. Back in France now, the old man fought tenaciously to save his life's work, and through his heroic efforts the *Revue* continued to appear throughout the years of the war. Always a prodigious worker capable of extremely rapid composition, during the same period P. Lagrange published his commentaries on the Epistles: *aux Romains* (1916) and *aux Galates* (1918).

In 1919 the venerable old man was again at Jerusalem surrounded by his old students. Many of them had long since acquired reputations in their own right, and the names Vincent, Abel, Savignac, and Jaussen were cited more and more frequently in scientific circles. This was certainly the happiest period of P. Lagrange's life. His huge commentaries on the gospels appeared with amazing regularity: *Saint Luc* (1921), *Saint Matthieu* (1923), *Saint Jean* (1925). During their composition he had necessarily to deal with textual criticism, with the theology of the New Testament, and with the pretended relations between Christianity and the Greek mystery religions. On all of these subjects he wrote articles which appeared in the *Revue Biblique.* Then, by way of synthesizing this vast inquiry, he published the first Catholic *Synopsis Evangelica* (1926), followed shortly by the crowning work of his genius: *l'Évangile de Jésus-Christ* (1928).[4] No other of his works ever reached such a large audience, and it has been translated into many languages. 1931 saw the publication of *Judaïsme avant Jésus-Christ,* describing the religious state of Jews at the dawn of the New Testament.

Old age only made him hasten. Now, at 78, P. Lagrange conceived the bold project of a vast introduction to the study of the New Testament. Thereupon a new series of works issued from his pen: *l'Histoire du Canon* (1933), adjudged at once "too advanced" and "too conservative"; *La Critique*

Textuelle (Rationelle) (1935); and *La Critique Historique, Les Mystères: l'Orphisme* (1937).

In 1935 the physicians informed P. Lagrange in no uncertain terms that he must leave Palestine at once. He returned to St. Maximin, but it was not to rest. There he completed the redaction of *l'Orphisme,* conducted a course or two in the house of studies, and gave frequent conferences to various groups in near-by districts. From St. Maximin, too, he watched eagerly over the continued progress of the *École Biblique,* and each year faithfully renewed his passport in the hope of returning once again. After all, he had spent forty-five years of his life in Palestine (ten more than St. Jerome at Bethlehem), and there he wished to die. But it was not to be.

Returning from a conference at Montpellier on March 4, 1938, he complained of a slight cold. The following day he remained in bed, where he sat propped up correcting the proofs of his last article for the *Revue Biblique.* On the ninth, being informed that it was the end, he replied simply, *"Je m'abandonne à Dieu,"* and was annointed. During the night he was restless; he attempted to speak but all that could be made out was "Jérus — Jérus — ." These were his last words. The next morning the great warrior-student died.

III

Fifty years from now, or perhaps even sooner, the name and works of P. Lagrange will have received their just appreciation. At present we live too close to the turbulent times in which he fought to be able to judge. But there can be no doubt of the verdict. That he aroused criticism, that many sincere men believed him to be a dangerous radical was almost inevitable, for he was a leader and a pioneer, and such things were to be expected. He bore them without bitterness. What does it matter, he used to say, if my reputation suffers a bit, if thereby the truth is spread? The passing years brought peace and international recognition and an ever widening circle of friends to the old master who did for modern criticism what St. Thomas did for Aristotle. Honors were heaped upon him. In 1903 the Academy of Inscriptions and Fine Arts had chosen him a member; later years saw him created a member of the Legion of Honor and of the Order of Leopold. An honor which particularly pleased him occurred in 1935, when one entire *Cahier de la Nouvelle Journée,* N° 28, was dedicated to him. In this book Cardinal Liénart and five other scholars paid him tribute in a synthesis of his tremendous labors in all scriptural fields, including Hellenistic studies and comparative religions. To open its pages gives one a glimpse of the staggering breadth of the man's inquisitive research.

The Greeks used to describe a perfect man with a single word: versatile. The term is an apt description of P. Lagrange. Students and visitors at St. Étienne and St. Maximin were astounded by the extent of his knowledge and interests. Speculative theological problems, politics, and labor conditions were subjects he was able to discuss with ease and accuracy. Best of all, he was able to find intellectual companionship with the lowliest of novices as well as with experts. In hours of relaxation he loved to read and reread Vergil, Seneca, and Cicero, the Greek dramatists and philosophers, especially Plato. Dante and Goethe and Shakespeare — all in their original languages — were old friends of his. Indeed nothing human was foreign to him.

And yet this man of "the Book" was a saintly man. Few have noticed how consistently he placed his great works under the patronage of Mary "who has always been so good to me." Each day long before time for Office he would be found in choir at a spot where his gaze could command both her altar and the tabernacle. In his desk, after his death, was found a slip of paper upon which he had written the wish that on his memento card there be, not his own picture, but that of the Vierge d'Autun. Throughout his career, even during the periods of intense activity, he fulfilled with meticulous care the demands of his religious life, and this was especially true during the periods when he was most bitterly attacked. During his long stay at St. Étienne he was several times elected Prior; but likewise he was many times a subject, and those who had any dealings with him in this latter capacity state emphatically that he was a most obedient subject, one who never showed the least resistance to authority.[5] He was devoted to conventual observance, and to the very end of his stay in Jerusalem he attended choir every day to recite the divine Office with the other professors of the school. To this childlike obedience and deep inner piety must be added a great humility. Needless to repeat here the many anecdotes which illustrate it; it is enough to say that whenever for one reason or another the censors of the Order (without whose permission nothing he ever wrote was published) criticized his articles, he never for an instant hesitated to change or amend the argumentation or statements brought into question.

But the picture of this great man is nowhere to be seen in better light than in his "spiritual testament":

I declare before God that it is my intention to die in the holy Catholic Church to which I have always belonged with my whole heart and soul since the day of my baptism, and to die there faithful to my vows of poverty, chastity, and obedience, in the Order of St. Dominic. To that end I commend myself to my good Saviour Jesus and to the prayers of His most holy Mother who has always been so good to me.

I declare also most expressly that I submit to the judgment of the Apostolic See all that I have written. I believe that I can add that I have always had the intention in all my studies, of contributing to the good — I mean to the reign of Jesus Christ, to the honor of the Church, to the good of souls.

RICHARD T. MURPHY, O.P.

NOTES AND REFERENCES

PREFACE

1. The *Revue Biblique* appeared under another title, *Vivre et Penser*, during World War II. Except for the name, it was exactly the same magazine; the old title was resumed in 1946. — *Trans.*

CHAPTER I

1. P. Lagrange set forth his views on inspiration in various articles published in the *Revue Biblique* (*RB*): "Une pensée de S. Thomas sur l'inspiration," *RB*, IV (1895), 563–571; "L'inspiration des Livres saints," *RB*, V (1896), 199–220; "L'inspiration et les exigences de la critique," *RB*, V (1896), 496–518; "Les sources du Pentateuque," *RB*, VII (1898), 10–32; in *La méthode historique* (Paris, 1903), pp. 71–109; and in various reviews (cf. *RB*, VI [1897], 324–327). *La méthode historique* is sometimes designated as the Conferences of Toulouse; English translation by E. Myers, now Bishop, and Vicar Capitular of Westminster: *Historical Criticism and the Old Testament* (London, 1905).

2. *Tractatus de divina Traditione et Scriptura*, 3rd ed. (Rome, 1882).

3. *RB*, V (1896), 206.

4. "Eos libros vero Ecclesia pro sacris et canonicis habet . . . proptera quod Spiritu Sancto inspirante conscripti, Deum habent auctorem" (*Denzinger*, 1787). M. Lusseau has seen fit to imagine that P. Lagrange interpreted the words "Spiritu Sancto conscripti" as a corrective which would temper the force of the affirmation "proptera quod habent Deum auctorem" (*Essai sur la nature de l'inscription scripturaire* [Paris, 1930], p. 48). To say the very least, Lusseau does not know how to read P. Lagrange, who never diminished the role of author played by God in the composition of the Bible. Certainly it is not diminishing God's role to understand His causality in a Thomistic sense.

5. A Roman theologian wrote to P. Lagrange: ". . . placing the causal propositions before the caused propositions, we have in logical order (*a*) Libri utriusque Testamenti Spiritu Sancto inspirante sunt conscripti. Ergo (*b*) iidem libri Deum habent auctorem. Ergo (*c*) ipsimet sunt sacri et canonici." Consequently the nature and truth of each consequence should be measured by its immediate antecedent, that is (*c*) by (*b*), and (*b*) by (*a*); *RB*, V (1896) 206. I once asked P. Lagrange who this theologian was, and he answered that it was P. Buonpensiere, then regent of the Minerva.

I do not see how P. Bea can object to this by writing, "Ceterum in Encyclica Providentissimus sicut iam in Conc. Vat., Deum esse auctorem S. Scripturae et per hoc eius inspiratorem clare enunciatur" (*De Inspiratione S. Scr.* [Rome, 1930], p. 17). It would be strange if the Vatican Council, and Leo XIII, departed from the Council of Florence: "Deum . . . profitetur auctorem quoniam eodem Spiritu Sancto inspirante utriusque Testamenti Sancti locuti sunt" (*Denz.*, 706). The text of the Vatican Council says exactly the same thing as that of the Council of Florence, and Leo XIII at the beginning of his encyclical cites the text of the Vatican Council (cf. *Enchiridion Biblicum* [*EB*], [Rome], 1927, No. 66).

6. *Propaedeutica*, I, 1.

7. *RB*, V (1896), 210.

8. *Ibid.*, 200.

9. Fr. Pesch, in his *De Inspiratione S. Scripturae* (Freiburg i. B., 1906, pp. 423–424), sounds at first like Franzelin: the book exists in the divine thought before being drawn from the thought of the inspired author ("idea libri debuit principaliter existere in mente divina et ex ea derivari in mentem humanam; non generalis tantum conceptus libri, sed singulae res et sententiae scribendae, eodem modo, quo liber prius exsistit in mente auctoris humani quam in charta"). This is Franzelin's anthropomorphism; but P. Pesch adds that this supernatural action of God, according to the strict concept of inspiration, is not a *communicatio specierum*. It is then question of a "supernaturale lumen indicativum quo homo sententias ad scribendum format ea plane ratione, qua Deus vult," which seems to resemble much the explanation of P. Lagrange.

Fr. Merck, who has recast the *Introduction* of Cornely, does not accept Franzelin's distinction of formal and material parts. Yet he admits suggestion, and even adds the adjective *litterarius* (which accentuates the anthropomorphism) to the word *author:* "Ita Deus vere auctor S. Scripturae, non qualiscumque sed litterarius, qui scilicet certas ideas ut suas (seu suo nomine) conscribit, id est concipit, ordinat, componit, scribendas proponit, litteris consignandas curat" (*Compendium introductionis in S. Scripturae libros* [1927], p. 966). Elsewhere, however, he is less firm. How did God suggest things which the author already knew, or could know by his own efforts? In two distinct manners: "sufficiebat ut Deus illas supranaturali operatione menti memoriaeque scriptoris velut scribendas objiceret," and this is the system of Franzelin; "aut eum ad illas quaerendas inveniendasque gratia sua impelleret et adjuverat" (which should be *adjuvaret*), and this is the system of P. Lagrange (*op. cit.*, p. 964).

P. Balestri aligns himself with P. Lagrange in a recently published work: *Biblicae introductionis generalis elementa* (Rome, 1932).

P. Bea in some parts of his work supposes a [divine] suggestion (cf. pp. 28, 31). Elsewhere, he notes, "Recentiores auctores consentiunt acceptionem rerum pertinere formaliter ad inspirationem, sed fieri posse et saepe fieri naturalibus viribus . . . vel saltem providentia" (*De Inspiratione S. Scripturae*, p. 34).

10. This is quite clearly seen in the work of P. Pesch, p. 478.

11. *RB*, V (1896), 505.

12. *La méthode historique*, p. 81.

13. *RB*, V (1896), 506.

14. "Uno verbo: vi inspirationis nihil ut verum credendum proponitur nisi quod Deus verbis hagiographi ut verum affirmare vult. . . . Potest etiam auctor inspiratus habere opiniones falsas; immo potest accidere ut ex eius loquendi modo conici possit quas opiniones veras vel falsas in mente habeat" (*De Inspiratione*, p. 459, n. 1).

15. *La méthode historique*, p. 105.

16. *Enchiridion Biblicum* (*EB*), 433.

17. ". . . Aliis verbis: dicta hagiographi quibus exprimuntur eius iudicia, cum ea modalitate qua ab ipso exprimuntur, sunt dicta Dei" (*De Inspiratione*, p. 56 f.).

18. *La méthode historique*, pp. 111–145.

19. *RB*, V (1896), 510 ff.

20. See below, n. 36, the decree of the Biblical Commission on literary genera. Catholic interpreters are generally agreed on principles; divergences come from the different ways of evaluating the arguments in favor of this or that literary genus.

21. *RB*, VIII (1899), 50–82. A second article of the same author, "Encore l'histoire du sage Ahicar," *ibid.*, 510–531.

22. *RB*, V (1896), 511.

23. Ignatius Guidi, "L'historiographie chez les Sémites," *RB*, XV (1906), 500–519; Msgr. E. Tisserant, "Fragments syriaques du livre des jubilés," *RB*, XXX (1921), 55–86, 206–232.

24. *RB*, VI (1897), 370–371. Following this, P. Lagrange proceeds to show that the best explanation of the beginning of Genesis is to admit two accounts of creation, the first account ending at 2:4. Other examples could be given, such as that of Balaam of whom he speaks elsewhere (*RB, VIII* [1899], 613): in one account Balaam consults God and obtains his permission before setting out (Num. 22:18–21), but in another he sets out without permission and is corrected by the angel (Num. 22:22–34). The death of Antiochus IV is related in different manners (2 Mach. 1:11–17 and 9:1 f.). In his *Manual* (Vol. II, 1906, 247–248), M. Vigouroux held that they were two different men; but it is generally admitted today that the first text is a citation and that both deal with the same king.

25. *RB*, V (1896), 216. P. Lagrange refers to Cardinal Zigliara, who held the same opinion (*Propaedeutica*, III, pp. 9, 4). Cf. also *RB*, VIII (1899), 610.

26. *RB*, VII (1898), 18.

27. *Ibid.*, 15.

28. P. Lagrange explained his views about dogmatic facts in a review of the writings of P. Nisius (*RB*, XV [1906], 135–142), where he says: "Apart from all historical proof, a Catholic exegete should hold the facts to be objective whenever they would be necessarily connected with dogma, and should recognize their character as dogmatic facts whenever this is sufficiently made known by the consent of the Fathers, on condition, however, that their consent concerns not merely the reality of the facts, but also the connexity itself" (141).

29. *RB*, V (1896), 512–517; *La méthode historique*, pp. 104, 106. Cf. *infra*, p. 30 ff.

30. *Historica et critica introductio in V. T. libros sacros* (Paris, 1885), I, p. 518 ff.

31. *Exegetische zur Inspirationsfrage* (Freiburg i. B., 1904), pp. 58–70 *passim*.

32. *EB*, 108.

33. He wrote to Lagrange on March 5, 1905: "As for your interpretation of the mind of Leo XIII in his encyclical, I think it is — as far as I am able to judge — exact" (cited in *RB*, XXVIII [1919], 598).

34. *Ibid.*

35. *EB*, 469–471.

36. *EB*, 474. The Biblical Commission had already stated that, under exceptional conditions and reserving always the judgment of the Church, there could be books or parts of books having the appearance of history. The text is as follows:

"Whether we may admit as a principle of sound exegesis the opinion which holds that the books of Holy Scripture which are regarded as historical either wholly or in part sometimes narrate what is not really history properly so called and objectively true, but only have the appearance of history and are intended to convey a meaning different from the strictly literal or historical sense of the words? Answer: *in the negative,* excepting always the case — not easily or rashly to be admitted, and then only on the supposition that it is not opposed to the teaching of the Church and subject to her decision — that it can be proved by solid arguments that the sacred writer did not intend to give a true and strict history, but proposed rather to set forth, under the guise and form of history, a parable or an allegory or some meaning distinct from the literal or historical signification of the words."

37. *RB,* IX (1900), 141–142. Six years later, P. Pesch wrote concerning this "sense": "Subesse saepe verbis Scripturae altiorem sensum, quam qui communibus interpretandi praeceptis inveniri possit, et ipsos hagiographos non semper totam amplitudinem sensus verborum inspiratorum comprehendisse" (*De Inspiratione,* p. 510 ff.).

38. *RB,* V (1896), 505–506. Cf. *ibid.,* XV (1906), 541.

39. August, 1897. Cf. *RB,* VII (1898), 10–32.

40. *RB,* V (1896), 381–407.

41. *RB,* VI (1897), 341–379.

42. *RB,* XII (1903), 27–51.

43. "La prophétie de Jacob," *RB,* VII (1898), 525–540; "Les Khabiri," *ibid.,* VIII (1899), 127–132; "Le cantique de Moïse, la chanson d'Hésébon," *ibid.,* 532–552; "S. Jérôme et la tradition juive dans la Genèse," *ibid.,* VII (1898), 563–566; "Histoire des Israelites au temps de Moïse," *ibid.,* VIII (1899), 623–632.

44. "L'historiographie chez les Sémites," *RB,* XV (1906), 500–519.

45. *RB,* VII (1898), 24.

46. *Ibid.,* 25.

47. *Conjectures sur les mémoires originaux dont il parait que Moïse s'est servi pour composer le livre de la Genèse* (Brussells, 1735). Astruc proposed the hypothesis as being "very advantageous, in that it would serve to do away with or clarify many difficulties prompted by a reading of this book, and which have up to the present almost overwhelmed some commentators."

48. *J* is the symbol for Jahvist (Jehovist); *E* for Elohist, from the divine name of Yahweh, Elohim, preferred in these texts; *D* for Deuteronomist; and *P* for Priesterkodex or Priestly Code. This last is chiefly represented by Leviticus.

49. At the time, a moderate Peripateticism (now evolved into Scholasticism) seemed to be a dangerous concession. St. Thomas Aquinas himself was condemned, on March 7 and 18, 1277, by the Bishop of Paris and Archbishop of Canterbury.

50. "The time seems to have come," he said at Fribourg, "when we can no longer remain inactive without compromising the salvation of souls and alienating from the Church her remaining intellectual forces. By advancing we can gain many more. Forward, then, but with respect." *RB,* VII (1898), 14.

51. *RB,* VIII (1899), 612; cf. *supra,* pp. 19–20.

52. *Commentarius in Numeros* (Paris, 1899), pp. 226, 321.

53. *RB,* VIII (1899), 612.

54. *RB,* VII (1898), 19.

55. Cf. *infra,* p. 31 and note 75.

56. *RB,* VII (1898), 137.

57. P. Lagrange had obtained the degree of doctor of laws before entering the Grand Seminaire, and the extent of his legal knowledge was remarkable.

58. *RB*, VII (1898), 19–21.

59. *Ibid.*, 21–23.

60. He cites Irenaeus, *Adv. Haer. III*, 21, 2; Clement of Alexandria, *Stromata*, I, 21–22; Tertullian, *De cultu feminarum*, I, 3; St. Basil, *Ep. ad Chilonem*; St. John Chrysostom, *Hom. VIII ad Hebraeos*; Origen, *II, 524 in Psalmos*; Léonce de Byzantium, *De Sectis*, p. 428; Isidore of Seville, *Origines*, VI, 3; *De vita et morte sanctorum*, LXI. Suffice it to quote St. Jerome: "Sive Moysen dicere volueris auctorem Pentateuchi, sive Ezram, eiusdem instauratorem operis, non recuso" in *Adv. Helvidium*, 7. Cf. *RB*, VII (1898), 23–28.

61. St. Jerome experienced great difficulties in translating the Hebrew text and producing the Vulgate, which was made the official text for the Latin Church by the Council of Trent; one of his difficulties was his preference for the Hebrew over the Greek of the LXX, which was almost unanimously held to be equally inspired. P. Lagrange wrote on this question in an issue of the *Bulletin de littérature ecclésiastique*, of Toulouse (February, 1899), and the article was reprinted in *Mélanges d'histoire religieuse* (Paris, 1915), pp. 167–184, under the title, "Saint Jérôme et saint Augustin, à propos des origines de la Vulgate."

62. *RB, VII* (1898), 27. St. Jerome felt the impact of Jewish tradition too. P. Lagrange points out seven faulty translations in the Vulgate version of Genesis, as a result of this influence, and five bits of faulty exegesis in *Liber quaestionum hebraicarum in Genesim* ("Saint Jerome et la tradition juive dans la Genèse," in *RB, ibid.*, 563–566). On this point cf. *infra*, p. 36.

63. *RB*, VIII (1899), 609.

64. *Ibid.*, 381.

65. *RB*, XII (1903), 377.

66. E.g., the prophecy of Jacob (Gen. 49:1–28), which is attributed by many authors to *J* rather than to *E*. This very ancient poem was not Jacob's work: "the ancient historians did not hesitate — nor incur the slightest reproach of error and falsity — to put speeches composed at leisure into the mouths of certain personages. It was enough for historical truth that they be appropriate." Cf. "La prophétie de Jacob," *RB*, VII (1898), 538, 540.

67. *RB*, VIII (1899), 626–632 *passim*.

68. *La méthode historique*, pp. 176, 68. P. de Hummelauer attributes Deut. 12:1–26:15 to Samuel, and regards the rest of the book as more or less worked over. Cf. *Commentarius in Deut.* [Paris, 1901], pp. 35, 119. Cf. the judicious review of this work by P. Lagrange in *RB*, X (1901), 609–616.

69. P. Lagrange admits that some bits of information go back to a source anterior to the Jahwist. Cf. *RB*, VIII (1899), 626.

70. *RB*, VII (1898), 28–32.

71. *RB*, X (1901), 615.

72. Cf. the posthumous article of P. Lagrange, "L'authenticité mosaïque de la Genèse et la théorie des documents," *RB*, XLVII (1938), 163–183. — *Trans.*

73. Cf. *supra*, p. 19, n. 24. What follows here is drawn principally from "L'hexaméron," *RB*, V (1896), 381–407.

74. The 50,000 years allotted to humanity by P. Koppel, S.J. ("Miscellanea biblica," *Biblica* [Rome, 1934], pp. 419–436) are unfavorable to this theory.

75. P. Lagrange rules out the cosmogony of the priest Berosus, who lived

at Babylon in the time of Alexander the Great. He concludes ("La cosmogonie de Bérose," *RB*, VII [1898], 395–402) that this cosmogony, posterior to the Bible, depends on Babylonian texts; the resemblances between Berosus and the Bible may be explained easily by supposing Berosus to be the imitator.

76. *RB*, VII (1898), 393–407 passim; *ibid.*, VI (1897), 375.

77. "L'innocence et le péché," *ibid.*, 341–379. The present analysis is a résumé of the conclusions of this important study.

78. *Ibid.*, 361, 362.

79. *Ibid.*, 365.

80. *Ibid.*, 377–379 *passim.*

81. *RB*, XI (1902), 270.

82. *La méthode historique*, p. 120. Text of the *Pensées*, II, 8.

83. *Ibid.*, 219. Pp. 183–220 deal with "L'histoire primitive."

84. *Ibid.*, 184.

85. *Ibid.*, 194.

86. *Ibid.*, 211.

87. In Arabic the name of Cain means an iron smith; thus Tubal-Cain was the inventor of hammered-out instruments, *ibid.*, 212.

88. P. Lagrange considered the deluge a partial inundation: the tower of Babel was an allusion to the gigantic temple of Borsippa which for long remained uncompleted. "It is no fancy to see in Babylon a proud village where all tongues met." The ruin of Sodom left traces in nature, *ibid.*, 214.

89. *Ibid.*, 216.

90. *Ibid.*, 57–58.

91. *Ibid.*, 58.

92. *Ibid.*, 57–65. Concerning the development of Israel's religion, P. Lagrange writes, "I do not hesitate to say that an attentive and critical historical study will reveal more and more the supernatural activity of God."

93. *RB*, VI (1897), 310; *La méthode historique*, pp. 60, 199.

94. *RB*, VIII (1899), 627.

95. *Ibid.*, 627–629.

96. *La méthode historique*, p. 173. Pp. 147–182 deal with the historical character of the civil legislation of the Hebrews.

97. *Ibid.*, 177.

98. *RB*, X (1901), 615.

99. "La loi de Hammourabi," *RB*, XII (1903), 27–51; cf. *La méthode historique*, pp. 156–182. The Code was found at Susa in the winter campaigns of 1901–1902, by the French expedition headed by Morgan, and is preserved in the Louvre. It is nearly eight feet in height, two feet wide, and eighteen inches thick, of finely polished black diorite. About 4000 lines of cuneiform writing cover the sides.

100. The reign of Hammurabi is generally put at *circa* 2000, while the exodus from Egypt took place around 1250 B.C. [The latest dates for the Hammurabi are now set at 1728–1686 B.C. by W. F. Albright in *The Westminster Historical Atlas to the Bible* (Philadelphia, 1945), p. 13. — *Trans.*]

101. *La méthode historique*, p. 169.

102. *Ibid.*, pp. 148–182 *passim.*

103. *Ibid.*, p. 175.

104. Cf. *supra*, p. 23 f.

105. Cf. *infra*, p. 46 for the decree of the Biblical Commission.

106. "El et Iahve," *RB*, XII (1903), 362–386; "Encore le nom de Iahvé," *ibid.*, XVI (1907), 383–386. The old pronunciation of "Jehovah" is due to a mistaken reading.

107. *RB*, XII (1903), 385–386.

108. "Les Khabiri," *RB*, VIII (1899), 127–132.

109. One by one the English, Americans, Germans, and the Custodians of the Holy Land opened their centers of biblical studies at Jerusalem. It was after World War I that the Roman Pontifical Biblical Institute, conducted by the Jesuit Fathers, opened a branch in Jerusalem. When the French government decided to establish an official school in Palestine, similar to the schools of the English, Americans, or Germans, it chose the Dominican school as its own. On October 15, 1920, the Academy of inscriptions and belles-lettres decreed that "the *École Biblique de S. Étienne* is by its location, sientific organization, and authority, wholly qualified to constitute the *École française archéologique de Jérusalem*."

110. Cited by P. Lagrange in *RB*, VII (1898), 112.

111. "De Suez au Sinai," *RB*, V (1896), 618–643; "Le Sinai; Du Sinai a Nahal," *ibid.*, VI (1897), 107–130; 605–625; "Ain Kedeis," *ibid.*, V (1896), 440–451.

112. "Notre exploration de Pétra," *RB*, VI (1897), 208–230.

113. "Inscription nabatéenne de Pétra," *ibid.*, 231–238.

114. "Recherches épigraphiques à Pétra," the report of P. Lagrange published by M. de Vogüé, *RB*, VII (1898), 165–172.

115. An Automobile can travel as far in an hour as a camel can in a whole day.

116. "Phounon," *ibid.*, 112–115; "Le Sinaï Biblique," *RB*, VIII (1899), 369–392; "Itinéraire des Israelites du Pays de Gessen aux bords du Jourdain," *RB*, IX (1900), 63–86; 273–287; 443–449.

117. At the time of the Turkish expedition against the Suez Canal.

118. This map is a geographical mosaic, dating probably from the time of Justinian. Cf. *infra*, n. 146.

119. *RB*, VII (1898), 114 ff.

120. *RB*, VIII (1899), 379.

121. He recalls this incident in a recent work, *M. Loisy et le Modernisme* (Paris, 1932), pp. 125–127. The few details given here are taken from Chap. VI, entitled, "L'initiative de Léon XIII," pp. 118–135.

122. This explains the "New Series" of the *Revue Biblique*, which ran from 1904 to 1919. In 1920 the original numbering of the volumes was resumed. — *Trans.*

123. *Op. cit.*, p. 127.

124. *Venticinque anni dopo l'enciclica "Providentissimus,"* Feb. 15 and March 1, 1919.

125. *RB*, XXVIII (1919), 593–600. The letter is cited on p. 599.

126. *M. Loisy et le modernisme,* pp. 164–246.

127. "Utrum argumenta a criticis congesta ad impugnandam authentiam mosaicam sacrorum librorum, qui Pentateuchi nomine designantur, tanti sint ponderis, ut posthabitis quampluribus testimoniis utriusque Testamenti collective sumptis, perpetua consensione populi judaici, Ecclesiae quoque constanti traditione necnon indiciis internis, quae ex ipso textu eruuntur, jus tribuant affirmandi hos libros non Moysen habere auctorem, sed ex fontibus

maxima ex parte aetati Mosaica posterioribus fuisse confectos? Resp. Negative" (cf. *EB*, 174).

128. "Utrum, salva substantialiter Mosaica authentia et integritate Penta-teuchi, admitti possit tam longo saeculorum decursu nonnullas ei modifica-tiones obvenisse, uti; additamenta post Moysi mortem vel ab auctore inspirato apposita, vel glossas et explicationes textui interjectas . . . ? Resp. Affirmative, salvo Ecclesiae iudicio" (cf. *EB*, 177).

129. *RB*, IX (1900), 414–423.

130. Edited by Gabalda-Lecoffre. Besides two small volumes, *La méthode historique* (Paris, 1903) and *Le sens du Christianisme d'après l'exégèse alle-mande* (1918). The second work was translated into English by Fr. W. S. Reilly, S.S., under the title, *The Meaning of Christianity According to Luther and His Followers in Germany* (London, 1920). P. Lagrange wrote thirteen large volumes; they appeared with impressive regularity. Nine were on the New Testament, and will be mentioned later. Four dealt with the Old Testa-ment or its milieu: *Le livre des Juges* (1903); *Études sur les religions sémitiques* (1903; 2nd rev. ed. 1905); *Le messianisme chez les Juifs* (1909); *Le Judaisme avant Jésus-Christ* (1931).

131. When it declared the Vulgate to be the authentic text, the Council of Trent likewise recommended a study of the original texts. P. Lagrange was the first Frenchman to attempt to comment directly on the original text. In Germany, Catholics had commented on the Greek, but not the Latin, text of the New Testament: Schanz for the Gospels, and Schoefer for the Epistles of Paul. [Cf. Pius XII, "Divino Afflante Spiritu," *Acta Apostolicae Sedis*, XXXV (1943), 297–325, especially 306–310. In this latest encyclical on the Study of Holy Scripture, the Holy Father warmly recommends Catholic studies and translations based on the original texts. — *Trans.*]

132. This is all explained in the article which announced the project, *RB*, 1900.

133. "Deux commentaires des Psaumes," *RB*, XIII (1904), 251–259.

134. "Esdras et Néhémie," *RB*, III (1894), 561–585; "La question Néhémie et Esdras," *ibid.*, IV (1895), 193–202.

135. "Les papyrus araméens d'Eléphantine," *RB*, XVI (1907), 258–271; "Les fouilles d'Eléphantine; Les nouveaux papyrus d'Eléphantine," *ibid.*, XVII (1908), 260–267; 325–349; "La colonie juive de l'île d'Eléphantine," *Le Cor-respondant*, March 10, 1912, reprinted in *Mélanges d'histoire religieuse*, pp. 1–31.

136. *RB*, XV (1906), 555.

137. "La Vierge et l'Emmanuel," *RB*, I (1892), 481–497; "Notes sur le mes-sianisme dans les Psaumes," *ibid.*, XIV (1905), 39–57; 188–202: "Notes sur les prophéties messianiques des derniers prophètes," *ibid.*, XV (1906), 67–83. He was also interested in Vergil, especially the IV Bucolic: "Le prétendu mes-sianisme de Virgile," *RB*, XXXI (1922), 552–572; "Le messianisme de Virgile," *Le Correspondant*, Sept. 25, 1933.

138. Alcan, Paris, 1905.

139. "Pascal et les prophéties messianiques," *RB*, XV (1906), 533–560.

140. "Les prophéties messianiques de Daniel," *RB*, XIII (1904), 494–520; "La prophétie des soixante-dix semaines de Daniel," *ibid.*, XXXIX (1930), 179–198.

141. *Judaisme avant Jésus-Christ*, passim.

142. *Ibid.*, 62 ff. There is not a single article dealing with the book of Daniel, in the *Dictionnaire Apologétique* of P. d'Ales, although many articles therein treat of the Bible.

143. *La méthode historique*, 35–69 *passim*.

144. "L'ange de Iahvé," *RB*, XII (1903), 212–225; "Le régne de Dieu dans l'A.T.," "La paternité de Dieu dans l'A.T.," *ibid.*, XVII (1908), 36–61; 481–499; "La Sagesse, sa doctrine des fins dernières," *ibid.*, XVI (1907), 85–104. Refutation of the insidious theories of Wellhausen and Renan on the history of Israel led to a study of Israelite religion in the times of Osee: "La nouvelle histoire d'Israël et le prophete Osée," *ibid.*, I (1892), 203–238. A further refutation of Renan: "Le panthéisme dans l'Histoire sainte," *ibid.*, 605–616. *Le Judaisme avant Jésus-Christ*, pp. 1–34, begins with a sketch of the religious history of Israel.

145. "La topographie de Jerusalem," *RB*, I (1892), 17–38.

146. "Le site de Sodome d'après les textes," *RB*, XLI, (1932), 489–514. Other studies of this nature: "Lettre de Jérusalem," *ibid.* (1892), 452–456; "Comment s'est formée l'enceinte du temple de Jérusalem," *ibid.*, II (1892), 90–113; "Excursion à Sibbé," *ibid.*, III (1894), 263–276; "Notes topographiques," *ibid.*, 139–140; 450–451: "Michmas," *ibid.*, IV (1895), 94–95; "La mosaique géographique de Madaba; Jérusalem d'après la mosaique de Madaba," *ibid.*, VI (1897), 165–184; 450–458; "Gézer," *ibid.*, VIII (1899), 422–427. In the *Conférences de Saint-Étienne* (Paris, 1911), "A la recherche des sites bibliques" (3–56), the general principles of topography are applied to the Holy Land. Noteworthy from an archaeological and historical point of view are two articles which appeared in *Le Correspondant:* "Palmyre" (Sept. 10, 1908), and "Les fouilles de Suse d'après les travaux de la délégation en Perse" (Jan. 10, 1913), reprinted in *Mélanges d'histoire religieuse*, pp. 32–68; 280–332.

147. The *Revue Biblique* has often been accused of partiality for non-Catholic works, and of severity toward Catholic books. A glance anywhere in the *Revue* is refutation of the charge, for nowhere else has the modernist, or rationalist, exegesis been disproved with more carefulness and vigor. It is true, the *Revue Biblique* honestly pointed out the good points of non-Catholic critics, but it never adopted the stand that a book was deserving of high praise simply because it was written by a Catholic. Works were judged on the basis of faith and science. It never pretended to be a mutual-admiration *Revue*. Complaints on this score came quite generally from authors who were not made much of. Granted, the *Revue* may lack diplomacy; that is high praise. Its frankness, which is all to its credit, is partly responsible for the authority of its judgments. At this juncture, it is most interesting to note that P. Maurice Claeyes Boúúaer, S.J., in the *Nouvelle Revue Théologique*, Vol. 61, May, 1934, 521 ff., holds that P. Lagrange did not insist enough on the deficiencies of Catholic criticism.

148. Cf. p. 29 ff. P. Lagrange was able to touch on so many subjects because of his profound knowledge of oriental languages. He could translate the cuneiform texts, spoke Arabic fluently, and read Hebrew as easily as he did French or German.

149. Cf. the dedication of the volume to Marquis de Vogüé, pp. vii–viii. [This book is described by Fr. Schmidt, S.V.D., as "The first dike against the flood of evolution." Cf. Barton, "Semitic Religions," *Studies in Comparative Religions*, II, 12, 31. — *Trans*.]

150. Cf. *supra*, 30 ff.

151. In the lengthy introductory chapter, P. Lagrange examines and rejects the system of evolutionary animism, which one school applies to the Semites, as well as to other peoples, in explanation of the origin of religion. He rejects the identification of the savages with the primitive man: "The savage is the end of an evolution that failed" (p. 5). Then he draws the important distinction between the religion which "acknowledges the existence of superior powers, good ones, to whom he pays homage," and mythology, which is an explanation of gods, the world, and man; for it especially attributes a soul to things. The immorality of some divine myths derives, apparently, from the social condition and from magical practices.

152. Cf. *RB*, I (1892), 275–281; 433–438; II (1893), 114–118; 220–222; 633–634; VI (1897), 104–106; X (1901), 66–72; XI (1902), 94–99; 515–526; XII (1903), 410–419. Especially to be noted are: "L'inscription de Mesa," King of Moab (very important), *RB*, X (1901), 522–545; and "La controverse minéo-sabéo-biblique," which treats of the relation of south Arabian epigraphy with biblical exegesis, *ibid.*, XI (1902), 256–272.

153. The Rabbins could not comprehend how the Messias, who, according to Daniel, appeared transcendent upon the clouds (7:12), could make His entry into Jerusalem on an ass, according to Zachary (9:9).

154. *Le Messianisme*, p. 265; cf. *La méthode historique*, pp. 55–56.

155. *La Revue catholique des idées et des faits* (Bruxelles, Dec. 22, 1934), p. 6.

CHAPTER II

1. In 1922 he published a small volume, *Évangile de saint Marc*, a popularization of his larger work.

2. *RB*, IV (1895), 5–20; V (1896), 5–38; and IV (1895), 160–185.

3. This orientation is clearly marked out in the conferences of Toulouse concerning *La méthode historique* (1st ed. 1903). The author's chief aim was to apply this method to the Old Testament. The second edition (1904) contained an appendix, *Jésus et la critique des Évangiles*, and dealt with the recently published works of Loisy. English translation: *Historical criticism and the Old Testament* (London, 1905).

4. *RB*, IV (1900), 414 ff.

5. *La méthode historique* (2nd ed.), p. 23.

6. To take another example from literary criticism, the historical bases of the dogma of the Virginal Conception vary much according as Luke 1:34–35 — which very clearly expresses this belief — belongs to the primitive source used by Luke, or if it was inserted into the actual text either by Luke or another interpolator. Cf. "Les récits de l'enfance dans saint Luc," *RB*, IV (1895), 192, and the commentary on Luke, p. 31 ff. Even in textual criticism, considerations of a dogmatic nature can sometimes be necessary for the Catholic research scholar in a discussion of the authenticity of a variant reading. In this connection, P. Lagrange cites Matt. 1:16, where the Syriac-Sinai manuscript, *sirsin*, has this ending to the genealogy of Christ: "Joseph, to whom the Virgin Mary was espoused, begot Jesus who is called the Christ." This reading cannot, without prejudice to the faith, be maintained; at least not if it means that Jesus was the true son of Joseph."

7. P. Lagrange's attitude toward the modernist crisis may be learned from

his *M. Loisy et le modernisme* (Editions du Cerf, 1932), which was occasioned by the appearance of Loisy's memoirs. [Cf. the foreword by Fr. Byrne. — *Trans.*]

8. *La méthode historique*, pp. 1–34.

9. *RB*, XVI (1907), 543–554.

10. Thus, for example, the 48th proposition of the decree *Lamentabili:* "Jacobus in sua epistola non intendit promulgare aliquod sacramentum Christi," cannot be condemned if it means only: the mere exegesis of the text forbids the affirmation that James promulgated a sacrament; but it is rejected because it is positive denial of the promulgation of the sacrament by James, and this is contrary to a definition of the Council of Trent.

11. *La méthode historique*, pp. 19, 33.

12. Loisy, here in step with the critics, writes: "From the beginning of its diffusion, Christianity was a religious sect notable for its cult of him under whose name and in whose faith the sect had been set up. Out of this situation was born its literature." *Les livres du Nouveau Testament* (1922), p. 8 ff.

13. Published by Gabalda in the collection, *Études Bibliques;* English translation: *The Meaning of Christianity*, by W. S. Reilly, S.S. (London, 1920).

14. *Le sens du Christianisme*, p. 13 ff.

15. *Ibid.*, xii.

16. An idea of his position relative to this problem may be obtained from lengthy reviews in the *Revue*, XXVIII (1919), 255 ff., of the works of Harnack and of Leipoldt, *ibid.*, XVI (1907), 450 ff. In 1933 he published his comprehensive *Histoire ancienne du Canon du Nouveau Testament* (Paris, Gabalda), a study of the formation and evolution of the New Testament canon up to the fifth century, when it was finally fixed. In this work, based upon documents gathered principally by Zahn, the learned German historian, P. Lagrange's thought on the canon of the New Testament can best be found.

17. The testimony of St. Irenaeus and Tertullian on this point is conclusive.

18. *Die Entstehung des neuen Testaments und die wichtigsten Folgen der neuen Schöpfung* (Leipzig, 1914), should be especially consulted.

19. Thus in the *Secunda Clementis*. Note, however, that St. Peter (2 Pet. 3:15–16) places the epistles of St. Paul among the *Scriptures*.

20. Paul's epistle to the Galatians, for example, which declared the abrogation of the old alliance, must have possessed at least the same authority as the writings of that alliance.

21. This rule was applied by Serapion, Bishop of Antioch, at the end of the second century when, after first having been favorable to the apocryphal gospel of Peter, because of the name it bore, he decided to reject it. He noted that this gospel was not received by "tradition"; consequently, this writing was not of apostolic origin, for if an apostle were actually its author, it would have been received with respect and handed down by the churches.

22. These are the so-called *deutero-canonical* books, a term distasteful to P. Lagrange because it seems to imply that there were inscribed in the Canon a number of second-rate writings, which gained only tardy admittance into the Canon or enjoyed only minor authority. Actually every composition recognized as apostolic and inspired has full authority; however, even if the apostolic authenticity of this or that book was, here or there, brought into question, there was never a time when the ensemble of disputed writings constituted a category of secondary rating.

23. It was also utilized by Theodore Beza and was the basis for the Authorized Version, published in London in 1611. Up to the end of the nineteenth century it was the official edition of the Anglican church.

24. *Introduction à l'étude du Nouveau Testament* (Paris, Gabalda): (1) *Histoire ancienne du canon du N.T.*, 1933; (2) *Critique textuelle:* I. The first part, by Msgr. Robert Devreese, is as yet unpublished. II. *La Critique rationelle*, 1935. When the present study was written, this volume had not yet been published, nor, of course, the following work: (3) *La Critique historique*. I. *Les Mystères: l'Orphisme*, 1937. This was the last book of P. Lagrange.

25. At least according to von Soden. P. Lagrange and other authors disagreed with this.

26. The term *Western* is misleading, for actually the Old Syriac version, as well as the Old Latin versions, is connected with this type.

27. The question suggests itself that there might have been other revisions of the New Testament in Greek besides those admitted by Westcott and Hort. Recent discoveries of documents at least permit the postulate of a special type of text called the *Caesarean*, which was the result of a different revision, and traces back to Origen.

28. Vaganay, *Initiation à la critique textuelle néotestamentaire* (Paris, 1934). English translation by B. V. Miller, *Introduction to the Textual Criticism of the New Testament* (Herder, 1937).

29. The method applied to current problems of textual study is now published as *La critique rationelle*. Many of his conclusions had been previously set forth in the *Revue Biblique*, XLIII (1934), 4–41, 161.

30. This may be verified by a glance at the various decisions given by the Biblical Commission on New Testament questions. As long as the traditional positions have not been demonstrated as false by internal criticism, or rendered untenable by discovery of new facts, the Commission reaffirms them.

31. Cf. the discussion of St. Irenaeus' opinion concerning the dates of the gospels in P. Lagrange's commentaries on Mark and Luke; and that of the famous text of Papias on the gospels, in his commentaries of Matthew, Mark, and John. Tradition attributes the second gospel to Mark, and adds that he wrote as Peter's disciple; P. Lagrange concludes: "The primitive tradition, distinguished from later additions by a study of the oldest texts, leaves the historian with no choice but to accept it, provided that the gospel itself does not contradict it" (*S. Marc*, 2nd ed., XXVIII). The commentary which follows shows that the content of the gospel itself does not destroy this tradition.

32. *RB*, IX (1900), 419.

33. These vary much from one author to another, and even in the lifetime of a single author. Interesting, from this point of view, to compare the extremely radical theories of Loisy in his work: *Les origines du christianisme* (Paris, 1934), dealing with the composition of the New Testament books, especially the gospels, with the much more moderate ideas advanced in his *Evangiles synoptiques* (1908).

34. Beginning in 1910, P. Lagrange opposed his own method to that of Loisy: "The differences in our methods comes to this: Loisy treats the texts as if they were condemned criminals, whereas I look upon them as witnesses. He is the examining magistrate; he questions the accused harshly, without sparing the torture, and only acquits them after an examination which is always rigorous, and occasionally even hostile" (*S. Marc*, 1st ed., IV).

35. Apropos of the critical theories concerning the gospel of St. Mark, P. Lagrange wrote: "When criticism leads to the declaration that some parts of Mark are secondary because they are miraculous, it substitutes the twentieth century prejudices of unbelievers for the criteria proper to literary analysis" (*S. Marc*, 2nd ed., L).

36. He notes this vice of method in M. Loisy, who declared that his guide in the critical study of the gospels was historical evolution, for the literary evolution of the gospel followed the evolution of primitive Christianity. "This would be excellent," wrote P. Lagrange, "but only on condition that the sequence of history be known; and as far as the origin of Christianity is concerned, this is known only from the books which are on the point of being dissected. . . . This resolve alone, to deduce the history of Christianity's origins from sources which have been cut up and rearranged to suit the supposed evolution of beliefs, indicates very well that the author is arguing with himself in a vicious circle" (*M. Loisy et le modernisme*, pp. 193-197).

As for the new German School of Form Criticism (*Formgeschichtliche Schule*), whose intention is to reconstruct the history of the tradition from which the gospels sprang, he warns of the same danger of the vicious circle, "if the authors suppose steps of tradition in order to cut up the sources, and then use this conjectural material to write history" (*ibid.*, p. 220).

37. Some have tried to identify this second source with the sayings (*Logia*) of the Lord, attributed to St. Matthew (who supposedly composed it in Aramaic) by Papias, Bishop of Hierapolis, in a famous passage. *Q* comes from the German word for *source: Quelle.*

38. "For the independent critics, the second gospel was the first in order of time. It is not our intention, in beginning with Mark, to give this hypothesis a decisive value from now on . . . but we intend to put the question as it is put today" (*Evang. selon S. Marc*, 1st ed., p. II).

39. P. Lagrange thought there were strong arguments against the primitive originality of the final verses of Mark (16:9-20) and preferred to look upon them, not as the work of an unauthorized editor (such an hypothesis is irreconcilable with the canonicity of the final verses, which every Catholic must hold), but as a fragment emanating, if not from an apostle, at least from a disciple of the Lord whose authority was recognized. In the second edition of the commentary, he added as possible the hypothesis of retouches, or an addition made by the author of the gospel.

40. When he examined the possibility of St. Mark's use of a hypothetical collection of discourses as supposed by the critics (in his commentary on the first gospel he proves that this was nothing more than Matthew Aramaic), P. Lagrange thought it more probable that Mark did not depend on it; in any case, if he used this source, it was with an author's liberty and not as a compiler. In his commentary on St. Matthew he formulates this conclusion with greater preciseness.

41. The "dogmatic character" of the second gospel has become, since Wrede's destruction (1901) of the classical positions of liberal exegesis, one of the axioms of the radical critics, who exaggerate it at will, in order to ruin Mark's trustworthiness as a narrator of true facts, and discover in it a preponderant influence of St. Paul. But P. Lagrange showed that Mark did *not* depend in a literary way on the epistles of St. Paul; the similarity of some of his expressions is sufficiently explained by the fact that they lived together.

He pointed out that what they had in common was not the characteristic points of the theology of St. Paul, but merely the doctrinal truths which the Apostle had taken from Christ's teachings, and upon which he built his own dogmatic structure. Finally, P. Lagrange showed that the bias attributed to St. Mark (favoring St. Paul while belittling the Apostles) is nonexistent.

42. "After their departure (that of Peter and Paul), Mark, disciple and interpreter of Peter, also transmitted to us in writing what Peter had preached." P. Lagrange holds that the *departure* can only mean the death of the two Apostles, and that other explanations in favor of another meaning are unsatisfactory.

43. Luke 4:31 to 6:19 parallels Mark 1:21 to 3:12; Luke 8:4 to 9:50 corresponds to Mark 4:1 to 9:41; and Luke 18:15 to 21:38, to Mark 10:13 to 13:37.

44. Luke omits entirely Mark 6:45 to 8:26.

45. "Luke is a great artist because he knows how to choose his details . . . each, chosen with care, contributing to the effect and all achieving their purpose. It is this that makes Luke so superior to Mark as a writer of Greek; Mark related what he saw, but single details are presented merely as fragments of reality, and are without literary significance. It is easy to see why Luke would eliminate these details, invoking the supreme rule of Greek art — at least in the most characteristic works — the rule of proportion and measure. Luke could have rehashed these fragments in his own style, but he did not; and this is a sign of his dependence and his remarkable fidelity" (*S. Luc*, p. LXVIII).

46. In his introduction to Luke, he merely sketched out the general lines of this solution, thinking he would be able to give it fuller consideration in his commentary on Matthew. In this last work he devoted himself to the problem of the relation of Mark and Matthew, of Matthew Greek and Matthew Aramaic, and simply remarked: "Nothing warrants our being more affirmative on the question of Luke's relation to Matthew than we were in the commentary on Luke."

47. The traditional theory was recalled and maintained by a decision of the Biblical Commission (June 26, 1912). P. Lagrange, even when using as a *working-hypothesis* the theory of two sources, always held for the essential value of this traditional statement. Concerning the hypothetical *Logia* attributed to St. Matthew, he wrote in the *Revue Biblique* (1896, p. 27): "If the *Logia* were an evangelical work containing only Christ's *words*, written in Aramaic and translated as such into Greek, given to the Church, and utilized by the author of the first gospel, who would have added *facts* to it, then I refuse to admit the existence of this primitive Matthew, for which I see no trace in tradition; internal criticism gives no critic the right to create it. But if the *Logia* are an evangelical work, containing the life, discourses, Passion, and Resurrection of the Saviour, written in Aramaic or Hebrew by the Apostle Matthew, then I do not refuse to call it, as Papias does, the gospel *Logia*. I have conceded, it is true, that it could have undergone a certain transformation in the Greek translation, and this would have given to the new work the character of a quasi-original writing. But I do not believe that internal criticism proves that these changes touch the substance, and hence, it does not contradict the traditional opinion." Cf., in this connection, *RB*, XXI (1912), 633–635.

48. According to Papias, it seems there were many Greek translations of

St. Matthew's *Logia;* Luke could have used one of these partial translations.

49. B. Weiss and A. Harnack attempted to reconstruct this source by extracting it from the texts common to both Matthew and Luke, and relying principally upon Matthew's order.

50. This is proved by a detailed, penetrating analysis of the content of the first gospel, which leads to the conclusion that there is hardly a phrase that may not be truly considered as having formed part of the primitive gospel.

51. There is not the same relation between Matthew and Mark as between Luke and Mark. "We perceive this essential difference between Luke and Matthew: Luke changes his words and turns of phrase with a great deal of liberty, in order to give some elegance to his Greek, but he includes all the details which give form to the facts, or, to put it differently, he has not only the essentials, but also the integrity of the accounts of Mark. On the other hand, there is Matthew, much closer to Mark in the choice and order of words, but much different in his manner of presenting things. The reason given for this important fact is that if Mark is not dependent on Matthew (which we rule out), it is Matthew who depends as a translator would, on Mark, but at the same time he was faithful to his Aramaic text" (*S. Matthieu*, p. LIX).

52. "Luke is more historical than Mark. Very deliberately he set out to write a more complete and readily recognizable biography. John himself, despite his doctrinal preoccupations, gave many chronological indications of the ministry of Christ. The tendency moved therefore toward historical literature. Matthew was a movement in the opposite direction, for even his account of the Nativity serves only to fill in his demonstration."

53. In the first few pages of *The Gospel of Jesus Christ,* P. Lagrange gives a simple, but suggestive, summary of how the gospels came to be written.

54. He draws this conclusion from the way in which Matthew places, in the same perspective, the external ruination of the ancient kingdom of God by the destruction of Jerusalem and the consummation of the world.

55. Except for the protestation of Caius, or of the Alogi at the end of the second century.

56. Proof of this is that neither the *Gospel of Peter* (despite its "I, Peter") nor the *Gospel of the Twelve Apostles* had any true authority.

57. Some of the details of the tradition (those of Irenaeus, for example) are not so certain. Obscure texts, like that of Papias, help to confuse the question. Because of Papias, P. Lagrange admits the existence of a John the Elder, distinct from John the Apostle; but he attributes to him only the modest role of a carrier of secondary traditions.

58. P. Lagrange thinks the real difficulty arising from the difference of the Greek of the Apocalypse (very corrupt) and that of the gospel (correct but of a Semitic color) may be answered by the hypothesis of a secretary; St. John would have dictated his gospel to him, but he would have retained some degree of freedom in the choice of forms and use of grammar without, however, destroying the particular character of John's style.

59. This one author, however, did not compose the pericope of the adulterous woman, or the verse about the angel of the pool, where the manuscript tradition is uncertain. P. Lagrange thought the gospel was written completely at one time, but admits the possibility of some alterations or transpositions.

He favored the changing of the order of chapters five and six, and likewise thought that chapters fifteen and sixteen (a second series of discourses after the Last Supper) were inserted afterward by the author as a complement to his work. Many critics consider chapter twenty-one as an appendix, but P. Lagrange was emphatically of the opinion that it was the work of the author of the gospel, except, of course, verses 24-25, which appeared to be the addition of a group, probably the elders of Ephesus, bearing witness to the truthfulness of the author.

60. "It is morally impossible that a work, *born* in Ephesus in a Greek milieu, would have so faithfully reflected the condition of minds and practices in Jerusalem sixty years earlier" (*S. Jean,* p. CXXXIV).

61. P. Lagrange was fond of quoting Renan, whose literary tact and independent spirit, in this regard, he praised. He only regretted that the author of the *Vie de Jésus,* in his evaluation of the historical worth of the discourses in the fourth gospel, took a position opposed to his own. Cf. *La vie de Jésus d'après Renan,* pp. 34-52.

62. There are many other problems of literary criticism in connection with the New Testament which have been discussed at more or less length in P. Lagrange's reviews in the *Revue Biblique.* It is impossible to point out all these reviews, but they often contain worth-while suggestions. Most critics admit the authenticity and integrity of the great epistles of St. Paul. Loisy gave his partial support to the ultraradical theories of Delafosse-Turmel; this means that one could distinguish numerous additions of Marcionite or Catholic tendency, from the authentic fragments in all the epistles attributed to St. Paul. P. Lagrange has dealt briefly with these points in his commentaries on Romans and Galatians. He admits as possible, but not probable, that the ending of Romans has been somewhat altered. As for Galatians, he merely explains the divergences between this epistle and the Acts of the Apostles; the Acts provide one of the principal arguments for those who attack the authenticity of the epistle.

63. In the introduction to his *Vie de Jésus,* Renan stated bluntly: "I do not reject miracles because anyone has proved to me beforehand that the evangelists do not deserve my absolute adherence. It is because they relate miracles that I say: 'the gospels are legends; they may contain history, but certainly not everything in them is historical.'" (Cited by P. Lagrange in *La vie de Jésus d'après Renan* [Paris, 1923], 61; English translation: *Christ and Renan* [Benziger, 1928], p. 54.)

64. No modern critic affirms that the evangelists deliberately tried to deform the historical truth. "Be it said to the honor of contemporary criticism," wrote P. Lagrange, "that it does not doubt the absolute sincerity of the evangelists." The doubt, or rather denial, has to do with the value of their testimony.

65. Historical skepticism led some authors to a denial of Christ's very existence. P. Lagrange and some of the most radical critics (Loisy, Goguel, and Guignebert) advanced decisive arguments against this theory, which Couchoud tried to popularize in France. However, neither Loisy nor Guignebert ascribe any historical value to the gospel account, in which, for wholly subjective reasons, they see only scattered fragments of historical truth; the gospel itself they held to be a total creation of the Christian community. Goguel, more moderate, draws back from ascribing such creative power to

the community; others maintain in principle a mistrust of the tradition, for they consider a gospel story as solid only if there are positive arguments for it which rule out creation by the tradition, e.g., if the incident or word are in opposition to the beliefs of the community. Cf. the reviews of P. Lagrange on Goguel, *RB*, XLI (1932), 508 ff., on Guignebert, *RB*, XLII (1933), 433, and on Couchoud.

66. At this point the argument becomes one of history properly so called, instead of remaining in the field of literary history. Cf. the many articles in the *Revue Biblique* which give various aspects of the discussion; cf. also *M. Loisy et le modernisme*, p. 217 ff. Quite improbable is any doctrinal evolution in which the Christology of the Synoptics is, because less precise, posterior to Paul.

67. Guignebert, *Jésus*, cited by P. Lagrange in *RB*, XLII (1933), 436.

68. Such is the defect of the otherwise excellent manual *Praelectiones biblicae* of P. Simon, C.SS.R., who multiplies the denials of Peter. Because he cannot see how the circumstances of the denials recorded by the gospels can be harmonized so as to number three, as Christ had predicted, P. Simon prefers to think that Christ's words had no such exact meaning. P. Lagrange's review in *RB* (1925), 134 ff., contains much food for thought on the harmonizing of the gospels.

69. *The Gospel of Jesus Christ*, xiv.

70. *Ibid.*

71. *Ibid.*, xiii.

72. P. Lagrange, *S. Mark*, p. CXXIII.

73. P. Lagrange compares the portraits of Luke and Mark as follows: "The descriptions given by Mark are as baked clay, bursting with life and beautiful in spite of a few rough edges; Luke copied them in white marble. The features are regular, but less expressive, the face is less animated; but what is wholly admirable is that Luke's picture does not lack resemblance" (*Evang. s. S. Luc*, p. LXI).

74. Some critics assume that the gospels are the projection of the life of the Church into the life of Christ.

75. *La méthode historique* (2nd ed.), p. 254.

76. *The Gospel of Jesus Christ*, xi.

77. The artificial framework of one year is that in which the primitive catechesis had disposed or arranged the principal events in Christ's career along with his principal teachings; these were the only points of vital interest to them.

78. The Goguel method. Cf. P. Lagrange's review of his *Vie de Jésus*, *RB*, XLI (1932), 599 ff. Goguel accused P. Lagrange of having less trust in the materials furnished by the gospels than he himself had, because he had given up all idea of writing a life of Christ. P. Lagrange considered this misrepresentation of his thought as malicious, and protested in all justice against it.

79. P. Lagrange had frequent occasion to discuss, particularly in reviews in the *Revue Biblique*, problems of historical criticism arising from other parts of the New Testament. The limited nature of our study does not permit us to mention them all.

80. Cf. *The Gospel of Jesus Christ*, II, 306–341, however, for his conclusions about the person and role of Christ as seen in the gospels. It is the solution of a believing historian.

81. Of these the principal works are *Le sens du Christianisme d'après l'exégèse allemande* (1918), and *M. Loisy et le modernisme* (1932). The second part of this latter work contains the evolution of Loisy's ideas, apropos of the new critical theories concerning the origin of Christianity; P. Lagrange discusses these theories and so completes his earlier work.

82. *Le sens du christianisme,* p. 226.

83. *Evangile s. S. Marc,* Introduction, Chap. VIII *passim.*

84. The founder of this school, Johannes Weiss, first proposed these ideas in his *Die Predigt Jesu vom Reiche Gottes,* published in 1892, and developed in a second edition, 1900. Loisy's *L'Evangile et l'Eglise* follows closely from this system.

85. P. Lagrange realized at once the real tendency of *L'Evangile et l'Eglise,* which was apparently a refutation of A. Harnack. In certain passages of his *Mémoires,* Loisy lets fall the suspicion that P. Lagrange was insincere, for — he insinuates — P. Lagrange had attacked him in order to cover himself. The real explanation, writes P. Lagrange, was simply that he waited as long as he possibly could to point out the divergences between his own and Loisy's position, "being reluctant to confer on myself the stamp of orthodoxy, at the expense of a writer whose destructive tendencies were not evident." He did not set forth his thought in this matter clearly until April, 1903, when the *Revue Biblique* carried his long review of *L'Evangile et l'Eglise.* At the end of the same year, in a letter to Msgr. Batiffol, published first in the *Bulletin de littérature ecclésiastique* (Dec., 1903, and Jan., 1904) and later reproduced as an appendix in the second edition of the *Méthode historique,* he again subjected Loisy's system to a critical examination in the light of the gospels. His purpose was to show that true historical method did not call for the profound transformation which the author of *L'Evangile et l'Eglise* thought necessary for the interpretation of the gospel.

86. *Le sens du christianisme,* p. 232.

87. Cf. *M. Loisy et le modernisme,* pp. 187–188. P. Lagrange cites Renan: "If Jesus' teaching had only been a belief in the imminent end of the world, it would today most certainly be buried in oblivion."

88. *Le sens du christianisme,* p. 244.

89. *Ibid.,* pp. 244–267. Cf. also *S. Matthieu,* pp. CLVI–CLXXII.

90. *M. Loisy et le modernisme,* p. 244: "Excellent proof," writes P. Lagrange, "that the end of the world was not to come after a short delay, is the fact that Jesus traced out a program to better the world. The Kingdom of God has come; it is the Church; and he prepared ministers for it by forming his disciples for their mission."

91. It is not surprising, then, that some critics who follow their principles to their logical conclusion think it much simpler to omit Christ altogether, for He apparently played no part in the beginning of Christianity. They have therefore struck Him out of history, and made Him a purely mythical character similar to the pagan deities, a God around whom a purely fictional human history has been fabricated.

This extremely radical theory had a certain vogue in Germany at the turn of this century. (Cf. *Le sens du christianisme,* pp. 308–315.) M. Couchoud popularized it in France in *Le Mystère de Jésus,* but was opposed, both by believing exegetes like P. Lagrange, and by radical critics like Loisy and Guignebert. These last two find it rather difficult to disown some of the conclusions which follow from their own negative attitude toward the historical value of the gospels. P. Lagrange pointed out as the only redeeming feature of the school which denies the historical existence of Christ: "It has clearly shown how utterly impossible it is to extract the highest religion, the purest morality, and the greatest spiritual power of the world from a routine entry in the *Gazette des tribunaux* in Judea" (*M. Loisy et le modernisme*, p. 245). [The *Gazette* would correspond to the daybook of our police courts, in which every occurrence involving the police is recorded. Since, by the theory in question, the gospels are bereft of all historical value, the whole story of Christ's passion and death would have been built up from an ordinary, unimportant entry in the police record. — *Trans.*]

92. "The only common denominator for all the gods and heroes of paganism lies in the fact that their so-called *Passions* concerned no one but themselves. Suffering or death was never accepted by the god in view of the salvation of men, nor regarded as useful to this salvation" (*Le sens du chrisianisme*, p. 291).

93. "To compare the Eucharist, which is the veritable eating of a god, with the ancient rite of Dionysus in which a bull was cut up into pieces and eaten raw (unless the victim was a human infant), is to confuse the flesh and the spirit, as St. Paul would say. In this case, the dependence is not between the two rites, but between the faith and the rite of both sides" (*M. Loisy et le modernisme*, p. 212).]

94. *Ibid.*, pp. 243–245; *Le sens du christianisme*, p. 332.

95. *Le sens du christianisme*, p. 333.

CHAPTER III

1. A. J. Festugière, *L'idéal religieux des grecs et l'Evangile* (Paris, 1932), preface of P. Lagrange, p. 9.

2. *II Apol.*, 13, 2–4.

3. *RB*, XVI (1907), 163–206; 325–348; 489–514. The third article concludes with a study of certain religious symbols, and evidently called for a continuation; but the expected conclusion never appeared in the *Revue Biblique*. Instead, in 1908, there appeared a book (only a small number of copies was printed) entitled, *La Crète ancienne*. In it we find the three above-mentioned articles, plus the completed chapter on religion, and an entirely new chapter on the origins: "La Crète ancienne et les Hellènes, la Crète et l'Egypte, la Crète et la Bible."

4. *La Crète ancienne* (1908 printing), p. 3.

5. *Ibid.*, *RB*, XVI (1907), 165.

6. *Ibid.* (1908 printing), p. 40.

7. Cf. the article on Greek art entitled, "Le miracle grec et les rythmes de l'art, à propos d'un livre récent," which appeared first in *Le Correspondant*, May 10, 1913, and was reprinted in the *Mélange d'histoire religieuse* (Paris, 1915), pp. 227–279. The study owes its birth to a work by W. Deonna, *L'archéologie, sa valeur, ses méthodes* (Paris, 1912). We give only these few lines from the article of P. Lagrange: "On the whole, the expression of suffering is (among the Greeks) dignified and restrained: they did not try to express their fear and cowardice at the thought of death. I cannot here shake off the strange impression I experienced when I saw at Père-Lachaise [famous Parisian cemetery] the famous bas-relief of M. Bartholomé. (I was

returning from Athens, where in the Ceramic and National Museums, there are so many funerary steles; not all of them are from the fifth century.) The pain or, rather the sadness of separation which found touching expression in them is tempered by the thought that all bond between the living and the dead has not been severed. If some doubt concerning the after-life finds expression in the anxious faces, none gives up to despair. Whereas the Greeks, miserable people, approached the somber portals like men condemned to the guillotine. . . . Sometimes, it is true, paganism did give to death a hideous appearance in order to move men to the quick enjoyment of goods which were all too fleeting. But these cases are rare. Of course, the Greeks did not understand the role of sorrow in the moral ascent toward perfection, and if they avoided expressing it, it was so as not to trouble the impassibility of the gods, and not to disturb the regularity of the traits of mortals. But that was part of their genius. . . . " (Art. cit. in *Mélanges d'histoire religieuse*, pp. 278–279.)

8. *La Crète ancienne*, p. 110.
9. *Ibid.*, p. 111.
10. "Le Logos d'Héraclite," *RB*, XXXII (1923), 96–107.
11. *Ibid.*, 96.
12. *Ibid.*, 107.
13. "Vers le Logos de Saint Jean," *RB*, XXXII (1923), 161–184.
14. *Ibid.*, 162.
15. *Ibid.*, 175.
16. "La philosophie religieuse d'Epictète et le christianisme. A propos d'un livre récent," *RB*, XXI (1912), 5–21; 192–212. "Marc-Aurèle: le jeune homme; le philosophe; l'empereur," *RB*, XXII (1913), 243–259; 394–420; 568–587.
17. Cf. J. Stelzenberger, *Die Beziehungen der frühchristlichen Sittenlehre zur Ethik der Stoa* (Munich, 1933), p. 473 ff. The manual of Epictetus was twice paraphrased by Christians, and often cited by compilers of poetic or moral anthologies.
18. *Discourses*, IV, 7, 6.
19. *Meditations*, XI, 3.
20. *Ibid.*, II, 17, 22; II, 19, 26.
21. *Ibid.*, IV, 1, 89.
22. *Discourses*, III, 5, 8 ff.
23. "La philosophie religieuse d'Epictète et le christianisme," *RB*, XXI (1912), 17–20.
24. "Marc-Aurèle, II. Le philosophe," *RB*, XXII (1913), 395–396.
25. Marcus Aurelius, *Meditations*, XII, 28.
26. *Ibid.*, IX, 28.
27. "La philosophie religieuse d'Epictète et le christianisme," *RB*, XXI (1912), 210.
28. *Ibid.*, 211. P. Lagrange there makes his reply to Renan, who had used the term "lay" to characterize the Stoic philosophy, saying that the school of Epictetus had ceased to be a lay school, and that its teaching saw all things in God. It may be so, but we would rather say, "in the God of the philosophers and savants, not in the God of Abraham, of Isaac, and of Jacob." Is the God of Epictetus the living God?
29. *Ibid.*, 212.
30. "Marc-Aurèle, III. L'empereur," *RB*, XXII (1913), 583.

31. R. P. Lagrange, Saint Justin (Les Saints) (Paris, 1914) xii–204. Cf. P. Lagrange, "Saint Justin, à propos de quelques publications récentes," Bulletin d'ancienne littérature et d'archéologie chrétienne, IV (1914), 3–15.

32. Saint Justin, pp. 202–203.

33. The following are the principal articles to which we shall refer. We have not attempted to draw up a complete bibliography, so there may be lacunae in the list: "Platon theologien," Revue Thomiste (1926), 189–218; "Comment s'est transformée la pensée religieuse d'Aristote, d'après un livre recent," ibid. (1926), 285–329; "La religion des stoiciens avant Jésus-Christ," ibid. (1928), 46–68; "La religion de Sénèque," ibid. (1928), 324–346; "Une morale indépendante dans l'antiquité: les Cyniques," ibid. (1929), 35–52; "Les doctrines religieuses successives de l'Académie fondée par Platon," ibid. (1929), 320–334: "Les cultes hellenistiques en Egypte et le judaisme," ibid. (1930), 309–328. To this list add "La religion de Cicéron d'apres le De natura deorum," Ephemerides Theologicae Lovanienses, July, 1928; "Les préliminaires historiques de la mystique catholique," La vie spirituelle, XXVII (May 1, 1931), 76–93.

34. Cf. "La religion des stoiciens avant Jésus-Christ," Revue Thomiste (1928), 46. "Stoicism in the Revue Thomiste! Plato will do! Honor to Aristotle! But does St. Thomas owe anything to the Portico?"

35. In this connection, cf. P. Lagrange's preface to Festugière, L'Idéal religieux. — [Trans.]

36. "Platon théologien," Revue Thomiste (1926), 189.

37. Ibid., 206.

38. Or Symposium, 211 d, 212 c.

39. "Platon théologien," loc. cit., 215.

40. L. Robin, Le Banquet de Platon (Paris, 1929), p. xlii.

41. W. Jaeger, Aristoteles: Grundlegung einer Geschichte seiner Entwicklung (Berlin, 1923).

42. Aristotle, Metaphysics XII, 7; 1072 b, 28.

43. "Comment s'est transformée la religion d'Aristote," Revue Thomiste (1926), 298.

44. Ibid., 326.

45. K. Reinhardt, Poseidonios (Munich, 1921), cited by P. Lagrange, "La religion des stoiciens avant Jésus-Christ," Revue Thomiste (1928), 63.

46. J. Carcopino, Le basilique pythagoricienne de la Porte Majeure (Paris, 1927), p. 190.

47. P. Lagrange, art. cit., 66 ff.

48. "La religion de Sénèque," Revue Thomiste (1928), 629.

49. "Une moral indépendante dans l'antiquité: les Cyniques," Revue Thomiste (1929), 51–52.

50. "Vers le Logos de saint Jean: Le logos de Philon," RB, XXXII (1923), 326–327.

51. This recalls to mind the famous letter of Claudius to the Alexandrians, dated A.D. 41, in which many historians are inclined to see an allusion to the troubles stirred up in the Alexandrian ghettos by the early Christians. The emperor probably had something else in mind than the Christians. Cf. M. J. Lagrange, "La lettre de l'empereur Claude et les Juifs d'Alexandrie," RB, XXIV (1925), 621–623; "La lettre de Claude aux Alexandrins," RB, XL (1931), 270–276.

52. R. P. Lagrange, *Le judaisme avant Jesus-Christ* (Paris, 1931), pp. 581–586, devotes a number of pages to the Therapeuti, and concludes: "In spite of all this, we cannot help thinking that the Therapeuti are mostly an allegorical fiction, whereby this great exponent of allegory expresses his ideal of Jewish scholarly contemplative life."

53. Cf. *Le messianisme chez les Juifs* (Paris, 1908), pp. 28–36; *Le Judaisme avant Jésus-Christ* (Paris, 1931), pp. 542–586; "Vers le Logos de saint Jean: Philon d'Alexandrie," *RB*, XXXII (1923), 321–371. Cf. also the important review of P. Lebreton's *Les origines du dogme de la Trinité*, *RB*, XIX (1910), 585–593, where the problem of the Logos is discussed at length.

54. "Vers le Logos de saint Jean," *RB*, XXXII (1923), 371.

55. *Ibid.*, 359. Cf. "L'ange de Jahvé," *RB*, XII (1903), 212–225.

56. E. Bréhier, *Les idees philosophiques et religieuses de Philon d'Alexandrie* (Paris, 1908), p. 310.

57. "Vers le Logos de saint Jean," *loc. cit.*, 346.

58. *Le judaisme*, p. 559.

59. W. Bousset, *Jüdisch-christlicher Schulbetrieb in Alexandria und Rom* (Göttingen, 1915).

60. "L'hermétisme," *RB*, XXXIII (1924), 481–497; XXXIV (1925), 82–104; 368–396; 547–574; XXXV (1926), 240–264. To these may be added the detailed reviews of W. Scott's *Hermetica*, *RB*, XXXIV (1925), 432–436; 593–597, and the study on "Hermeticism" in *Le Correspondant*, March 10, 1927.

61. *RB* (1924), 481.

62. *Ibid.* (1926), 262–264.

63. Zozimus, in a fragment of uncertain authenticity, is perhaps the oldest witness of the first Corpus. Clement of Alexandria had already mentioned "forty-two very important Hermetic books, thirty-six of which deal with the entire Egyptian philosophy and must have been studied by the prophets; the other six deal with medicine" (cf. *Stromata*, VI, 4). These books have not been identified. Cf. P. Lagrange, *RB*, XXXIII (1924), 491.

64. Cyril of Alexandria, *Contra Iulianum*, I, 30, *PG*, 77, 548.

65. *Poimandres*, 32.

66. *Corpus hermeticum*, IX. W. Scott holds that the Christians could have been the persecutors of the Hermetists. But as P. Lebreton remarks (*Recherches de science religieuse* [1926], 361), it is unlikely that the Christians at Alexandria, at the end of the third century, were strong enough to terrorize their pagan adversaries. P. Lagrange (*art. cit.*, *RB*, XXXIV, 595) thinks that the author is simply beating the air, considering the evil treatment often meted out to the philosophers.

67. J. Carcopino, "Le tombeau de Lambridi et l'hermétisme africain," *Revue archéologique* (May–June, 1922).

68. Cf. P. Lagrange's review of the above-cited article, *RB*, XXXII (1923), 311–312. R. Reitzenstein, *Poimandres* (Leipzig, 1904), p. 146 ff., believes he can reconstruct in its broad outlines the history of the Hermetic communities. His description is pure imagination.

69. W. Bousset, *Kyrios Christos, Geschichte des Christusglaubens von den Anfängen des Christentums bis Irenaus* (2nd ed.; Göttingen, 1921), p. 174 ff.

70. *RB*, XXXV (1926), 251–252.

71. P. Lagrange, "L'hermétisme," *ibid.*, 264. Cf. "Ce que fut d'apres M.

Lasserre le prétendu drame de la metaphysique chrétienne," *Le Correspondant,* Oct. 25, 1925.

72. No need to speak here of the important and penetrating studies of P. Lagrange on the mysteries of Eleusis. In the following chapter the reader will find an appreciation of these studies. It goes without saying that they must also be taken into account if one would have a well-rounded judgment of P. Lagrange's contribution to Hellenism.

To be complete, we should at least mention P. Lagrange's studies on "Le prétendu messianisme de Virgile," *RB,* XXXI (1922), 552–572, which ought to be completed by a reading of his long review of the work by J. Carcopino, *Virgile et le mystère de la IVe Eclogue, RB,* XXXIX (1930), 446–452. Cf. also what he had to say about the Pythagorean basilica of the Porta Maggiore, and Pythagoreanism in *RB,* XXXVI (1927), 599–608.

CHAPTER IV

1. These lines are from P. Lagrange's review of H. Gunkel's (German) work, *L'intelligence du N.T. du point de vue de l'histoire des religions* (Göttingen, 1903), *RB,* XIII (1904), 271.

2. Review of Deissmann's *Licht vom Osten* (Tübingen, 1908), *RB,* XVIII (1909), 627–628.

3. *RB,* XXIX (1920), 296. The work of M. Clemen to which reference is made is: *Die Reste der primitive Religion im altesten Christentum* (Giessen, 1916).

4. Review of Carl Clemen's *Religionsgeschichtliche Erklärung des Neuen Testaments* (Giessen, 1909), *RB,* XVIII (1909), 281.

5. *RB,* XIII (1904), 271.

6. Review of Loisy's *Les Mystères paiens et le Mystère chrétien* (Paris, 1919), *RB,* XXIX (1920), 446.

7. Opening lecture of his course on the history of religions at the *Collège de France,* Dec. 5, 1931, reproduced at the end of his work, *Le mandéisme et les origines chrétiennes* (Paris, 1934). Text cited, p. 174.

8. Review of *Orpheus, Histoire générale des religions,* Solomon Reinach (Paris, 1909), *RB,* XIX (1910), 138–139.

9. *RB,* XL (1931), 151.

10. *RB,* XVIII (1909), 281.

11. *RB,* XIX (1910), 131. The two citations from M. Van Gennep are taken from the *Revue de l'histoire des religions,* LVIII (1908), pp. 51, 48, note 1.

12. *Ibid.,* p. xii.

13. P. Lagrange, *Mélanges d'histoire religieuse* (Paris, 1915), pp. 73–74.

14. Cumont, *Les religions orientales dans le paganisme romain* (ed. 1929), p. ix.

15. Cumont, *ibid.,* p. ix, I.

16. P. Lagrange, *M. Loisy et le modernisme* (Juvisy, 1932), p. 206.

17. Cf. the study of M. Vénard in this volume, pp. 54–93.

18. P. Lagrange, *Le sens du christianisme d'après l'exégèse allemande* (Paris, 1918), Chaps. 7 and 8.

19. *Theologisch Tidjschrift* (1917), p. 228.

20. P. Lagrange "La gnose mandéenne," *RB,* XXXVI (1927), 321.

21. *Die hellenistichen Mysterienreligionen, ihre Grundgedanken und*

Wirkungen (Leipzig and Berlin, 1910), with frequent re-editions.
22. *Kyrios Christos* (1913).
23. *Mémoires*, III, 231.
24. *Les Mystères paiens et le Mystère chrétien*.
25. *La nouvelle journée* (May 1, 1920), pp. 451–452.
26. Cf. *Les Mystères paiens et le Mystère chrétien*, pp. 209, 231–232.
27. *RB*, XXIX (1920), 426.
28. *Ibid.*, 435.
29. Also known as Koré or Persephone.
30. Adonis, Attis, Osiris, etc.
31. *RB*, XXVIII (1919), 206.
32. *Ibid.*
33. *Ibid.*, 199.
34. *Ibid.*, 200–201.
35. *Ibid.*, 203–205, text and notes.
36. *Ibid.*, 208–215.
37. *Ibid.*, XXXVIII (1929), 63 ff. and 201 ff.
38. *Ibid.*, 212.
39. "Attis et le christianisme," *RB*, XXVIII (1919), 423.
40. *Ibid.*, 437.
41. *Ibid.*, 423.
42. Franz Cumont, *Les religions orientales* (2nd ed.), p. 86.
43. *Ibid.*, 433.
44. *RB*, art. cit., 434–435.
45. *Cohortatio ad gentes*, I, 2.
46. *RB*, XXVIII (1919), 454.
47. *Dict. des antiquités grecques et latines* (Darenberg et Saglio), "Taurobole."
48. *RB*, *ibid.*, 438.
49. *Ibid.*, 442.
50. *Ibid.*, 433.
51. *Ibid.*, 453.
52. *Ibid.*, 466.
53. Translation of Loisy, *Mystères* (2nd ed.), 148.
54. *De Iside et Osiride*, p. xxvii.
55. *RB*, XXIX (1920), 436.
56. *Ibid.*, 439.
57. *Ibid.*, 440.
58. *Histoire du culte des divinités d'Alexandrie*, p. 127.
59. *RB*, loc. cit., 440.
60. *Ibid.*, 436.
61. *Ibid.*, 437.
62. Loisy, *op. cit.*, p. 151.
63. *RB*, loc. cit., 438.
64. *Ibid.*, 441.
65. Lagrange, *Mélanges d'histoire religieuse*, p. 103.
66. *Ibid.*, pp. 105–106. At this point in the work, Lagrange's article in *Le Correspondant*, July 25, 1910, is reproduced. Mention has previously been made of it.
67. Résumé of P. Lagrange's exposition, loc. cit.
68. *Orpheus*, p. 102.

69. *Mélanges*, pp. 107–108.

70. *RB*, XXIX (1920), 441.

71. *Mystères*, 202.

72. *RB, ibid.*, 442.

73. *Mystères*, 197.

74. *RB, ibid.*

75. *RB*, XIX (1910), 135.

76. *Kyrios Christos* (1913), p. 166.

77. M. J. Lagrange, *M. Loisy et le modernisme* (1932), p. 203.

78. *RB*, XXIX (1920), 421–422.

79. *RB*, XXI (1912), 126–127.

80. *Ibid.*, XXIX (1920), 444.

81. *Ibid.*, 442.

82. *Ibid.*, 443.

83. *Ibid.*, 421.

84. *Ibid.*, 446.

85. *Ibid., loc. cit.*

86. *Mélanges*, pp. 119 and 121. (The article of 1910.)

87. *Ibid., passim*, pp. 121–129.

88. *Histoire de la Littérature grecque chrétienne* (Paris, 1928), I, p. 294. See page 141 on the gospel of St. John, and page 311 for the idea of Christ in St. Paul.

89. *Bibliothèque de Synthèse historique*, directed by H. Berr.

90. *Op. cit.*, 515–517. Cf. Chaps. I and II of the Third part, *Vers l'universalisme*, which were contributed by M. Boulanger.

91. In the collection *Christianisme*, directed by P. L. Couchoud.

92. *Orphée* (Paris, 1925), pp. 168–170.

93. *Jésus* (1933).

94. *Dieux et Religions*, conferences given by different authors at the Union of freethinkers and free-believers for moral culture (Paris: Rieder, 1926), p. 84. Otherwise his conference is interesting. See declarations of the same kind in *Jésus* (Index, *Mystères*).

95. H. A. Kennedy, *St. Paul and the Mystery Religions* (London, 1923), reviewed by Jacquier in *RB*, XXIV (1915), 272.

96. *RB*, XXIX (1920), 297. The Bulletin is signed *L*, and refers to Harnack's articles of 1916.

97. *Die Mystik des Apostels Paulus* (Tübingen, 1930), reviewed by Lagrange in *RB*, XLII (1933), 115.

98. *Die Religionsgeschichte und das Urchristentum* (1932). Review in *Revue des sciences philosophiques et théologiques* (1934), 2*.

99. *Revue archéologique* (1920), 150. Cited in *RB*, XXXI (1922), 312.

100. Vol. I of the *Compte rendu du Congrès* of his jubilee (Rieder, 1928). See A. Loisy, *Les origines de la Cène eucharistique*, p. 77 ff.; 2nd ed. of *Mystères paiens et le Mystère chrétien* (1930), and *Naissance du Christianisme* (1933).

101. P. Lagrange, *M. Loisy et le modernisme*, p. 217 ff.

102. Articles in the *Revue Biblique*.

103. *RB*, XXXII (1923), 153.

104. *Judaisme*, p. 405.

105. *Ibid.*, p. 402.

106. *Ibid., loc. cit.*
107. *RB*, XIII (1904), 192.
108. *Judaisme*, p. 403.
109. *RB, loc. cit.*, 410.
110. *Judaisme*, p. 404.
111. *RB, loc. cit.*, 208 f.
112. *Judaisme*, p. 405.
113. R. Reitzenstein, *Das iranische Erlösung-mysterium* (Bonn, 1921). R. Reitzenstein and H. H. Schroeder, *Studien zum antiken Syncretismus aus Iran und Griechenland* (Leipzig and Berlin, 1926).
114. *Judaisme*, p. 406.
115. *Ibid., loc. cit.*
116. Writing in 1931, P. Lagrange could not refer to the important Egyptian discovery of the writings of Mani himself, of historical references about him, and of the persecutions undergone by his sect, all of which were made public in 1932. *RB*, XLII (1933), 619–621.
117. *RB*, XXXI (1922), 282–286.
118. *Judaisme*, pp. 406–409.
119. *RB*, XXXVI (1927), 330–335.
120. *RB*, XXXVII (1928), 17.
121. *Judaisme*, p. 426.

CHAPTER VI

1. Reprinted from the *Catholic Biblical Quarterly*, 1941, pp. 134–144.
2. The reader may consult the following articles of appreciation which appeared after the death of P. Lagrange:
   R. De Vaux, in *La Vie Intellectuelle* (1938), 9–26
   M. Humeau, in *La Vie Spirituelle*, LV (1938), 60–76
   P. Levie, in *Nouvelle Revue Theologique* (1938), 466–472
   A. McLoughlin, in *Dominicana* (1938), 108–117
   H. Vincent, in *Revue Biblique* (1938), 321–354
   —— Transl. in *Blackfriars* (1938), 397–411; 475–486
   J. Vosté, in *Angelicum* (1938), 245–261
   C. J. Kearns, in *Irish Eccles. Record* (1938), 611
   R. T. Murphy, in *Catholic Biblical Quarterly* (1941), 134–144
3. Since this decree emanates from the Consistorial Congregation and *not from the Holy Office*, there is no question of orthodoxy involved; nor has there ever been. The decree was merely disciplinary, limiting the use of his writings (none is mentioned by name) to seminary professors. At any rate, this decree was abrogated by the Code of Canon Law (6,6°), in 1918.
4. The letter of Cardinal Pacelli acknowledging in the name of the Pope, Pius XI, the receipt of a copy of *L'Évangile*, and which is reproduced on page iv of the 1936 printing, was considered by many in Europe to be a declaration that the last vestiges of suspicion had been removed from the name of P. Lagrange. Cf. Vosté, *loc. cit.*, p. 256, for an expression of the esteem in which Pius XI held P. Lagrange.
5. Cf. the letter addressed to the whole Order by the V. Rev. S. M. Gillet, O.P., Master General, written in New York upon hearing of the death of P. Lagrange. It is reproduced in *Dominicana* (1938), pp. 112–115.

Date Due

FEB 10 '54			